QUEEN ALEXAND

Georgina Battiscombe

Georgina Battiscombe was educated at an Anglican convent school and at Lady Margaret Hall, Oxford. She comes of a North Country family with a strong political tradition. Married to Christopher Battiscombe, Grenadier, Colonial Civil Servant and archaeologist, she has lived in Zanzibar, in Durham and for a time in Windsor Castle.

Her first serious book was a biography of the Victorian writer 'Charlotte M. Yonge', to be followed by 'Mrs. Gladstone' and 'John Keble'. The latter, published in 1963, received the James Tait Black Prize.

To Ruth

Queen Alexandra

GEORGINA BATTISCOMBE

SPHERE BOOKS LIMITED
30/32 Gray's Inn Road, London, WC1X 8JL

First published in Great Britain in 1969 by
Constable & Co. Limited

First Sphere Books edition, 1972

TRADE
MARK

Printed in Great Britain by
Hazell Watson & Viney Ltd,
Aylesbury, Bucks

The would-be biographer of Queen Alexandra is faced by a surprising shortage of material. By his will King Edward VII directed that all his personal and private papers, including, of course, his letters from Queen Alexandra, should be destroyed. In her turn, Queen Alexandra expressed a wish that after her death all her private papers should be likewise destroyed, a request which was most scrupulously carried out by her faithful friend and companion, Miss Charlotte Knollys.

Fortunately, Queen Alexandra's correspondence with King George V and with Queen Mary escaped this holocaust. By gracious permission of Her Majesty the Queen I have been given unrestricted access to these letters and to all other relevant material now in the Royal Archives at Windsor Castle. Since the material available in the Royal Archives forms the basis of this book, my thanks are due first of all to Mr Robert Mackworth-Young, Librarian at Windsor Castle, for his invaluable help and advice, and to the Registrar, Miss Jane Langton, and the various members of her staff for their unfailing kindness and patience.

The Rigsarkivet at Copenhagen might have been expected to be a valuable source of material. However, in spite of the kind co-operation of the staff, and in particular of the Director, Rigsarkivar Mr Johan Hvidfeldt, research there proved disappointing. It would appear that on the death of any of her Danish relatives Queen Alexandra asked that her letters should be returned to her to be subsequently destroyed with the rest of her papers. The only exception seems to have been her correspondence with her youngest brother, Prince Waldemar, who did not die until 1939. Unfortunately, therefore, these letters must remain inaccessible until 1989.

The Archives of the October Revolution in Moscow form another and somewhat surprising source of important material. Here are to be found Queen Alexandra's letters to her sister, the Empress Marie, a correspondence covering the fifty years from 1867 to 1917. Forty volumes of letters, housed in Moscow, and written in Danish in a hand which is very difficult to decipher, obviously present a formidable problem. By the courtesy of the Russian authorities and of Mr Michael Kauffman of the Victoria and Albert Museum, I was allowed to read the one volume (1878–1881) which was among the exhibits at the Anglo-Russian Exhibition in April 1967. Unfortunately it contained nothing of any interest. The authorities in Moscow have now undertaken the lengthy task of deciphering and translating these volumes; until this work is completed the letters cannot be made available for research or publication. I hope that later on it may be possible to publish some of these letters in a separate volume; meanwhile, I would wish to thank all those who have so generously helped me in this matter, in particular Mr G. Belov, Head of the Central Archives Department of the U.S.S.R. Council of Ministers, Sir William Hayter, Professor Alexander Guber, Mr Ivan Koulikov of the U.S.S.R. Embassy, and Mr John Morgan of the British Embassy in Moscow.

Much valuable material is to be found in private collections of papers. I wish to thank most warmly all those who have given me access to such material, especially the Hon. Geoffrey Bridgeman (Macclesfield Papers), Lord Ponsonby of Shulbrede (Ponsonby Papers), Mr Victor Montagu (Sandwich Papers), the Duke of Hamilton (Fisher Papers), Brigadier A. W. P. Llewellen Palmer (Lincolnshire Papers), Miss Amicia Carroll

(Knollys Papers), Mrs Campbell Ellis (Probyn Papers) and to Mr Keith Mason (Beresford Correspondence). I am indebted to the Hon. Lucy Holland for permission to use the Knutsford Papers, and to Mr Felix Hull, Kent County Archivist, for similar permission as regards that section of the Knollys Papers to be found in the Maidstone County Library. The Haig Papers, the Haldane Papers, and the Rosebery Papers are now in the National Library of Scotland; I am very grateful to the Assistant Keeper, Mr Alan Bell, for his help and co-operation. My special thanks are also due to H.R.H. Prince Ernst August of Hanover, who kindly allowed me to use papers in his family archives at Gmunden, and to his archivist, Mr G. M. Willis, who translated these letters for me. I am grateful, too, to the Estate of the late Sir Frederick Treves and the President and Council of the Royal College of Surgeons of England for permission to quote from the unpublished account of King Edward's illness by Sir Frederick Treves.

To give a detailed bibliography would seem to me neither helpful nor necessary. The first and most essential printed source of information is, of course, Sir Philip Magnus's invaluable biography of King Edward VII. Other books which I have found specially useful are Lady Longford's *Victoria R.I.*, Sir Harold Nicolson's *George V*, Mr James Pope-Hennessy's *Queen Mary*, and two volumes of letters, *Dearest Child* and *Dearest Mama*, edited by Mr Roger Fulford, who has given me much valuable help.

Many people have been kind enough to give me their personal reminiscences of Queen Alexandra. In particular I wish respectfully to thank H.R.H. the Duke of Windsor, H.R.H. Princess Alice of Athlone, H.R.H. Princess Margrethe of Bourbon Parma, and Lady Patricia Ramsay. Information of special value came from Blanche, Lady Lloyd, Lady Alexandra Trevor-Roper, Mrs Whitehouse, Mrs Sofka Skipwith, and Captain Michael Laing, R.N.

I would have liked to thank here by name all those kind persons who have helped me in many and various ways. To all of them I am profoundly grateful; a list, however, would be so long as to be meaningless. Nevertheless, I wish to make special acknowledgments to Sir Terence Cawthorne for his help over the questions connected with Queen Alexandra's deafness, to my daughter, Aurea Morshead, for research on Lady Geraldine Somerset's diaries, and also to Mr R. C. Marrington, Tapissier at Sandringham House, Major B. M. Mitchell, Curator, QARANC Museum, Dame Beryl Oliver, Miss Josephine Barnes, and Sir Owen Morshead. Mr Ralph Arnold has been my counsellor throughout the writing of this book; to him for his encouragement and for his wise and humorous advice I owe my last and perhaps my deepest debt of gratitude.

Chapter one

DANISH CHILDHOOD

'Saxon and Norman and Dane are we, But all of us Danes in our welcome to thee' – so run the familiar lines of Tennyson's *Welcome to Alexandra.* Hers was a genuine case of 'dual nationality'; though she became deeply attached to her adopted country of England, she remained ineradicably Danish in sympathy and outlook, and her personality is only to be properly understood when seen against the background of the land where she was born and brought up.

The Denmark of the first half of the nineteenth century was a simple and unsophisticated country. Its energy was given to the task of making good the havoc of the Napoleonic Wars, which had left it almost totally impoverished, its fleet destroyed and its maritime trade ruined. The union with Norway, which had endured for four hundred and fifty years, had been dissolved in 1814 and Denmark proper, with the Duchies of Schleswig and Holstein and a few unimportant colonies overseas, was all that remained of the once extensive possessions of the Danish Kings. Frederick VI (1808–39) ruled over his diminished territory for all the world as if he were an old-fashioned country squire and Denmark his private estate. Every evening, for instance, the keys of the gates of the city of Copenhagen were brought to him to be placed on his private writing-table. Before the Second World War there still existed a few semi-independent states – Zanzibar and Sarawak are two which spring immediately to mind – so small that ruler and ruled could and did know each other personally. Everybody had unhindered access to the sovereign who was expected to concern himself as much with the personal problems of his subjects as with the political affairs of the state. Frederick VI was just such a sovereign. When that gawky country youth, Hans Andersen, found himself penniless in Copenhagen it was to the King that he appealed, and it was the King himself who made the necessary arrangements for his education. This close connection between sovereign and subject, and the fact that anyone, regardless of social status, could have direct personal contact with the sovereign, meant that although the constitution of Denmark was an autocratic one, the Danish way of life was essentially democratic. No great gulf yawned between royalty and the rest of mankind; to this day the Danish Royal Family can walk the streets of Copenhagen and shop in its popular stores without exciting any particular stir or comment. The whole nation, in fact, behaved rather like one big family in a country where, as in Scotland, family ties counted – and still count – for very much. People were intensely proud of their family connections; they were also prepared to take their family duties and responsibilities seriously. The family was the basic unit, and vast family gatherings the typical form of entertainment.

This tiny nation was fiercely patriotic. After the losses of the Napoleonic Wars and the secession of Norway, 'Denmark's position among European nations had sunk so low,' writes Mr Palle Lauring, 'that she hardly counted as a nation any more.'[1] To the Danes themselves, however, their country still counted for very much and they were determined to see her restored to something like her old position and prosperity. In particular they were determined not to be forced into ceding any more territory, which meant, in effect, that they were determined to hold on to the Duchies of Schleswig and Holstein. The connection between Denmark proper and the Duchies had always been a troubled one, complicated by the unfortunate fact that although Holstein was predominantly German in language and culture, and Schleswig Danish, a decree dating as far back as 1481 declared that these two provinces must always remain united, '*up ewig ungedeelt*'. Many Danes would have been prepared to acquiesce in the cession of German-speaking Holstein but the two Duchies were apparently inextricably linked together and the whole nation was resolved that Schleswig must remain Danish. For that principle Denmark was prepared to fight, and it was becoming clear that with Holstein eager to break free from Danish rule, and with Prussia casting greedy eyes on both Duchies, before very long the fighting would begin. It was equally clear that, left to herself without assistance from the Great Powers, Denmark would stand no chance against the might of Prussia.

The Great Powers, however, were not particularly interested in the affairs of a small country which seemed to have drifted out of the main stream of European history. Denmark was a long way away and few people knew or cared very much about what went on there. Posted to Copenhagen, diplomats, and more especially their wives, sighed to find themselves exiled to a small town where the shops were bad, the food boring, the language unintelligible, and the fashions several years behind those of Paris. Yet, remote though the country was from the great centres of culture, the Romantic Movement had reached Denmark and its influence had sparked off what can fairly be described as a Danish renaissance. Kierkegaard was its philosopher, Thorwaldsen, then the most famous of European sculptors, its most notable artist, Hans Andersen its chief literary figure. Denmark might be facing great financial and political difficulties but culturally she was very far from bankrupt.

All these Danish characteristics and traditions went to the making of Princess Alexandra's personality, whilst the hard facts of Danish history influenced both her opinions and her prejudices. Her natural simplicity, her childlike – almost childish – tastes and habits, the delightful ease with which she could make herself at home with the man in the street, all came to her from her unsophisticated Danish upbringing. From Denmark she learnt the fiery patriotism typical of a small and struggling nation and the undying hatred of all things German that was to characterise her few excursions into politics. So, too, her clannishness, her lasting attachment to her old home and to her own relations, the tenacity with which she fought their battles and upheld their interests, sprang from the deep family feeling which formed the base of the structure of Danish society. Only the Danish cultural revival left her untouched. She came of a family almost wholly lacking in intellectual interests; the French ambassador at Copenhagen described her father, Prince Christian of Schleswig-Holstein-Sonderburg-Glücksburg, as having 'a mediocre mind and very little education'.[2] Prince Christian, however, had many good qualities; upright, dutiful and affectionate, he made an excellent husband and father and, when his time came, a popular and reasonably successful monarch.

Although his connection with the reigning house of Denmark was a distant one Prince Christian was indubitably royal, since no morganatic blemish marred his pedigree. When his father died, the old King, Frederick VI, as a matter of course assumed responsibility for his upbringing. He was brought up, however, in a very simple manner, and in due time he was given a captaincy in the Guards where he had to make his own way like any other officer with very little to live on beyond his army pay, the young prince having neither estates nor income to correspond with his high-sounding string of territorial titles.

The most interesting episodes of Prince Christian's youth were his two visits to England, one in 1837 as the bearer of the Danish King's congratulations to Queen Victoria on her accession, the second a year later as the official representative of Denmark at her coronation. By English standards Prince Christian was something of a country bumpkin – his first calls in London had to be on a tailor and a hatter to make him fit to appear in Society – but nevertheless he cherished the dream that he might be considered as a suitor for Queen Victoria's hand. Nobody took his pretensions very seriously except his relative Augusta, Duchess of Cambridge, wife to Queen Victoria's uncle Adolphus, Duke of Cambridge, to whom he had naturally confided his hopes. However, in 1840 Queen Victoria married Prince Albert of Saxe-Coburg-Gotha and two years later Prince Christian himself married the Duchess of Cambridge's niece, Princess Louise of Hesse-Cassel.

Princess Louise, or Princess Christian as she now became, was an altogether more lively and forceful character than her husband. As a wife she was something of a *maîtresse femme;* but her marriage was a happy and prosperous one and both her husband and her children were devoted to her. Her daughter Princess Alexandra inherited her slim, exquisite figure, her gaiety, her taste for music and also her simple, unswerving religious faith, in which Prince Christian shared. To judge from her letters Princess Christian's beliefs were of a very definite, almost dogmatic nature, in contrast with the equally genuine but much less clearly defined religious views, sometimes amounting to little more than deism, held by most members of the English Royal Family. Unfortunately together with all these good gifts Princess Alexandra also inherited from her mother a serious and frustrating physical handicap in the shape of a hereditary form of deafness known as otosclerosis.

Such was Princess Alexandra's heritage from her native land and her parents, two influences which were to retain a permanent hold upon her. Devoted wife and mother though she became, in spirit she never left her childhood home. As Queen Victoria wrote, referring to the disunion so common in royal families, 'one remarkable exception is the Danish Royal Family; they are wonderfully united – and never breathe one word against each other, and the daughters remain as unspoilt and as completely Children of the Home as when they were unmarried', adding, rather wistfully, 'I do admire this.'[3]

Alexandra Caroline Marie Charlotte Louise Julia, a name usually shortened to 'Alix', was born in Copenhagen on 1 December 1844 in the Yellow Palace, a house palatial only in name. Her childhood home was well suited to her family circumstances, being at one and the same time definitely royal but completely ordinary. The Yellow Palace is neighbour to the magnificent Amalienborg Palace, the King's official residence, but in itself it is no more than a pleasant and unpretentious house in a quiet street, distinguished from the neighbouring houses only by its colour. The front door opens directly on to the pavement so that the house lacks privacy and passers-by can glance in at the ground-floor windows. The Amaliengade, the street in which the Yellow Palace stands, runs from the splendid square of the Amalienborg towards the Nyhavn, only some five minutes' walk away. This old harbour reaches right into the heart of the city and the ships tie up beside the road, opposite a row of picturesque houses where, a hundred years ago, rich and respectable merchant families lived next door to warehouses, sailors' taverns and brothels. From the windows of the Yellow Palace itself you might see the masts of ships sailing up and down the Sound, so that from their earliest infancy Prince Christian's children were familiar with the sight and smell of the sea and the business of seafaring men.

These children were six in number. Princess Alexandra was never so deeply attached to her eldest brother Prince Frederick (born 1843) as she was to Prince William or 'Willi' (born 1845) and to her sister Princess Dagmar or 'Minny' (born 1847). Within this exceptionally united and affectionate family these three children formed a still more closely-knit inner circle. A long gap in age separated Princess Thyra (born 1853) and Prince Waldemar (born 1858) from the rest of the family so that, devoted though all six children were to each other, of necessity no great intimacy existed between the young ones and their elder brothers and sisters.

After the passage of more than a century it is difficult to make any clear picture of the family life or to differentiate one child from the other by taste, temperament, or even by appearance. Photography was as yet in its infancy and Prince and Princess Christian were so badly off that they could not afford to spend much money on portraits and miniatures. Princess Christian attempted to remedy this situation by sketching the children for herself, but unfortunately she had none of Queen Victoria's artistic gifts and her efforts compare very badly with the Queen's charming sketches of her own children. Princess Christian in fact was so incompetent an artist that whenever possible she drew her subject from behind, thus avoiding the necessity of tackling the horrid complexities of the human face. Not merely, therefore, are her drawings useless as likenesses but as the back view of one small child is very like the back view of any other, it is impossible even to say which child they represent. One large oil portrait by a professional artist does indeed exist, showing the young Princesses Alexandra and Dagmar aged about ten and seven. Although in reproduction the picture is pleasing enough, the original is totally devoid of artistic merit, but it at least confirms the often expressed opinion that Princess Alexandra was the prettier and Princess Dagmar the more lively of the two little girls.

If we know little about the appearance of these children we know next to nothing about their individual characters or the incidents of their childhood. No lesson books, no childish letters, no diaries of parents or governesses have survived to help us reconstruct daily life in the nurseries of the Yellow Palace or the long, happy summers spent at Bernstorff, an eighteenth-century hunting-lodge a few miles from Copenhagen, which the King had put at the disposal of Prince Christian and his family. Bernstorff is a small but very elegant white-stuccoed house. Over the handsome front-door is inscribed a Latin motto particularly suited to a holiday home, *Honesto inter labores otio sacrum*. Around this charming house is a large park, well-wooded and undulating, a pleasant place where the children could wander at large with their donkey and their dogs.

The first real glimpse that we get of Princess Alexandra is neither at the Yellow Palace nor at Bernstorff, but in the gardens of the Rosenborg, another Royal property in Copenhagen. Here, one day in 1854, a young Englishwoman, Miss Bessie Carew, who had arrived in Copenhagen on board a yacht belonging to Sir Henry Wynne, chanced to be strolling in company with her host. Although her English snobbery was outraged by the sight of 'a lot of rather dirty little children playing about' she was much enjoying the beauty of the gardens when her attention was caught by the sight of a rather unusual equipage:

> 'We saw a go-cart drawn by a goat, which was led by a very smart-looking footman in a green and gold livery, with another one behind. Someone who looked like a ladies' maid or nurse was walking beside the cart. Seated in the cart was the most beautiful little girl about eight years old' – she was in fact nine – 'wearing a little fur bonnet. "That", said Sir Henry Wynne, "is the little Princess

Alexandra of Denmark." She waved to us gaily as she went by.'[4]

Here already is a mention of those two characteristics which were always to cause wondering and delighted comment, Princess Alexandra's superlative beauty and her gay, spontaneous courtesy. The comparative pomp of two liveried footmen in attendance may have been due to the altered position of her father. Prince Christian's patron, the old King Frederick VI, had died the year before Princess Alexandra was born. He was succeeded by his cousin, King Christian VIII, who reigned nine years and was in his turn succeeded by his son, King Frederick VII. Because he gave the country a democratic constitution King Frederick is still something of a popular hero to the Danes, but in private life he was anything but an estimable character. After having been twice married and twice divorced he set up house openly with his mistress, a onetime milliner with a disreputable past whom he created Countess Danner and with whom he later contracted a morganatic marriage. This much-married man was, however, incapable of begetting children; when one of his wives was erroneously reported to be pregnant King Louis-Philippe exclaimed, 'Well, God bless the father, whoever he may be.' It therefore became necessary to decide who should succeed him upon the Danish throne. The nearest heir was Princess Alexandra's uncle, Prince Frederick of Hesse-Cassel, but added to other difficulties was the fact that in the inconclusive war between Denmark and Holstein which broke out in 1848, Prince Frederick had admitted his German sympathies by taking the Holstein side. Prince Christian, on the other hand, had been the only member of his family to remain loyal to Denmark, and he had fought with some distinction in the Danish Army, thereby adding greatly to his popularity. By descent Prince Christian's wife Louise was nearer than he to the Danish throne but her candidature was barred because the Salic Law ran in the Duchies, though not in Denmark itself. On 8 May 1852 the London Protocol, a settlement guaranteed by Russia, France, England, Prussia, Austria and Sweden, affirmed the indivisibility of Danish territory and designated Prince Christian as heir to the Danish throne.

This access of dignity, however, brought little or no increase of income and the family in the Yellow Palace still had to struggle hard to make ends meet. Money was too short to allow of many luxuries, even educational ones. Princess Christian herself taught music to her daughters, whilst Prince Christian took their physical education in hand, putting both boys and girls through a strenuous course of gymnastics, a form of exercise in which these athletic children delighted. Dancing they also enjoyed, and in after years Princess Alexandra could sometimes be persuaded to demonstrate her acrobatic skill by performing that extremely difficult ballet-step, *le grand jeté*. Outdoor sports were their pleasure, in particular riding, and Princess Alexandra grew up to be a thoroughly proficient horsewoman.

Their intellectual attainments, however, lagged sadly behind their physical prowess. The children had English nurses and so learnt to speak that language from their earliest years. Somehow or other the girls became fairly fluent in French and German; they received careful religious instruction, but of other education they had little or none. Perhaps this mattered the less because these were not children with artistic or intellectual tastes but a healthy and happy gang of good-looking extroverts. They were well known for their rough-and-tumble humour and for their liking for practical jokes. Embarrassing though this habit might be to their more sophisticated friends, it was never allowed to overstep the bounds of politeness, their parents being insistent on the necessity for good manners.

Of the girls only Princess Dagmar showed the slightest liking for books and literature. Princess Alexandra's time was almost entirely spent in the company of this sister, with whom she shared a small and barely-furnished bedroom since the accommodation at the Yellow Palace was too cramped to allow the children to have rooms of their own. These two girls were always simply, not to say plainly, dressed and they soon learnt that the best way to get a new evening frock or a smart bonnet was to make it for themselves. In her early youth Princess Dagmar was both pretty and piquant, but Princess Alexandra was a genuine beauty. A quick-tempered, passionate creature, she was deplorably unpunctual and something of a tomboy, but she was also deeply affectionate, transparently honest, and possessed of an instinctive wisdom beyond her years which made her a peacemaker in the rare family quarrels.

In spite of the lack of money, every second year the family would set out on a journey, or perhaps it would be more accurate to say a pilgrimage, to Schloss Rumpenheim near Frankfurt. This pleasant, white-painted house on the bank of the Main was the property of Princess Christian's relations, the Hesse-Cassel family. Here it was that an English Princess, Mary, daughter of George II, had withdrawn herself and her outraged Protestant susceptibilities when her husband, the Landgrave of Hesse-Cassel, unaccountably and inconveniently lapsed into the errors of the Roman Catholic faith. Princess Mary's son, the Landgrave Frederick, left Rumpenheim to his six children on the understanding that it should become the centre every two years of a great gathering of the family.

The Landgrave Frederick who made this interesting bequest was grandfather to Princess Christian, and her family thus stood at the very centre of the Rumpenheim cult, for a cult it very soon became. To breathe a word of criticism of Rumpenheim was blasphemy and to admit to less than complete satisfaction with its furnishing, its amenities, or even with its *cuisine* was to show oneself to be an inferior person unworthy of a place within the charmed circle of true devotees. All physical inconveniences, even the mental inconvenience of boredom, were part and parcel of the Rumpenheim *ethos*, which was compounded of childish jokes, family affection, much flirtation and a vast amount of gossip. Sophisticated Rumpenheim certainly was not. To be royal is not necessarily to be smart and the Royalties who assembled at Rumpenheim were definitely dowdy. Some few among these rather dim figures of Archdukes, Landgraves, and minor Royalties must have possessed intellectual or artistic interests but there was very little cultural flavour to the interminable conversations in the Rumpenheim *salons* or under the shade of the *platanenallee*. And if the company there assembled was not interested in culture, neither was it primarily concerned with politics. Whatever intrigues went on at Rumpenheim were matrimonial rather than political, thereby fulfilling the intention of the Landgrave Frederick who, believing that good things should be kept within the family, had hoped that the Rumpenheim gathering might be the means of promoting as many marriages as possible among his descendants.

Nor was the Rumpenheim gathering in any true sense cosmopolitan. This may seem surprising since to Rumpenheim came connections of the Hesse-Cassel family from nearly every country in Europe. Royal personages, however, formed a caste apart which had little to do with nationality; the visitors to Rumpenheim lived like goldfish enclosed within the glass bowl of royalty, looking out at the world but not of it, and for all the chance that the young Princess Alexandra had there of learning something about the people and customs of countries other than her own she might as well have stayed at home in her native Denmark. To the outsider Rumpenheim society would have seemed very limited and life there extremely dull, but for those who had known the place since their childhood it was a centre radiating family warmth and cosiness, the epitome of all that is implied by that untranslatable word, *gemütlichkeit.*

Princess Alexandra herself had known and loved Rumpenheim for as long as she could remember. As a very small child she had been pushed in a pram along the garden paths by her plump and pleasing cousin, Princess Mary Adelaide, daughter of that Duchess of Cambridge who had befriended Prince Christian during his visits to England. A year or two later she and her sister Princess Dagmar played there with a small boy who grew up to become the Chancellor of Prussia. The meeting between the three children was not altogether a success; years later von Bülow recounted how he had been set upon and scratched by the two little girls, an episode which is perhaps the earliest example of Princess Alexandra's belligerent attitude towards the Germans. Princess Alexandra he remembered as already blossoming into beauty; her sister had seemed the more lively and clever of the two but she had impressed the boy as being 'desperately hard-headed'.[5]

Childhood ended for Princess Alexandra with her confirmation, which took place on 20 October 1860, a few weeks before her sixteenth birthday. This occasion was an important and rather awe-inspiring one, especially to a girl as sincerely religious as she was. The ceremony was all but marred by the behaviour of Countess Danner who claimed her right to be present. Although the lady was now the King's morganatic wife she was still looked on very much askance, and Princess Alexandra's parents were greatly relieved when, having made her point, she failed in the end to put in an appearance. The confirmation service was followed by a reception given by the King himself, a function which was for the Princess something in the nature of a 'coming-out' party. From henceforth she counted as a grown-up young lady but in fact the course of her life was very little altered. True, she had fewer lessons to do – she had never had very many – but she did not go out at all in Society, for Society there was none to speak of in Copenhagen. In normal circumstances, as the daughter of the heir to the throne, she would have moved freely in Court circles but her parents did not consider a Court presided over by Countess Danner to be a desirable *milieu* for their daughter. They themselves attended Court functions only when attendance was absolutely necessary, and Princess Alexandra's party-going was limited to such innocuous gaieties as a small family dance or a concert at the home of the elderly Queen Mother.

The Princess could not but know the reason why she was forbidden to appear at Court. All Denmark was humming with scandal about Countess Danner and it is impossible that the children in the Yellow Palace should have grown up in ignorance of what went on literally next door to their home. Innocent Princess Alexandra certainly was, but presumably not ignorant. Her parents were models of virtue and propriety but some of her relations were less reputable. 'The mother's family are bad, the father's foolish,'[6] Queen Victoria wrote of these same parents and though Princess Christian's Hessian relatives were probably not as immoral as Queen Victoria imagined them to be, nevertheless the family gossip at Rumpenheim may sometimes have been less than edifying. Princess Alexandra had, besides, the good fortune to have three brothers and one at least of the three was not remarkable for a high standard of sexual morality. We have no direct evidence to show how much or how little she knew about these matters but, taking into account the reputation both of the Danish King and of some members of her own family, it is reasonable to suppose that by the time she grew up she was well aware that the married happiness of her own parents and of Queen Victoria and the Prince Consort was the exception rather than the rule in the royal households of that generation, and that fidelity was a virtue not usually to be expected of a royal husband.

Such was Princess Alexandra at the age of sixteen; a young and lovely girl, probably not ignorant but certainly unsophisticated and, because of the circumstances of her upbringing, of necessity inexperienced in the ways of the great world. The gaps in her education were lamentable and obvious; academically, she was an almost complete ignoramus. At first sight it would hardly seem to be an upbringing likely to fit her for high position or for a life spent much in the public eye. She had, however, enjoyed the great advantage of a happy childhood; growing up surrounded by love, sympathy and appreciation she had never known what it was to feel insecure. But indulgent though her parents were, the hard facts of finance had made it impossible for them to spoil their children by showering presents upon them or pampering them physically, although it must be admitted that some people considered these children to be 'spoilt' in other and more subtle ways. Princess Alexandra's lack of social experience might have been a real drawback to her had she not been blessed with natural tact and dignity and a bewitching physical grace. As a child she had been a tomboy but never a hoyden; now at sixteen it would have been as impossible for her to make an awkward movement or ungainly gesture as it would have been for her to utter a tactless or blundering remark. This charm of manner and genuine sympathy with other people went a very long way towards covering up the intellectual barrenness of her conversation. People forgot that Princess Alexandra could be a little bit of a bore; they remembered her only as an entrancing creature who combined a fairy-tale beauty with that rare and endearing quality of heart which the French call *bonté*.

Chapter two

THE PRINCE OF WALES

During the happy years of Princess Alexandra's Danish childhood across the North Sea another royal child was growing up in circumstances very different from hers. This boy was her fourth cousin, both of them being descended from King George II of England. Albert Edward, Prince of Wales, always known to his family as 'Bertie', was born on 9 November 1841, the second child and eldest son of Queen Victoria. He was thus from birth destined to succeed to the throne of what was then the greatest and most prosperous country in the world and his upbringing was designed with a view to fitting him for this high destiny. Inevitably from his earliest years he lived surrounded by royal pomp and protocol; his life was a progress from one stately home to another, Buckingham Palace, Windsor Castle, Osborne, Balmoral. He never had any personal experience of poverty in any shape or form, never knew what it meant to be obliged to do anything for himself of necessity and not from choice.

Much has been written about the system of education to which the unfortunate boy was subjected.* One point, how-

* An admirable and detailed account can be found in the first chapter of *Edward VII*, by Sir Philip Magnus.

ever, is too often forgotten; mentally and physically the Prince was pre-eminently his mother's child. Queen Victoria and the Prince Consort were loving and conscientious parents, too conscientious in fact, for it would have been better for their son had they occasionally indulged in a little judicious neglect. Of the two, his father loved him the best but understood him least; his mother may not have loved him so warmly but she understood him only too well. He had her bulging blue Hanoverian eyes, he had her receding Hanoverian chin – contrary to general belief a weak chin is often allied with a very strong character – he also had the vitality, the positiveness, the warm humanity, the phenomenal memory, the impatience of theory and the passion for concrete detail which were among her more notable characteristics. Baron Stockmar hit the nail squarely on the head when he described the Prince of Wales as an exaggerated copy of his mother, and Queen Victoria herself declared, 'he is my caricature'.[1] For this reason she never felt really at ease with him; he was the living ghost she was always trying to lay, the ghost of her unregenerate Hanoverian self, the Victoria she might have been had she never married Albert.

Unfortunately the system of education devised for the Prince of Wales took no account of his remarkable resemblance to his mother. It had been arranged with much thought and care by the Prince Consort himself, acting with the advice of Baron Stockmar, the *éminence grise* of the Saxe-Coburg-Gotha family. It might have worked admirably had the boy chanced to take after his serious-minded Germanic father, with his love of the abstract, his taste for music and art, his insatiable intellectual curiosity and his detachment from the interests and ways of thought of the common man. For the Prince of Wales as he in fact was this education proved to be a disaster. An academic, unimaginative and quite inflexible system persisted in ruthlessly day after day, year after year, clean contrary to the natural bent of the boy's mind and character, produced a result which almost amounted to a case of split personality. His first tutor, Henry Birch, remarked significantly that it was very difficult to follow any rigid system of education because 'the Prince of Wales was so different on different days'.[2] The baffling contradictions of his nature continue to puzzle posterity; few historical figures provoke such contrary feelings and judgments. At one moment he appears admirable, wise, charming; at the next, almost wholly repulsive. All human beings are inconsistent but such a Jekyll-and-Hyde personality is a rarity. In later years the Prince of Wales's natural gifts and his great good sense helped him to minimise, or at least to disguise, the psychological damage done to him by his education but he was never to develop into a properly integrated character.

After nine years of strict and almost solitary education following his seventeenth birthday in November 1858 came the first indications that his parents considered the Prince to have attained to something like responsible status. He was freed from the supervision of an uncongenial tutor, his income was increased to £500, he was created a Knight of the Garter and, much to his embarrassment, for he had wished to work his way up like any other young officer, he was gazetted a lieutenant-colonel in the British Army. More significantly still, in December 1858 there occurs the first written reference to the question which was soon to cause so much trouble and anxiety, the problem of finding him a wife.

On 22 December Feodore, Princess of Hohenlohe-Langenburg, wrote to her half-sister, Queen Victoria, a description of Princess Augusta of Meiningen, 'undeveloped, quite a child, but I should say she will be a very nice, clever, good girl'.[3] Wisely, the Queen decided that an undeveloped child, however nice, good and clever, would not make a suitable wife for her son and that she must look elsewhere. Lists were drawn up of possible princesses and as most of these princesses were German, Victoria naturally enlisted the help of her eldest child, 'Vicky', the Princess Royal, now married to the Crown Prince Frederick of Prussia. In 1859 the Crown Princess was nineteen and Walpurga or 'Wally' Hohenthal, her lady-in-waiting and chief helper in the quest for a bride for the Prince of Wales, only a year older. Many delicate and difficult negotiations were necessarily left in the hands of these two girls hardly out of their teens.

In the autumn of 1859 Wally Hohenthal accompanied the Crown Princess on a visit to England, where they found the Queen and the Prince Consort much occupied with the question of their son's marriage.* The most favoured candidate was now Elizabeth of Wied, afterwards Queen of Rumania and better known as Carmen Sylva. Stockmar, who was nevertheless inclined to favour her claims, described her as being 'to use a homely English expression, rather dowdy',[4] and the Crown Princess wrote, 'I do not consider her at all *distinguée* looking – certainly the opposite to Bertie's usual taste'. However, she remained on the *tapis* for more than a year whilst the Crown Princess and her mother discussed and dismissed 'the Weimars – very nice girls but delicate and not pretty',[5] the little Princess of Sweden, 'a dear little girl but much too young',[6] Marie of the Netherlands, Hilda of Dessau, Princess Alexandrine of Prussia, 'poor Addy, *not* clever or pretty',[7] and the almost unknown Princess Marie of Altenburg, 'shockingly dressed and always with her most disagreeable mother'.[8] Certainly the field was not a promising one. The only attracttive candidate appeared to be Princess Marie of Hohenzollern-Sigmaringen 'who is *quite lovely* and strikes everyone; all eyes are upon her when she comes into a room she is so *distinguée* and lady-like'.[9] This paragon, however, could not be considered as a possible bride for the Prince of Wales as she was by religion a Roman Catholic.

The search for a princess possessed of the qualities which Queen Victoria required of a daughter-in-law, 'good looks, health, education, character, intellect, and a good disposition',[10] was proving a dispiriting and all but impossible business. 'I think of our English Ladies,' the home-sick Crown Princess wrote wistfully, 'and their manners and appearance; and how much Bertie admires them, and of what use would cleverness be without some attractions to capture him?'[11] Mother and daughter agreed on the desirability of good looks although the Crown Princess could write in a moment of despondency, 'beauty is rare, and not really a necessity, only a pleasant ginger-bread'.[12] As well as demanding beauty, or at

* In her memoirs Walburga Paget specifically states that on the way home to Berlin after this visit, she toured Germany with the Crown Princess in search of a possible bride, ending their quest at Düsseldorf where they attended 'a huge supper-party with every available young German princess'. The correspondence between Queen Victoria and her daughter makes no mention of this improbable episode, and in fact goes to show that the Crown Princess returned from England straight to Berlin.

least attractiveness, the Queen stressed the necessity for good temper, cheerfulness, and a certain determination. She did not expect that any bride would find her position either an easy or a comfortable one and she pointed out, with some truth, that the Prince would be certain to tyrannise over a character in which feminine gentleness was not allied to firmness of will.

Both on political and personal grounds the Queen and the Crown Princess had from the very beginning ruled one Princess right out of court. No Danish bride could be considered. Tension was increasing between Denmark and the German Confederation, headed by Prussia, over the question of Schleswig-Holstein. The Crown Princess was, of course, married to the heir to the Prussian throne, whilst Queen Victoria was always pro-German in sympathy; both of them were against any Danish marriage. As far back as February 1858 the Queen had written, 'There have been more attempts to encourage an arrangement for a future marriage of one of your younger sisters with the Prince of Denmark's son, but we won't hear of it and have poured cold water upon it. It would never do.'[13] Not merely did the Queen object to the political implications of a Danish marriage; she also dreaded the influence of Princess Christian's relations. The Princess herself was beyond reproach; not so her family. As Queen Victoria was to write a year later, 'not a word can, I believe, be breathed against the mother, but against her mother and sisters, plenty!!'[14] As well as disapproving of Princess Christian's Hesse-Cassel relations the Queen also disliked the idea of a close connection with the Danish Royal Family which, according to Mr Roger Fulford, 'at this time was conspicuously decadent'. Clearly enough, Princess Alexandra would not be a welcome daughter-in-law.

One of Queen Victoria's chief objections to marriage with any of Princess Christian's children was the close link existing between the Danish family and the Cambridges, those cousins whom she viewed with such mixed feelings. For George, Duke of Cambridge, she had genuine affection and she cherished a dutiful love for her Aunt Augusta, the Dowager Duchess, but she neither liked nor approved of the Duchess's two daughters, the Grand Duchess Augusta of Mecklenburg-Strelitz and Princess Mary Adelaide. In particular, she was irritated almost beyond endurance by Princess Mary Adelaide's irresponsibility. She would have been less than pleased had she known that already the Duchess of Cambridge and Admiral van Dickum, the Danish Minister in London, were putting their heads together in an attempt to arrange a marriage between the Prince of Wales and the Duchess's great-niece, Princess Alexandra. For the moment, however, nothing came of their scheming. The first person, apparently, to put forward Princess Alexandra's name seriously was Wally Hohenthal, who, in October 1860, married Augustus Paget, British Minister in Copenhagen. During her wedding tour of England she was bidden to dine at Windsor where she found herself seated next the Prince Consort. Greatly daring, she broached the subject of the Prince of Wales's marriage – 'I told him that Mr Paget had often seen Princess Alix and thought her the most charming, pretty, and delightful young Princess it was possible to imagine.'[15]

Wally Paget must have been a persuasive advocate since both the Prince and the Queen, who had previously been so firm against a Danish marriage, now took up the idea with some enthusiasm. Apparently the Crown Princess was asked to collect information for on 7 December she wrote to her mother in some detail about this new candidate:

> 'I send you now a photograph of Prince Christian's lovely daughter. I have seen several people who have seen her of late – and who give such accounts of her beauty, her charm, her amiability, her frank natural manner and many excellent qualities. I thought it right to tell you all this in Bertie's interest, though I as Prussian cannot wish Bertie should ever marry her. I know her nurse who tells me she is strong in health and has never ailed anything. . . . I must say on the photograph I think her lovely and just the style Bertie admires, but I repeat that an alliance with Denmark would be a misfortune for us here.'[16]

The photograph won the day for Princess Alexandra. Immediately, the Prince Consort capitulated to her beauty; 'from the photograph,' he exclaimed, 'I would marry her at once.'[17] 'The one of Princess Alexandra is indeed lovely,'

Queen Victoria wrote, 'what a pity she is who she is!'[18] The Crown Princess herself must have been equally impressed because on sending a second photograph she cautioned her mother not to let the Prince of Wales see it 'or he *must* fall in love with it, for it really is most fascinating, charming'.[19] As a good Prussian, however, she was bound to oppose the idea of a Danish marriage and she continued to canvass the claims of other candidates, picturing herself as turning over the leaves of the *Almanach de Gotha* in the vain hope of discovering the name of a suitable princess who had somehow or other so far escaped her notice.

Queen Victoria now inclined towards the idea of Princess Alexandra as a possible bride, despite all drawbacks. 'You ask me whether I heard any more about the Danish beauty,' the Crown Princess wrote rather tartly on 19 February 1861. 'I hear almost every week about her but never mentioned it as I thought you did not wish to hear more about her and were determined not to give her another thought.'[20] The Queen, however, was prepared for second thoughts and as soon as she had recovered a little from her grief at her mother's death, which took place on 16 March, she reverted to the subject, with the more earnestness now that other suitors were reported to be in the field. 'It would be dreadful', the Crown Princess wrote in reply, 'if this pearl were to go to the horrid Russians.'[21]

Everybody was now agreed that the Prince of Wales's happiness must take precedence over all other considerations and that the only bride with whom he was likely to be happy was Princess Alexandra. Even the Queen of Prussia, who of all people might be most certainly expected to oppose such a match, agreed with this point of view. 'The Queen taxes her brains all day long on this subject,' the Crown Princess wrote, 'and has arrived at the same conclusions as I have – that is, that the accounts of Princess Alix sound better than those she could give of any other German princess she knew, but that she is of course much against the match for other reasons.'[22] As yet the Crown Princess was only going on hearsay for she had never set eyes on Princess Alexandra. Obviously the next step was to invite Prince and Princess Christian and their daughter to Berlin, but both the Crown Princess and the Queen of Prussia advised against this plan. Berlin was too full of unmarried Princes; 'the lovely daughter may be snapped up before we are aware of it'.[23] The only other place which suggested itself for a meeting was Mecklenburg-Strelitz, the home of Queen Victoria's cousin, the Grand Duchess Augusta, daughter of the Duchess of Cambridge. Above all, the Queen wished to prevent the Cambridge family from having any hand in this business of the Prince of Wales's marriage. In an oddly expressed, undated memorandum from Osborne she noted two points to be especially avoided:

'1. That it should be a political marriage – the young Princess must put strong Danish feelings, if she has any, in her pocket.
2. That the parents should in any way owe it to the Cambridges and that any negotiations or arrangements should be through them.'[24]

Now, however, at the very beginning of the negotiations Queen Victoria was obliged to jettison the second clause of this memorandum and to put herself under an obligation to the cousins of whom she disapproved so much. The Crown Princess wrote the Grand Duchess Augusta of Mecklenburg-Strelitz a somewhat disingenuous letter, proposing a visit at the end of May but making no mention of any Danish princess, although she very well knew that on the suggested date Princess Alexandra and her mother would be staying at Strelitz.

Cousin Augusta proved co-operative and to Strelitz the Crown Princess and her husband 'Fritz' accordingly went on 29 May. At once they were both captivated by Princess Alexandra's beauty and charm of manner – 'I never set eyes upon a sweeter creature than Princess Alix; she is lovely!'[25]

The Crown Princess's attempt to describe this loveliness shows how impossible it is to convey beauty by compiling a catalogue of beautiful features; her uninspired description is, however, worth quoting as giving the actual facts about Princess Alexandra's appearance:

'She is a good deal taller than I am, has a lovely figure but very thin, a complexion as beautiful as possible. Very fine white regular teeth and very fine large eyes – with extremely prettily marked eyebrows. A very fine well-shaped nose, very narrow but a little long – her whole face is very narrow, her forehead too but well shaped and not at all flat. Her voice, her walk, carriage and manner are perfect, she is one of the most ladylike and aristocratic looking people I ever saw.'[26]

Oddly enough, she says nothing about Princess Alexandra's colouring, the deep blue of her eyes, the soft brown of her hair, her skin like peaches and cream, so different from the pink and white tints and extreme blonde fairness of the English Royal Family.

The Crown Princess was enchanted not only by Princess Alexandra's appearance but also by her unstudied charm of manner, 'she is as simple and natural and unaffected as possible – and seems exceedingly well brought up'.[27] Though Alexandra was the younger by five years she appeared to be quite at her ease, which was the more surprising since the two princesses had in fact very little in common. The Crown Princess was essentially intellectual; except for her maternal passion for babies and small children, a subject that could hardly be of much concern to the sixteen-year-old Princess Alexandra, all her interests were on the intellectual level. Some of her portraits show her to be a very attractive young woman by modern standards but in her own day she was praised for her brains rather than for her beauty.

Clever girls do not always take kindly to noted beauties, but after this meeting at Strelitz the Crown Princess was writing to her mother in almost extravagant terms; 'graceful', 'bewitching', 'indescribably charming' are only a few of the epithets which she bestows on Princess Alexandra. Her enthusiasm certainly ran away with her judgment on some points, for she declared that Princess Alexandra spoke English without the slightest accent; in fact she spoke it with a very heavy Danish accent and continued to do so until the day of her death. Even so, she did not go so far as to pronounce Princess Alexandra clever; all she would say was that she could not 'perceive the slightest thing to make me think the contrary'.[28]

To her father, the Crown Princess wrote that Princess

Alexandra's education 'seems to have been a very good one, i.e. a *natural* one – and one of the heart',[29] the opposite, therefore, of the education which had been inflicted on the Prince of Wales. In this same letter to the Prince Consort she couples Princess Alexandra's name with that of the royal personage who was always to be her friendly rival for the palm of beauty, 'I never saw a lady since the Empress Eugénie who made such an impression upon me.' That a sixteen-year-old girl, straight from the seclusion of the schoolroom, could stand comparison with the Empress Eugénie is sufficiently surprising. What is still more remarkable is the fact that this girl's beauty, charm and character were enough in themselves not merely to reconcile both the Crown Prince and the Crown Princess of Prussia to a match so contrary to Prussia's interests that the Crown Prince could describe it as 'the very worst that could happen to us',[30] but also to turn these two people into ardent propagandists for such a marriage.

'You are I know perhaps a little inclined to be carried away if you are pleased with a person,' Queen Victoria wrote in very gentle criticism of her daughter's outpourings, 'but Fritz is not and as he so entirely coincides with what you say about Princess Alix (why is she called so?) I feel quite sure she really must be charming in every sense of the word – and really a pearl not to be lost.'[31] Immediately the Queen set about the business of securing this pearl for the Prince of Wales, fearing lest any long delay might further the chances of other suitors. The chief rival at that moment was the Prince of Orange, whose mother, the Queen of Holland, had lost no time in making approaches to Prince and Princess Christian. It had not been possible to keep the purpose of the Strelitz visit a complete secret although many people supposed that the Crown Princess had gone there on behalf of her husband's cousin, 'Abbat', Prince Albrecht of Prussia.

The other party to the proposed marriage had already been informed of the plans being made for his future. As early as April 1861 the Prince Consort had taken his son into his confidence. The Prince of Wales's reaction was one of tempered enthusiasm; he pointed out the dangers of proposing in haste and repenting at leisure – 'in these days if a person rashly proposes and then repents, the relations, if not the lady herself, do not let him off so easily".[32] Queen Victoria was less than pleased with the behaviour and appearance of her eldest son; commenting on his 'sallow, dull, heavy, blasé look' she exclaimed, 'May he only be worthy of such a jewel! There is the rub!'[33] She even had moments when she doubted whether Princess Alexandra would accept him. Otherwise nobody seems to have troubled very much about the girl's reactions, taking for granted that a penniless princess would be delighted to marry the Prince of Wales. Meanwhile, the Prince's Comptroller, General Bruce, had no hesitation in commending the proposed bride; 'the description is indeed most captivating,' he wrote to the Prince Consort, 'and to my eyes has shed a bright gleam of light upon a somewhat dark future.'[34]

Other people were not so enthusiastic, especially if their political sympathies happened to be with Germany. Chief among the objectors were Stockmar, now a very old man, and the Prince Consort's brother, Ernst of Saxe-Coburg-Gotha, a character perfectly cast for his role of Wicked Uncle.

Stockmar set out his arguments against the proposed marriage in a typically ponderous letter:

> 'Since the affair is based on the condition that one party has the solid features of character that the other party is missing, the certainty of the existence of such features would have to be a *conditio sine qua non*. What we know for certain, however, is only youth and beauty. I am wondering whether the important moral powers that we need are available as well? And if they are, may we assume from the up-bringing and the family conditions, that they have brought about development and fundamental satisfaction?'[35]

It was now that the Crown Princess first referred to a small matter that was later to be magnified into a large objection. She had noticed on Princess Alexandra's neck a scar which could have been caused by scrofula and might therefore be a sign of a tubercular tendency. Happily these fears proved groundless, both Wally Paget and the Grand Duchess Augusta assuring her that the mark was merely the result of a neglected cold. The scar which might have altered history by preventing the Princess's marriage in fact influenced nothing more serious than the course of fashion. As a very young woman Princess Alexandra wore her hair in ringlets; later, when she wished to dress it high, thus exposing her neck, she invented the jewelled 'dog-collar' to hide the unsightly mark. These dog-collars became the rage and for fifty years or more every fashionable woman wore one when in evening dress.

The Prince of Wales had expressed a natural wish to meet his proposed bride. This summer of 1861 he was in camp at the Curragh near Dublin, temporarily attached to the Grenadier Guards. It would not therefore seem surprising that he should visit German Army manœuvres in the Rhineland and then join his sister the Crown Princess at Baden, which was conveniently near to Rumpenheim where Princess Alexandra and her family would be staying. A 'chance' encounter could be arranged, Princess Christian meanwhile doing her utmost not to attract 'the attention of the 43 members of our Rumpenheim family'.[36] With this meeting in view Queen Victoria sent a lengthy questionnaire to the Crown Princess, who returned a series of curiously negative answers:

1.	*Question*	If the young people seem to like each other, what is to be done?
	Answer	Nothing.
2.	*Question*	Should the Mother (Princess Christian) not be told that the impression has been favourable?
	Answer	Not necessary.
3.	*Question*	What should be the next step?
	Answer	To wait until Bertie has reported home.
4.	*Question*	How long should the visit (of Princess Christian's) last?
	Answer	Left in our hands.
5.	*Question*	Should the impression be made known to Princess Christian by writing (after she has left) or verbally?
	Answer	(None)
6.	*Question*	How long should Bertie stay?
	Answer	Left in our hands.
7.	*Question*	May Bertie's coming to Germany be spoken of?

Answer	Yes.
8. *Question*	Supposing the Princess Christian wishes to know if the favourable impression produced by her daughter would lead to anything further what is to be said?
Answer	(None)
9. *Question*	Is the Princess Christian after this visit or interview to be put in direct correspondence with *us* or whether all letters are still to go through Vicky?
Answer	Through me (Vicky).
10. *Question*	If Princess Christian asks what she is to say to her husband, what is to be answered?
Answer	Nothing.
11. *Question*	Should the Princess Christian not be told (supposing that the Parties like each other) that the marriage can only succeed if it is *not* a political one; – that Princess Alexandra must not have any political views; – that she ought to come to Germany for a time to Vicky, and then later to us for some time, that, however, in the *latter* case, she must be *entirely with us*, that I should have the *entire* control over her; that she should *not* go out with the Duchess of Cambridge and Mary and the Princess Christian ought to know, that the Duchess of Cambridge and Mary, though very kind to us and ours, are *not* fit to give a young Princess advice as to society and behaviour in it for that they unfortunately have done themselves *much* harm by the way in which they have gone about everywhere and by the familiar tone which Mary has been allowed to have with gentlemen as well as with ladies?
Answer	To be borne in mind. Can be.[37]

With this inconclusive missive as guide, clear in nothing but its condemnation of the Cambridges, and with the answer to the vital Question Eight left significantly blank, the Crown Princess set about making her arrangements. The attempt at secrecy, of course, failed; whilst the Prince of Wales was on holiday in Scotland he was much annoyed by paragraphs appearing in the English press on the subject of his marriage whilst a German paper actually mentioned the proposed meeting in the Rhineland.

One person, however, was still in complete ignorance. On the morning of 24 September a very puzzled Princess Alexandra knocked at the door of Princess Mary Adelaide's room at Rumpenheim. That day, she explained to her cousin, she was to go with her parents on an excursion to Speyer. In 1861 railway journeys were an extremely dusty and dirty form of travel and she had naturally thought to put on an old dress, a spoilt frock being a serious matter to a girl as badly-off as she was. To her surprise her mother, usually so careful and thrifty about clothes, had ordered her to wear her very best outfit. What could be the reason for this unprecedented command?

As Prince and Princess Christian with their family were admiring the beauties of Speyer Cathedral in the chapel of St Bernard they came upon the Crown Princess and her husband. With them, of course, was the Prince of Wales. He had perhaps been told too much about Princess Alexandra's beauty for his first reaction was one of disappointment. Her nose was too long, her forehead too low. She proved, however, to be such a lively and charming companion that at the end of a quarter-of-an-hour's conversation he was prepared to overlook these defects and recognise that she was indeed lovely – 'the reverse of indifference on both sides soon became quite unmistakeable'.[38] Meanwhile the Crown Princess talked to Princess Christian whom she was delighted to find 'so quick and sharp', in spite of the handicap of deafness. The Prince Consort, she thought, would have enjoyed a conversation with this lively woman, so quick of apprehension that she might almost 'hear the grass grow'. Princess Christian agreed, or pretended to agree, with Queen Victoria's opinion of the Cambridge family; she had been so shocked by Princess Mary Adelaide's flirtatious manner that she had warned her own daughter not to behave in similar fashion unless she wished to have her ears boxed. Prince Christian, 'handsome in appearance and a perfect gentleman', was especially to be commended for the tactful way in which he refrained from embarrassing the Prince of Wales with over-pressing attentions.[39]

The two parties travelled together as far as Heidelberg where again they 'chanced' to be spending the night in the same hotel. Before saying goodbye the two young people exchanged signed photographs. Both the Crown Princess and her husband were delighted at the results of the meeting; the Prince of Wales however would commit himself no farther than to write, 'We met the Prince and Princess Christian and the young lady of whom I had heard so much, and I can now candidly say that I think her charming and very pretty.'[40]

The Prince's unaccountable lack of enthusiasm now appeared as the chief obstacle in the way of the proposed match. He had been undoubtedly attracted by Princess Alexandra; it was not the proposed bride but the idea of marriage itself which seemed to dismay him. 'A sudden fear of marriage, and, above all, of having children which for so young a man is so strange a fear, seems to have got hold of him,'[41] Queen Victoria wrote in bewilderment. The Crown Princess found it incomprehensible that 'that sweet lovely flower which would make most men fire and flames' should have made so slight an impression – 'If she fails to kindle a flame none will ever succeed in doing so.'[42]

On 7 October the Prince Consort addressed a ponderous memorandum to his son in an attempt to put an end to this strange hesitancy. The Prince of Wales had expressed a desire to marry young, a desire 'based on the conviction that it would be impossible for you to lead with any chance of success or comfort for yourself a protracted bachelor life'. A meeting had therefore been arranged with a charming princess and on his return the Prince had given his parents 'a most favourable report of the Princess, whose beauty appears to be almost perfect, whose manners and deportment you report as very distinguished and refined, and whose education appears to have been remarkably good'. Why, then, this hesitation? The Prince, of course, could not be sure of knowing his own mind after so short an acquaintance, 'unless you had actually fallen in love (which, after this apparent hesitation, can hardly be supposed to be the case)'. Another meeting would therefore be arranged but 'you must clearly understand that this interview is obtained . . . in order that you may propose to the young Lady if she pleases you on further acquaintance as much as she did at first'. The Prince must not indulge in 'a general vague apprehension that you might someday meet someone else you might like better', and thereby lose 'positive and present advantages for the hope of future chances which may never occur'.[43] A beautiful princess in the hand was in fact worth any number of possible paragons in the bush.

Seldom has a more peremptory pistol been held at the head of a reluctant lover. Then, suddenly and catastrophically, the reason for this hesitancy became painfully clear. A story which had been going the round of the London clubs at last reached the Prince Consort's ears; the previous summer, when in camp at the Curragh, his son had indulged in a love-affair with an actress called Nelly Clifden.

Such an entanglement was perhaps only to be expected. Months earlier General Bruce had hinted broadly at such a possibility: 'there are elements of moral danger which we must take into account and which may hereafter be productive of difficulty and embarrassment.'[44] The Prince of Wales was behaving as most of his companions behaved; fornication was the fashionable thing among smart young men and especially among smart young army officers. The average father would not have been unduly shocked. The Prince Consort, however, was anything but an average father. In that robust and not particularly squeamish age he fondly hoped that his sons would enter marriage virginal and unspotted by any previous sexual experience. Remembering their position, exposed to all the temptations that beset the path of princes, remembering too their ancestry on both sides, the reputation of the Prince Consort's own father and brother and Queen Victoria's monstrous regiment of uncles, this hope would seem pathetically unrealistic and unreasonable, but where sexual morality was concerned the Prince Consort, that eminently reasonable man, became blind and deaf to reason. He now wrote his son a long letter which would have been a piece of gross and deliberate cruelty had the writer's own suffering not been apparent in every line. Even so, the letter reveals a lack of sympathy so complete as to explain, and therefore partly to excuse, some of the least attractive features in the Prince of Wales's character.

The Prince of Wales replied with what Sir Philip Magnus describes as 'heartfelt and pellucid simplicity'. He had indeed yielded to temptation but the affair was now finished and he could only express his contrition for what had occurred. The Prince Consort relented sufficiently to go down to Cambridge to see his son and returned feeling much relieved but physically exhausted. In a letter to the Crown Princess dated 29 November he admitted that he was at 'a very low ebb'. On 2 December he collapsed with typhoid fever and on 14 December he was dead.

Chapter three

ENGAGEMENT AND MARRIAGE

Queen Victoria was convinced that distress over the Nelly Clifden affair had fatally undermined the Prince Consort's strength; she believed that the Prince of Wales was the direct cause of his father's death. Her obsession on this point was so powerful that she even urged the Crown Princess to say something on the subject to Princess Christian: 'Quite in ignorance of the character of Bertie the Mother must not be – for were the poor girl to be very unhappy I could not answer for it before God had she been entrapped into it.'[1] Princess Christian in fact heard of the Prince of Wales's escapade from her cousin, the Duke of Cambridge. She was deeply distressed, not so much by the Prince's lapse from virtue as by the not altogether accurate news that there was very serious discord between the Queen and her son. Wally Paget found her in floods of tears over the Duke's letter, declaring that she feared her daughter's position would be a very difficult one since if the Queen really disliked her son so intensely she was bound also to dislike his wife.

Queen Victoria, however, was determined that the plans for the marriage must go forward, although mourning had put a stop to any idea of an immediate engagement. The Prince

Consort had approved the match and with her his wishes now had the force of law. 'The marriage is the thing and beloved Papa was most anxious for it,' she wrote to her daughter; 'I feel it is a sacred duty he, our darling angel, left us to perform.'[2] She was touched to hear that Princess Alexandra had spoken 'so prettily and feelingly' about the Prince Consort's death, with a special word of sympathy for the Prince of Wales himself.

The Prince's own attitude, however, was far from clear. The Queen planned to send him on a tour of the Middle East in order to avoid 'a constant contact which is more than ever unbearable to me',[3] and when he left England on 6 February she still professed herself uncertain as to his matrimonial intentions. But if the Prince of Wales would not have Princess Alexandra his brother Prince Alfred was willing and anxious to do so. 'Affie' made no secret of the fact that he would like this beautiful girl whom, incidentally, he had never seen, for his own bride. 'If Bertie turns obstinate,' the Queen wrote, 'I will withdraw myself altogether and wash my hands of him. Affie would be ready to take her at once and really if Bertie refuses her (which no one thinks he will) I would recommend Affie's engaging to marry her in three years.'[4]

In Denmark the uncertainty of the situation was not unnaturally preying upon Princess Christian's mind (significantly enough, all negotiations were done by the mother, the father remaining silent in the background). Without consulting her daughter Princess Christian had on her own responsibility refused a tentative proposal from Russia, thinking a Prince of Wales a more eligible *parti* than a Czarevitch. Now, fearing that after all the English marriage might come to nothing, she wished, as the Crown Princess expressed it, 'to have the Czarevitch in reserve'.[5] She therefore became so reluctant, where previously she had appeared all enthusiasm, that Queen Victoria could only suppose that the stories about the Prince of Wales had reached her ears by way of the Cambridge family: 'Has perhaps Princess Christian heard of poor wretched Bertie's miserable escapade and thinks him a regular *mauvais sujet*?'[6] the Queen wrote in great alarm, forgetful that two months previously she herself had been insistent that Princess Christian should be told about his bad behaviour. She was so fearful lest Wally Paget should be spoiling the simple Princess Alexandra that apprehension made her quite incoherent:

'One word about Princess Alix; don't encourage too much dressing or smartness; great quietness and simplicity – going to the opposite of loud or smart dress – like our foolish English girls; for God's sake don't let Wally try to encourage them to catch the poor Boy by that – fashionable dressing – anything but that.'[7]

The Queen had completely failed to understand her son's reaction to the Prince Consort's death. Stunned and distressed by the tragedy, he had not been able to turn his mind immediately to thoughts of marriage. Now, however, he had had time to recover from the shock. On his way back from the East he broke his journey in Paris where he spent his time buying jewels and pretty trinkets for his intended bride, and when he arrived in England the Queen found him 'immensely improved' and most anxious for marriage.

Other people, however, were equally anxious that the marriage should not take place. Both Stockmar and Ernst of Coburg were still hot against the scheme and scandal about Princess Alexandra and her family circulated freely. The old story of the scrofulous origin of the scar on her neck was revived, whilst far more damaging tales were repeated on every hand. On hearing of the meeting at Speyer, the Crown Princess's sister-in-law, Louise of Prussia, had insisted that both Prince and Princess Christian were most undesirable characters: 'the father is a drunkard and for some time the mother bore a very bad reputation.'[8] In January 1862 the Crown Princess wrote: 'Monsieur de Roggenbach, Doctor Meyer, Fritz Holstein, and Uncle Ernst all repeated verbally and by letter the story that Princess Christian had had illegitimate children and Princess Alix had had flirtations with the young officers, one of whom had been removed from the neighbourhood in consequence.'[9]

Wally Paget and her husband had no difficulty in exposing these tales as fabrications but, virtuous though Princess Christian and her daughter might be, some of their relations were not so blameless. The old Landgravine, Princess Alexandra's grandmother, was said to be 'wicked and very intriguing, besides not respectable', whilst, according to the

Crown Princess, the story about an illegitimate child properly belonged to Princess Alexandra's aunt, the Princess of Dessau. Another aunt, Augusta, 'married to Monsieur (Baron) Blixen, was separated from him and not at all respectable; her husband, you know, is an adventurer'.[10] This same Baron Blixen was causing much alarm to his sister-in-law, Princess Christian. He was determined to put a stop to the proposed marriage and with that end in view he was on his way to England, where she feared that he might make great play with his position as Princess Alexandra's uncle and do much harm by his untrue stories. The Queen might well shrink from the thought of the Prince of Wales marrying into such a family.

It was left to Sir Charles Phipps, Keeper of the Privy Purse, to point out that the Prince was not marrying Princess Alexandra's family, but the Princess herself: 'Were the choice between the Princess and another, in other respects as desirable, the misconduct of the relations might have well been considered a bar to seeking this Princess for the Prince of Wales. But this is not so; there is no other princess whose charm and agreeable manners can compare with those of Princess Alexandra.' Sir Charles pointed out that 'it is of the *first importance* that the Prince of Wales's wife should have beauty, agreeable manners, and the power of attracting people to her, and these the Princess Alexandra seems to possess in a remarkable degree'. He made the sensible observation that 'with a virtuous and well-educated girl, the ill-repute of some members of her family usually adds to her horror of vice'.[11] Clearly, this seventeen-year-old girl had so high a reputation for goodness, charm and beauty that, in spite of scandal and gossip, sensible men considered her to be not merely a possible but an ideal wife for the heir to the throne.

Somewhat reassured on the question of Princess Alexandra's family the Queen fell to tormenting herself about the Prince of Wales's attitude. She feared that he was embarking on marriage solely with a view to self-gratification, without giving proper thought to his responsibilities towards his future wife. In a touching and transparently sincere letter he tried to reassure his mother, stressing his desire to be of service to her and to his country, and above all, his determination that, should the Princess accept him, he would do his very best to make her happy.

From the mass of existing evidence it is easy enough to discover the Prince's reactions and those of his family but it is far more difficult to ascertain what Princess Alexandra's feelings may have been. She remained completely silent about the impression made on her by the meeting at Speyer, a silence which her mother interpreted favourably. Not till the New Year of 1862 did the rumours of an impending marriage come to her ears and then her first reaction was one of anger that gossip should have made so free with her name. Her mother, however, pointed out that rumour had not been so very wrong since another meeting between her and the Prince of Wales had already been suggested. Princess Christian left her daughter's choice nominally free whilst making very clear to her the advantages of such a match and Princess Alexandra, for her part, appeared anything but unwilling to meet the Prince of Wales again. She may not have had much say in deciding her own fate but she was very far from objecting to the fate arranged for her.

Queen Victoria was about to visit Germany on pilgrimage to the Prince Consort's childhood home and, being anxious to see Princess Alexandra for herself, she arranged to visit her uncle Leopold, King of the Belgians, at Laeken, which was conveniently near to Ostend where Prince and Princess Christian would be staying with their family. When Queen Victoria left for Germany the Prince of Wales was to come to Laeken in order that he might propose to Princess Alexandra.

Queen Victoria arrived at Laeken on 2 September. The following day came the meeting with the Danish family. This was an awkward occasion since nervousness made Princess Christian more than usually deaf whilst the Queen remained constrained and shy, missing the support of her husband. After an exchange of polite sentiments, Prince Christian, whose part had hitherto been a completely passive one, remarked that his daughter was 'a good child, not brilliant, but with a will of her own'.[12] In this pedestrian but truthful summary of Princess Alexandra's character Prince Christian stressed the two qualities which Queen Victoria specially desired to see in her son's wife, genuine goodness and the spirit to stand up for herself when and if necessary.

Queen Victoria admitted to finding the parents 'not very

sympathique', adding, however, 'Alexandra looks as if she were quite different and above them all.'[13] No wonder then that she should describe this interview as most trying to her. Princess Alexandra's own trial was still to come. Difficult as the situation was for Queen Victoria it was far more alarming for the seventeen-year-old girl brought to be inspected by this formidable monarch. However, Princess Alexandra showed no undue trepidation but only a sufficiently becoming shyness when she came later that evening to pay her respects to her future mother-in-law. In tactful recognition of Queen Victoria's mourning she wore a plain black dress without any jewels. Her hair was simply turned back from her forehead to fall in long ringlets to her shoulders. The effect was one of breathtaking simplicity and loveliness, and at once the Queen's heart warmed towards this exquisite young creature who was to be her son's wife. She spoke kindly to her and presented her with a sprig of white heather picked by the Prince at Balmoral, saying that she hoped it would bring her luck. Princess Alexandra was much moved and her emotion showed in her face – 'the dear child looked so affectionately and kindly at me'. In her turn the Queen was entirely captivated and she praised the girl in the highest terms possible, 'How He would have doted on her and loved her!'[14]

Meanwhile the Prince of Wales had made a special journey to Windsor, and there, with the simple piety that was one part of his contradictory nature, he laid a wreath on his father's coffin 'and prayed for dear Papa's blessing for the step which I am about to take'.[15] The next day he left for Ostend. Princess Alexandra had now to face the meeting with her future husband, whom she had seen but once in her life and then only for a few brief hours.

On their arrival at Ostend, the Prince's Comptroller, Sir William Knollys, was struck by his charge's unaccustomed air of happiness and enthusiasm; he was equally delighted by Princess Alexandra's simple dignity and her total lack of affectation. She was looking her loveliest; in spite of Queen Victoria's strictures Wally Paget had seen to it that she was equipped with a few more sophisticated and fashionable frocks than those which Princess Christian had thought suitable. The Prince of Wales left that evening for Brussels with his mind made up; he was determined to ask this beautiful girl to be his wife. The next day, when the Danish family visited him at Brussels, he took the opportunity to tell Prince Christian of his intentions; 'I never saw anybody so pleased as he',[16] was his naive comment on the reactions of his future father-in-law. On 9 September the whole party met again at Laeken. King Leopold tactfully suggested a walk in the gardens where it was easy enough for the Prince and Princess to fall behind the rest of the party. She gave him an opening by showing him the Queen's sprig of white heather. He proposed and at once she accepted him. He asked her not to be too hasty but to consider the matter carefully. That, she replied, she had done long ago. Was she indeed sure that she liked him well enough to become his wife? Yes, she answered, and kissed him.

One question inevitably arises – were these two young people, who were so slightly acquainted, in love with one another? Sir Charles Phipps had no doubts on the subject; he was certain that the Prince of Wales at least was not. Writing from Brussels on the very day of the proposal he commented to Queen Victoria, 'It would be absurd to suppose that a real feeling of *love* could as yet exist for a person whom His Royal Highness has only seen in all for a few hours.'[17] But, given the smallest excuse for so doing, the Prince was ready and anxious to fall in love with the girl who had been selected as his bride. Ever since the discovery of the Nelly Clifden episode he had been told over and over again that his only hope of salvation lay in an early marriage. Both the Prince of Wales and Princess Alexandra had been brought up to expect that their marriages would be arranged for them, and for him at least the choice of a partner was very limited. As a writer in the *Saturday Review* remarked, 'a man who can only marry seven women may count himself singularly fortunate if one of the seven unites so many recommendations as the Princess Alexandra'. The Prince of Wales was clearly delighted by the enthusiastic praise of Princess Alexandra which met him on every side; it gratified his pride to know that someone in whom he already felt a proprietary interest was so universally admired. He had a connoisseur's eye for a pretty woman and here was one of the loveliest women in the world willing and anxious to marry him. She was not only beautiful; she was also warmhearted, ready to give him the affection that he so badly needed. It is not surprising that, three days after he had been accepted by the Princess, he could write to his mother in words which have the unmistakeable ring of truth, 'I frankly avow to you that I did not think it possible to love a person so much as I love her.'[18]

Princess Alexandra's own feelings are much more difficult to assess. At Brussels, before the actual proposal, both Wally Paget and Countess Reventlow had reported her as being 'very much taken' with the Prince of Wales, and it seems as if at this stage she was the more in love of the two. The Prince's letter to his mother describing the proposal scene reads as if even at that eleventh hour he had remained a little uncertain whilst Princess Alexandra had no doubts or hesitation. How should it have been otherwise? A young girl, brought up in seclusion and comparative poverty, is wooed by the most eligible young man in the world, and, should he choose to exert himself, one of the most attractive – 'he turns most ladies' heads',[19] wrote the Crown Princess of her brother. The favourite author of Princess Alexandra's childhood, Hans Andersen, might have invented just such a story; it is the classic fairy-tale situation worked out in real life.

To measure love is fortunately an impossibility but, whatever may have been the exact nature of the Prince and Princess's feelings, those who saw them together in the days following their engagement were in no doubt as to their happiness. They went riding and the Prince of Wales was filled with admiration for her iron nerve; she played the piano and sang to him in her peculiarly sweet voice. Queen Victoria had laid down that even after the engagement the lovers should only be allowed to see each other alone 'in a room next to the Princess's mother's with the door open, for a short while',[20] but it seems that Princess Christian may have been a little more lenient.

Princess Alexandra was at particular pains to make herself pleasant to the elderly invalid King Leopold, who was not unnaturally flattered by the attention paid him by this lovely young girl – 'the dear child is very kind to me'.[21] King Leopold was an extremely shrewd judge of character and one of his remarks to Queen Victoria is especially penetrating and prophetic: 'There is something frank and cheerful in Alix's character, which will greatly assist her to take things without being too much overpowered or alarmed by them.'[22] In another letter he writes, 'I have no doubt *qu'elle se formera bien.*'[23] As yet, however, the Princess was quite unformed, a fact which never seems to have struck either Queen Victoria or her daughter, the Crown Princess, eager as they were to entrust the Prince of Wales to such very inexperienced hands. Perhaps they were misled by Princess Alexandra's manner, which was poised and dignified beyond her years. As for the Prince, he was still very immature; 'his is a nature which develops itself slowly,' his sister wrote, 'I think you will find that he will go on improving and that his marriage will do a great deal for him in that way.'[24] Development was to be a keynote in this marriage, or so his family fondly hoped. The question was, in what direction would husband and wife help each other to develop?

The lovers were only to be allowed a short time together in which to enjoy their happiness. 'Tuesday will be a very trying time for us,' the Prince wrote to Queen Victoria on 14 September, 'as it will be our first parting, but I hope not for very long.'[25] Any such hope was doomed to disappointment for the Queen had determined that her son was not to visit Denmark. The Schleswig-Holstein problem was growing more and more acute and war between Denmark and Germany seemed inevitable. In these circumstances a visit to Copenhagen by the Prince of Wales might be construed as a political gesture, and even if it could be shown to have no political significance it would be certain to exacerbate the feelings of the Prince's German relations. The Crown Princess's part in arranging his Danish marriage had already made her so unpopular in Prussia that she and the Crown Prince deemed it prudent to absent themselves on a Mediterranean cruise and the Queen decided that the Prince of Wales should accompany them on this tour.

Political expedience, however, was not the real motive behind the Queen's decision; as General Grey wrote, 'it is the fear, I might almost say the horror, the Queen has of the Princess's mother's relations.'[26] The Prince was not to be allowed to go to Copenhagen for fear of 'family influence';

instead, Princess Alexandra was to come over to England in November to stay with the Queen. By that time, however, he would be far away on his Mediterranean cruise. The prospect was a bleak one both for Princess Alexandra, who complained that she was being sent to England 'on approval', and for the Prince of Wales, who was by now head over heels in love. 'Just interrupted by our "lover",' wrote the Queen's lady-in-waiting, Lady Augusta Bruce, 'in a state about his bride and all her affairs, too tender and so very, very dear, a love-letter of twelve pages brought forward to be quoted and held crumpled up for fear that the zephyrs should blow upon it!'[27] But the Queen was adamant; she wanted her future daughter-in-law all to herself.

Prince Christian was to escort his daughter to Osborne but it was made clear to him that he was only to stay two nights. As soon as the party stepped on board the British ship *Black Eagle,* Princess Alexandra sat down to write the Prince her very first letter from British territory. A quarter-of-a-century later she vividly remembered how 'terribly frightened' she had been at the prospect of spending weeks alone with Queen Victoria in the gloomy seclusion of Osborne without even a lady-in-waiting of her own in whom she could confide.[28] None of her alarm, however, showed in her face or bearing as she landed late on the foggy but moonlit evening of 5 November, to be greeted only by Princess Helena, known as 'Lenchen', and the little Prince Leopold, aged nine. 'The great representative of the House of England,' to use Lady Augusta's phrase, had been much worried about the bouquet entrusted to his care. All anxieties were forgotten, however, the moment Princess Alexandra appeared. Graceful, smiling, and apparently entirely at her ease, she immediately took the little boy in her arms and gave him a big kiss, thus initiating a loving brother-and-sister relationship which was to bring occasional flashes of brightness into Prince Leopold's short and deeply overshadowed life. The Princess always had the gift of shedding brightness around her; Queen Victoria admitted in her journal that as she welcomed her future daughter-in-law 'a gleam of satisfaction for a moment shone into my heart'.

In the weeks which followed the Queen found herself charmed by the girl's companionship and delighted by her grace and beauty. Princess Alexandra made great friends with the Queen's daughters, and especially with Princess Helena, although in later years Princess Louise was to be her favourite. She took drawing lessons, she worked hard at English, which she already spoke fluently, she read the books she had brought with her, 'all serious, pious old books, most of them well-read, underlined old copies',[29] and, wonderful to relate, every night she went to bed punctually at ten.

It was clear that her great object was to learn all she could so that she would be the better able to make herself of use to her future husband, with whom she appeared to be 'quite devotedly in love', writing to him constantly and at great length – 'the drift of letters is fearful'.[30] Of an evening she would sit alone with the Queen, listening to stories about the Prince Consort and the happy days now gone for ever and one evening, when they had been speaking of his last illness, she was so moved that she suddenly burst into tears and wept bitterly upon the Queen's shoulder. No wonder then that Queen Victoria should be in raptures, describing her as 'a pearl', 'a real blessing to me' and as 'one of those sweet creatures who seem to come from the skies to help and bless poor mortals and to brighten for a time their path'. Among all these exaggerated paeans of praise one phrase stands out in charming simplicity, 'she is so pretty to live with'.[31]

The good effect of the Princess's visit was very noticeable. 'Her bright joyous young presence has done much to rouse the poor dear Queen who seems doatingly [*sic*] fond of her and has her a great deal with her,' wrote Princess Mary Adelaide; 'we found a great change in the Queen who is able to smile and even laugh cheerfully at times.'[32] The only difference which Princess Alexandra had with her future mother-in-law was over the question of the suite she would bring with her when she returned to England as a bride. Queen Victoria refused to consider the possibility of a 'foolish little Danish girl' coming as lady-in-waiting, and she would not even allow a Danish maid – 'it would not be for the dear young couple's happiness if Alix had a maid to whom she could chatter away in a language her Husband could not understand'.[33] The Queen suggested a German maid, a proposal which was hardly likely to meet with Princess Alexandra's approval; she even urged that the engaged pair should write to each other in German instead of in English. 'The German element is the one I wish to be cherished and kept up in our beloved home,' she told the Crown Princess; 'it is doubly necessary in this case, as Alix's parents are inclined to encourage the English and merge the German into Danish and English and this would be a dreadful sorrow to me; the very thing dear Papa and I disliked so much in the connexion is the Danish element.'[34]

The Queen was much put out when Prince and Princess Christian insisted that their daughter must return in time to spend her eighteenth birthday in her own home. Princess Alexandra and her father journeyed back to Denmark by way of France, where the Prince of Wales met them at Lille on his way home from the Mediterranean and travelled with them as far as Hanover. 'It was a happy thing to witness the happiness of the young couple in the society of each other,'[35] wrote General Knollys.

The two were not to meet again before the wedding, which was fixed for 10 March. This choice of a date in the middle of Lent shocked High Churchmen and Low Churchmen alike. Queen Victoria vetoed April because the birth of Princess Alice's first baby was expected during that month. May was out of the question, the Royal Family being surprisingly superstitious about May marriages – 'we all have a very strong objection to a marriage in May.'[36] The Prince of Wales could not be expected to wait till June for his bride; the wedding, therefore, must be in March regardless of the Lenten fast. In vain did Archbishop Longley point out that 'the light in which Lent is viewed by our Church has led her intelligent members generally to refrain from fixing that period for their marriages;'[37] the implied appeal to the Queen's intelligence went unheeded. Although the Archbishop was supported by her dear friend and counsellor, Dean Wellesley, she demolished their objections with one of her heaviest broadsides:

> 'The objection rests merely on fancy or prejudice and one in this case based on no very elevated view of one of God's holiest ordinances. . . . She would be very glad of an opportunity of breaking through a custom *only* in use among the *higher classes* and which she can't help considering as very

Catholic. . . . Marriage is a solemn holy act *not* to be classed with amusements.'[38]

The months before the wedding were full of difficulties and disagreements. The Danes felt that because they were a small nation they were being treated with scant consideration and took great offence that no formal demand for Princess Alexandra's hand had been sent to the Danish King. Wedding invitations were another source of trouble; Queen Victoria refused to have any of the Princess's relations present except her immediate family. She also gave great offence by omitting to invite many of her own German relations, in particular the Hanoverian cousins and the Grand Duchess Augusta of Mecklenburg-Strelitz. The worst disagreement of all arose over Queen Victoria's proposal that although the wedding was not to take place till March the Princess should leave Denmark as early as January and pay a visit to King Leopold on her way to England, a plan which Princess Christian not unnaturally vetoed, wishing to keep her daughter at home as long as possible.

All these disputes of course served to increase the dislike which Queen Victoria had always felt towards Princess Christian but they in no way altered her affection for Princess Christian's daughter. She remained enchanted with her future daughter-in-law, whom she described as 'this sweet bright being whose soul seems (like that of our blessed precious Prince) very like the lovely robe which envelopes it'.[39] With her son she was less satisfied, finding him 'a very unpleasant element in the house'.[40] The sooner his marriage took place the better but, as she wrote to Uncle Leopold, 'I am *very anxious* for the result; I fear dear Alix is under a complete delusion.'[40]

Meanwhile wedding presents were showering in upon the Princess whose possessions had previously been so few and so simple. King Frederick sent a magnificent necklace, the pendant being copied from the thirteenth-century Dagmar Cross, the most famous jewel in Denmark. All manner of precious objects came from Danish friends and European royalties, whilst in England a still more magnificent array of presents awaited her arrival. Princess Alexandra herself was busy with her trousseau, a slow business a century ago in Copenhagen where good dressmakers were scarce and fashionable materials hard to come by. When asked for advice Lady Augusta Bruce replied, 'three or four trains and *grandes toilettes*' – the Princess had never before owned a *grande toilette* – 'will, the Queen thinks, be sufficient'.[41] King Leopold wished to give the wedding-dress, which was to be of exquisite Brussels lace. Among all this new-found splendour Princess Alexandra still kept her old simplicity; when at last the day came to leave for England she travelled in a very smart bonnet she had made herself.

The ship in which the party sailed to Hamburg was an uncomfortable one; everybody was soon looking dirty and unkempt and Wally Paget's husband, Augustus Paget, reported the Princess as seeming, not unnaturally, 'rather down in the mouth'. She cheered up on arrival at the *Schloss* near Kiel belonging to her uncle, the Duke of Glücksburg, where she was welcomed by a bevy of girls all dressed alike in white muslin with rose-pink scarves. From now onwards her journey assumed the character of a royal progress. Everywhere she was greeted by huge crowds, shouting 'as loud as their lungs would let them'; she was toasted and fêted and serenaded, whilst at stopping places all along the route royal personages appeared to greet the Prince of Wales's lovely bride. The reception at Brussels, planned as the climax of her journey, was, however, slightly marred by King Leopold's ill-health and by the fact that Princess Alexandra herself had prosaically caught a cold which forced her to take to her bed.[42]

Meanwhile, in England, the nation was preparing to welcome the future Princess of Wales. For the first time a break appeared in the clouds of official gloom which had enveloped the country ever since the Prince Consort's death. After fifteen months of black garments and long faces, with no official functions more cheerful than the unveiling of a memorial, here at last was an occasion for national rejoicing rather than national mourning. Queen Victoria, very understandably, thought otherwise. There was to be no break in Court mourning, and at the wedding, although the invited guests could wear what colours they pleased, members of the Royal Family were only allowed the small concession of lilac and white, or white and grey. The Queen herself, of course, would appear in deepest black. The ceremony itself was not to be in London but in the comparative privacy of St George's Chapel, Windsor, a decision which much annoyed the general public. *Punch* declared that as the wedding was to be in an obscure Berkshire village, noted only for an old castle with no sanitary arrangements (a hit, this, at the notorious badness of the Windsor Castle drains which had been the real cause of the Prince Consort's fatal illness), the only notice should appear in the marriage column of *The Times* and should be worded thus:

> 'On the 10th inst, by Dr Longley, assisted by Dr Thomson, Albert Edward England K.G. to Alexandra Denmark. No cards.'

The people of London, however, were not to be thwarted. If they were not to greet Princess Alexandra on the wedding-day itself they would nevertheless welcome her to England with a welcome such as no royal bride had ever received before. No matter what the official attitude might be, this was to be an occasion for the nation at large.

When the royal yacht bringing the wedding-party to England anchored off the Kentish coast the Mayor of Margate came on board to present an address of welcome. The Princess accepted the scroll with becoming seriousness, but she was afterwards seen using it as a weapon with which to belabour her brother Prince William. As the yacht steamed up the Thames estuary to the accompaniment of the boom of guns from the batteries at Tilbury and the Nore it seemed as if half London were there to welcome the Princess, so vast was the crowd upon the water. These were not the rich or the noble but the common citizens in wherries, in rowing-boats, in paddle-steamers, all out to make a day of it and to shout themselves hoarse in greeting to the Prince of Wales's bride.

The Prince himself, arriving twenty minutes late, positively ran up the gangway at Gravesend in his haste. Soon afterwards the bride and bridegroom disembarked to drive through streets festooned with evergreens and orange-blossom to the station where a special reception-room was ready for them. The pictures on its walls had been almost too carefully chosen, one being *The Measure for the Wedding Ring* by Maclise, the other, *Mine Own*, by Halliday.

All along the railway-line from Gravesend to London every barn and cowshed had its flag and even the haystacks were decorated. Although the day was bitterly cold the London streets were packed with a crowd so great that the procession was several times brought to a halt, and it was only with the greatest difficulty that it succeeded in making its way through the press of people to the Mansion House. Here the crowd was at its thickest, the people surging round the carriage where the Prince and Princess sat with her parents, some of those nearest to her even attempting to kiss her hand. Suddenly the charger ridden by an officer of the Household Cavalry escort began to plunge and kick and by an odd mischance its hoof caught in the rear wheel of the carriage. A nasty accident seemed inevitable when Princess Alexandra, who was never fearful of horses, leant out and, taking hold of the animal's hoof, extricated it from the wheel.

The windows of the great houses in Piccadilly were filled with aristocratic spectators, among them the Prime Minister Lord Palmerston, Lord John Russell, and the richest woman in England, Miss Angela Burdett-Coutts. The only conspicuous absentees were the Prince's brothers and sisters; gossip had it that the Crown Princess in particular had wished to watch the procession but that her mother forbade her. Piccadilly drawing-rooms hummed with criticisms of the official arrangements, the poor taste of the decorations, the absence of outriders, the extraordinary shabbiness of the Royal equipages. No one, however, had anything but praise for Princess Alexandra herself, her beauty, her composure, the charm of her bearing. As her carriage passed Gloucester House, the Cambridge mansion, she blew kisses to her aunt the Duchess and to her cousin Princess Mary Adelaide. With the Duchess at Gloucester House was her lady-in-waiting, Lady Geraldine Somerset. Devoted, affectionate, prejudiced, and suffering from a hopeless passion for the Duchess's son, George, Duke of Cambridge, Lady Geraldine deserves a word of introduction. In the absence of any contemporary diarist of the calibre of Creevey or Greville her artless *Journal*, as yet unpublished, is one of the best available sources of gossip and comment. On this occasion she describes Princess Alexandra with typically gushing enthusiasm:

'*Charming* she was! bowing so prettily, so gracefully, right and left incessantly; winning *all* hearts by the gracious cordiality of her manner, that fascination she so really possesses combined of dignity, simplicity, grace and geniality! Poor Child! seven miles she had of this incessant bowing! *so* tired she must have been.'[43]

The Princess had to face yet more welcoming crowds at Slough and Eton before, in darkness and pouring rain, her carriage at last arrived at Windsor Castle where the young princes and princesses rushed down to the door to greet her. The Queen lingered behind but as her son led his bride forward, 'looking like a rose', and beautiful in her half-mourning dress of grey frock, white bonnet and violet mantle, on an impulse of affection she came forward and kissed the girl warmly. Later, as Queen Victoria sat alone in her room struggling with tears of emotion, 'dear gentle Alix knocked at the door, peeped in and came and knelt before me with the sweet loving expression that spoke volumes. I was much moved and kissed her again and again.'[44] Thus the Queen took her daughter-in-law to her heart and though the bond between the two was often to be strained it was never to be broken.

That evening the Princess found on her dressing-table a copy of a poem by Martin Tupper, *A Greeting to the Princess Alexandra*, printed on white satin and placed there by order of the Queen. It is a pity that the length of this enjoyable effusion makes it impossible to quote more than one verse:

'She comes! the Maid of Denmark,
  The Raven, – No! the Dove!
The Royal Maid of Denmark,
The darling child of Denmark,
  To be our Queen of Love;
She comes! His young and beauteous Bride,
Behold her at the Prince's side,
His truest crown, his joy and pride, –
  She comes! All blessings on her!
Our ALBERT-EDWARD's happy choice,
Making the World's great soul rejoice
  That such a Prince has won her;

For, searched we all the nations round
No fairer, better, could be found,
None in whose lot more hopes abound
  Of joy and peace and honour!
Then, shout again with heart and voice
And let the startled welkin sound
  From echoing shore to shore,
A hundred thousand welcomes!
A hundred thousand welcomes!
  And a hundred thousand more!'

Princess Alexandra had little time to rest during the two days that remained before the wedding. Three months previously the Prince Consort's body had been moved to the new mausoleum at Frogmore. There she and the Prince accompanied the Queen who joined their hands together standing before her husband's tomb and saying solemnly '*He* gives you his blessing'. Not surprisingly, the Princess appeared much moved. A less trying occasion was a drive through Eton where she was greeted most enthusiastically by the boys. Some half-a-dozen of them ran beside the carriage for nearly a mile and so obtained 'a stunning view' of the beautiful Princess. One was bold enough to hand her a bunch of violets, another wrote home afterwards that 'she grinned away like beans and so did her mother'.[45]

Meanwhile, the wedding-guests were arriving at the Castle where they admired the temporary room built on to St George's Chapel and, in Victorian phrase, 'lionised' the wedding presents. The Prince's gift of a *parure* of pearls and diamonds was specially admired and so were the diamonds and opals which the Queen had given not only in her own name but in that of her dead husband. The trousseau came in for less favourable criticism; '*some* of the gowns are pretty, all the wreaths hideous', wrote Lady Geraldine, but at least she admitted that the bride was supplied with beautiful handkerchiefs. On the evening before the wedding there was a dinner-party of a hundred guests, at which Princess Alexandra charmed the highest dignitaries of the land as easily as she had charmed the Eton boys. 'The descriptions you have read of her beauty and sweetness of manner are not at all exaggerated,' the Archbishop of Canterbury wrote to his niece, Catherine Longley; 'we exchanged a few words which were quite enough to leave the most favourable impression.'[46]

The next day, 10 March, pale and a little tremulous, Princess Alexandra went to her wedding in St George's Chapel.

The occasion was one to focus the attention of the whole nation and endless descriptions were written of the scenes inside and outside the Chapel. Of them all, one letter is particularly entertaining in its unstudied liveliness. It is written by one of the Eton boys who had run so gamely beside Princess Alexandra's carriage:

> 'On Tuesday morning we assembled at 10.30. Everyone had white kid gloves and a swell favour. When we got into the Castle we were led into a capital place to see. [First came] the Danish family, a thinnish Prince, one nice-looking young chap, and two girls; the youngest, Thyra, stood and looked out of the window and seemed awfully confused and astonished. The Princes and Princesses came, the little chaps had kilts on; Princess Helena looked very nice; last came the Princess Royal who got awfully cheered. The next lot was Mayors and Councillors and Sheriffs, with gorgeous footmen; then came the Prince in a blue coat and cocked hat.* Next bridesmaids – all one saw was petticoats sticking out of the window and the tops of their heads. At last came the Princess Alexandra. She looked regular nailing but was in a carriage all by herself. She was dressed in white – I don't know the French name for it but it looked like muslin. She was a little pale but her eyes weren't red.'[47]

The frock which young Liddell took to be of muslin was not the wedding-dress of exquisite Brussels lace which had been King Leopold's gift. For patriotic reasons it had been decided at the last moment that the Prince of Wales's bride must wear an English-made dress. The one chosen for Princess Alexandra was of silver-tissue trimmed with Honiton lace in a pattern of roses, shamrocks and thistles, the skirt garlanded with orange-blossom – '*tres bon gout*, light, young, and royal, made by Mrs James'.[48] Such was Lady Geraldine's verdict but Lord

* He was in fact wearing Garter robes.

Granville thought the dress 'too sunk in greenery'. Lady Geraldine described the bridesmaids, who were all of them English, as 'eight as ugly girls as you could wish to see' and Lord Granville wrote, 'the bridesmaids looked well – when their backs were turned'.[49] Since he was writing a description for the benefit of the Duchess of Manchester, who had been pointedly omitted from the list of invited guests, he may have deliberately made the worst of things; an engraving shows eight pretty young creatures looking quite delightful in white crinolines garlanded with pink roses.

Queen Victoria watched the service from the privacy of Catherine of Aragon's closet. She recorded that she had felt 'horribly overcome' and Lady Geraldine noted that the singing of a chorale composed by the Prince Consort 'upset his poor family terribly and they all, the Princesses as well as the Queen, cried much'.[50] The Prince Consort's ghost indeed seemed to haunt the wedding festivities. After the service the Archbishop remarked to the Crown Princess how calm and self-possessed the bride had been. 'Yes,' the Princess answered, and as she spoke the tears came into her eyes, 'she may well be – she has a *Father* and a Mother – but here are *we nine* without a Father.'[51]

Whoever was responsible for the seating arrangements in the Chapel had been tactless enough to place Mr and Mrs Disraeli face to face with Mr and Mrs Gladstone. On the shockingly overcrowded train which took the guests back to London Disraeli had to sit upon his wife's knee, whilst the Duchess of Westminster, wearing half a million pounds' worth of jewels, pushed her way into a third-class carriage with Lady Palmerston. Even so, she was luckier than Count Lavradio, who had his diamond star torn off and stolen by roughs. Meanwhile after a wedding-breakfast which Queen Victoria refused to attend – '*I* lunched alone' – the bride and bridegroom left for a short honeymoon at Osborne, the new Princess of Wales exquisite all in white with orange blossom in her bonnet. Looking down from a window in the Grand Corridor, the Queen saw their open carriage halt below her for a moment, 'Bertie standing up and both of then looking up lovingly at me.'[52]

A YOUNG WIFE AND MOTHER

Before returning to Germany the Crown Princess paid a brief visit to her brother and his bride at Osborne. She wrote to the Queen to give her impression of the honeymoon pair:

> 'It does one good to see people so thoroughly happy as this dear young couple are. As for Bertie, he looks blissful. I never saw such a change, his whole face looks beaming and radiant. Dear Osborne is in its greatest beauty and all breathes peace and happiness. Darling Alix looks charming and lovely and they both seem so comfortable and at home together. Love has certainly shed its sunshine on these two dear young hearts and lends its unmistakable brightness to both their countenances.'[1]

The week's honeymoon over, the Prince and Princess of Wales took up temporary quarters at Buckingham Palace in order to see something of her family before their return to Denmark. The Queen was more than ever enchanted with her new daughter-in-law – 'To look at darling Alix and into those eyes is a satisfaction; and then she is so quiet, so placid, that it is soothing to one, and I am sure that must do Bertie good.'[2]

On 20 March a great reception was held at St James's Palace; 'the Princess too charming,' wrote Lady Geraldine, 'it really is *wonderful* how well she did it all, when one thinks of the quiet, domestic home she has had! She has such perfect grace, dignity, affability combined! and held her little conversations most bewitchingly, winning all hearts.'[3]

Similar opinions came from other, less prejudiced observers. Three days after the reception the Prince and Princess visited the Zoological Gardens in company with her Danish relations. The Princess, still in half-mourning for the father-in-law she had never known, was wearing a dress of silver grey moiré silk trimmed with violet velvet, a white bonnet and veil, and 'a very handsome shawl'. The elegance of this outfit and the charm of the bride who wore it captured the heart of a casual passer-by: 'She is quite as tall as the Prince of Wales, and in a very long dress and a high bonnet looks more important than he does, and is so elegant that she need not fear the competition of the other beauties, the Empress of France and the Empress of Austria.'[4] Elegance was not a quality to be expected in any young woman brought up in Copenhagen a century ago. The Princess, however, was one of those fortunate beings who are elegant by nature; she did not have to feel her way, as most girls do, by a system of trial and error but emerged from her Danish school-room fully capable of taking her place as a leader of European fashion.

At a farewell party for the Princess's family the assembled royalties did their best to raise their drooping spirits by making an appalling din on a 'piano-organ'; 'the whole evening,' Lady Geraldine commented, 'was so unlike Buckingham Palace' – and therefore, perhaps indicative of things to come. It was not to be expected that the life of this young and vivacious couple would be conducted after the model provided by Queen Victoria and the Prince Consort. When the Queen married she was already a reigning sovereign much occupied with official business; in later life, when she was also the mother of nine children, she had even less time or inclination for social pleasures. The Prince of Wales, on the contrary, had nothing whatsoever to do. Although his mother continued to believe that she was not long for this world she gave her heir no opportunity to learn anything about the duties of the position which, in her opinion, he was so soon to occupy. Even apart from matters of state, he was not encouraged to undertake any of the public functions which his father had performed. His future presented an almost total blank. In spite of his idle hands and the proverbial interest which Satan takes in such cases the Prince of Wales must keep out of mischief; more positive occupation the Queen had none to offer.

One traditional function of royalty, however, remained for him to perform. Society, in those days rightly spelt with a capital S, had always looked to the Royal Family for a lead, but no such lead had been forthcoming since the long-ago days of King George IV. The Court of King William IV and Queen Adelaide had been definitely dowdy and, although much had been hoped of the young Queen Victoria as a leader of Society, all such hopes were extinguished with her marriage. The Prince Consort had both disliked and been disliked by the British aristocracy; in any case he was not a man to set store by the doings of Society. In this respect, as in so many others, the Prince of Wales bore no resemblance to his father. He loved parties and he loved people, and the chief thing he asked of people was that they should be entertaining. The Princess too had all a young girl's natural delight in dances and pretty clothes and innocent admiration – 'she behaves as though she likes admiration and was perfectly well-pleased to dispense her smiles all around'.[5] This spring of 1863, for the first time in her life the Princess had money to spend and smart clothes to wear. Few girls have ever enjoyed such a wonderful season of gaiety as now opened before her. At the age of eighteen she emerged from her Danish chrysalis to find herself immediately acclaimed as the Queen of Society.

Today it is hard even to imagine the brilliance of London Society a hundred years ago. In this small and compact group of people everybody knew everybody and nearly everybody was worth knowing. The people who belonged to this group were rich enough to entertain lavishly and cultivated enough to make these lavish entertainments both beautiful and amusing. Society now went mad – the expression is not too strong – over this lovely young princess. Middle-aged statesmen and men of the world, characters such as Gladstone,

Clarendon, Disraeli, were rapturous in her praise, Disraeli, of course, paying her the most perspicacious compliment of all, 'She has the accomplishment of being gracious without smiling; she has repose.'[6] Mrs Gladstone remarked, 'the Princess is so pretty it is quite a pleasure to be in a room with her.'[7] Lady Waterford was charmed by 'the graceful young Princess of Wales', whilst Mr Gladstone's young niece, Lucy Lyttelton, went into ecstasies over 'the loveliness of the Princess, her noble innocent and peculiarly dignified expression, her winning grace and her most beautiful smile'.[8]

The rigid rules of English Society were very different to the simplicity of Denmark, yet this 'child Princess', as Lord Esher called her, never seemed to put a finger wrong. Of course one or two critics made themselves heard. Some of the older generation complained that the Prince and Princess did not know what it was to be quiet; they were never still for an instant and, like children, they could not live without amusement. Others criticised the lack of formality and the disregard for royal etiquette which marked their style of entertaining; 'they receive too much *comme particuliers*', wrote Lady Geraldine, 'they are charming *maîtres-de-maison* but *too little* royal'.[9] But however careless of etiquette she might be the Princess never lost a certain natural dignity; nobody would dream of taking liberties with her in spite of her uninhibited taste for fun and frolic. She had a great capacity for enjoying herself, thus adding greatly to the enjoyment of those around her. Perhaps the most memorable of all the parties which took place this memorable summer was a ball given by the Brigade of Guards, when the officers stood in two long lines and crossed their swords overhead whilst the Prince and Princess danced down the room under this glittering archway, he happy and boyish, she radiantly beautiful.

The functions at which the Princess appeared were innumerable. She held drawing-rooms, deputising for the Queen, a position which filled her with such alarm that Lucy Lyttelton commented on her unusual pallor and Lady Knightley wrote of her as 'a bit of a thing, with a white gown and a white face, two curls and a tiara'.[10] At the end of this function the Princess was completely exhausted, which was not altogether surprising, since there had been more than three thousand presentations to be made. Half way through the function the doors had had to be closed in order to give her a few moments of rest and relaxation. With her husband the Princess attended the balls and Commemoration ceremonies at Oxford where the royal programme was so strenuous that Lord Derby remarked 'I think they are taxing him and still more the Princess's good nature and *powers* rather highly.'[11] She was shown over the Crystal Palace by Joseph Paxton himself, afterwards lunching in the Royal Apartments there and attending a grand concert. In lighter vein she went to Chiswick House for a 'breakfast', which at that date meant an evening party, and danced country dances on the grassy lawn. Wherever she went and whatever the occasion her beauty and charm turned all heads; the remarkable thing was that her own remained unturned.

Two factors helped to steady her. One was her interest and pleasure in her new homes, Marlborough House and Sandringham. Much as she enjoyed social activities she was in essence a domestic creature and home was always to be the real centre of her life. Marlborough House she loved from the first moment she set eyes on it, and she soon came to have an equal affection for that undistinguished house which had been acquired for the Prince of Wales in the remote country near the Wash. Old Sandringham House was remarkable only for an extraordinary porch and conservatory added to the original building by that wild-cat among Victorian architects, Samuel Saunders Teulon. The Princess's first visit at Easter 1863 was an uncomfortable one. The house was already in the hands of the builders, whilst the surrounding countryside was bleak in the extreme at that time of year. 'No fine trees, no water, no hills, in fact no attraction of any sort or kind,' moaned the Princess's Lady-of-the-Bedchamber, Lady Macclesfield:

> 'There are numerous coverts but no fine woods, large unenclosed turnip fields, with an occasional haystack to break the line of the horizon. It would be difficult to find a more ugly or desolate-looking place, and there is no neighbourhood or any other countervailing advantage. The wind blows keen from the Wash and the Spring is said to be unendurable in that part of Norfolk. It is of course a wretched

hunting country and it is dangerous riding as the banks are honey-combed with rabbit-holes. As there was all England wherein to choose I do wish they had had a finer house in a more picturesque and cheerful situation.'[12]

The young couple, however, found nothing to grumble about at Sandringham. The Princess felt at home in the flat Norfolk country, which reminded her of her own Denmark, and she was delighted with the charming decorations of the room which had been allotted to her as her personal sitting-room. Above all both husband and wife rejoiced to find themselves in a home of their own, able to do what they pleased without comment or interference. One of the guests on this first visit was Canon Stanley, specially invited because the Prince had spent the previous Easter with him on the shores of the Sea of Galilee. On Easter Eve the Princess brought her new English prayer book down to the drawing-room and asked the Canon to explain to her the unfamiliar English Communion Service, which he did by comparing it carefully with the Danish Lutheran liturgy. 'She was most simple and fascinating,' he wrote afterwards, describing her as 'so winning and graceful, and yet so fresh and free and full of life.'[13]

This simple but heart-felt religious faith was the second factor which prevented the Princess from being spoilt by the perpetual adulation which surrounded her. It was a faith in which her husband joined although he did not perhaps share it to the full. Sir Philip Magnus writes of the Prince's 'unclouded and humble religious faith', and describes him in later years as 'a convinced and practising Anglican'.[14] Unlike Queen Victoria, both the Prince and the Princess inclined towards High Church beliefs and practices. One of the Prince's personal friends at this date was Charles Wood, afterwards Lord Halifax, a famous leader of the High Church party. Incidentally, Charles Wood was also one of the Princess's most devoted admirers; 'he quite raves of her beauty', his sister Emily wrote this spring of 1863, 'every time he sees her he comes back in fresh raptures'.[15] The Prince was deeply impressed by his friend's earnestness; 'if ever I become religious,' he was heard to remark, 'I shall be of Charley Wood's religion.'[16]

The Princess was religious already and 'Charles Wood's

religion' appealed to her greatly. It must be admitted that she was attracted more by the beauty of the services and by their musical setting than by any more weighty reasons of history or doctrine. Church history and doctrine were intellectual matters, and things of the intellect meant nothing at all to her. She had beauty, she had goodness, she had intuition and sympathy and charm, but she had very little brain. This was her irredeemable defect, a root from which a vast amount of trouble was to spring. The Prince was in no sense an intellectual but he enjoyed the company of clever people. In particular, he enjoyed the company of clever women; for instance, he had always been particularly attached to his two clever sisters, the Crown Princess and Princess Alice of Hesse. He looked to women for two things; first, the satisfaction of his physical desires, the second, deliverance from the spectre of boredom which haunted him incessantly. Beyond everything else, he hated to be bored and in the long run a stupid woman, however beautiful, was bound to prove a bore. For the moment, however, his young wife was all he needed or desired. Physically she was one of the most beautiful and attractive of women; as a companion she was gay and engaging, sharing in his taste for schoolboy humour and practical jokes. At the age of twenty-one this was all that he appeared to require to keep him happy.

The only person to be less than satisfied with the situation was Queen Victoria. At first she was all joy and satisfaction; 'the effect of his sweet wife has already been most favourable on Bertie',[17] she informed King Leopold on 17 March. To the Crown Princess she wrote in similar strain; 'I love her more and more and she quite understands Bertie and shows plenty of character.'[18] The Queen, however, had already made the significant observation, 'very clever I don't think she is',[19] and all too soon she was writing in different and disillusioned tones:

> 'She [the Queen of Prussia] thinks Alix very pretty and nice but she says Alix must try and get Bertie to occupy himself – unfortunately she never does anything but write! She never reads – and I fear Bertie and she will soon be nothing but two puppets running about for show all day and night.'[20]

Although the Princess wrote so much the Queen complained that 'she does not write well', adding 'I fear the learning has been much neglected and she cannot either write or I fear speak French well.'[21] She described the Princess as 'looking so sallow and losing her *fraicheur*' and for the very first time she remarked on the handicap which was later to prove so serious, 'Alas! she is deaf and everyone observes it, which is a sad misfortune.'[22]

In fairness to Queen Victoria it should be made clear that her objections were not those of a mere kill-joy. She was seriously alarmed lest the ceaseless round of gaieties might affect her daughter-in-law's health: 'Bertie and Alix left Frogmore today, both looking as ill as possible. We are all seriously alarmed about her. For although Bertie says he is so anxious to take care of her, he goes on going out every night till she will become a skeleton, and hopes there cannot be.'[23]

The last sentence explains the real fear behind the Queen's anxiety. She was not to be disappointed in her hopes of an heir; by the end of June the Princess was pregnant. This fact made little or no change in her way of life which the Queen stigmatised as 'a whirl of amusement'. In a letter written to Lord Granville a week or so before the Prince's marriage the Queen had made perfectly clear her own idea of the proper social life for a Prince and Princess of Wales – 'The Queen thinks that with the exception of Lord Granville, Lord Palmerston and possibly Lord Derby and three or four other great houses in London, Westminster House, Spencer House, Apsley House, the Prince and the future Princess should not go out to dinner, and further, not to *all these* in the same year.'[24]

Formal dinners in the houses of the more elderly and respectable nobility had little in common with the type of entertainment which was soon to be associated with the name of Marlborough House. The cheerful atmosphere there was naturally very attractive to a young man; it was therefore not surprising that the nineteen-year-old Prince Alfred spent as much time there as possible in company with the charming sister-in-law whom he had half hoped to have as his own bride. Queen Victoria treated this infatuation *au grand serieux*, on 18 May writing to the Crown Princess, 'We do all we can to keep him from Marlborough House as he is far too *épris* of Alix to be allowed to be much there without possibly ruining the happiness of all three, and Affie has not the strength of mind or rather of principle and character to resist the temptation and it is like playing with fire.'[25] Prince Alfred's embarrassing admiration for the Princess of Wales continued to weigh on the Queen's mind; a year later she was writing to King Leopold, 'He *cannot* live *en tiers* with Bertie and his wife, whom he only likes and admires *too much*.'[26] No jealousy over the Princess, however, was able to destroy the warm affection between the two brothers, who were always to remain good friends.

The London Season over, the Prince and Princess planned a holiday in Scotland, intending in mid-September to travel all the way to Rumpenheim to spend a week with her relations and then return to Scotland again. This scheme Queen Victoria rightly stigmatised as 'mad and very imprudent', writing to King Leopold, 'I mean to refuse permission for really they ought to be quiet and that Rumpenheim party is very mischievous for my poor weak boy's head.'[27] Of necessity therefore they remained at Abergeldie where they could relax and enjoy the simple pleasures of picnics without attendant servants, when Charles Wood would boil the potatoes and the Princess collect wood for the fire. In November they were back at Sandringham entertaining a succession of guests, including Lord Granville, who rather improbably described the household at Sandringham as reminiscent of Balmoral in the happy days of the Prince Consort. The Queen wrote to tell her son how delighted she had been by Lord Granville's letter:

> 'I naturally rejoice truly to hear this, as I know that our *court* and life were thought a *pattern* from its *right dignity without stiffness* and the Country has looked and longed to see *you both* follow that course with great anxiety and how they will rejoice to see this realised! Let us hope that in serious subjects such as *reading* this will gradually follow. This letter is meant for beloved Alix too naturally.'[28]

Another visitor was the Princess Royal, who wrote to Queen

Victoria describing the house and commenting on her sister-in-law's unusually easy pregnancy:

> 'This seems a charming place so quiet and country-like, and a delightful house furnished with great taste and comfort. Bertie and Alix seem to like it very much and to be very happy and comfortable. Dear Alix seems very thin but looking well; she shows her condition very little though her figure is much changed already – she seems perfectly well, has not an ailment of any kind or sort to complain of and has a very fresh colour. When I think of what I was the first time I cannot help thinking that she is wonderfully lucky.'[29]

All through this autumn the Princess was consumed by anxiety for her family and for her native country of Denmark. Much had happened in the months which had passed since her wedding. In June her favourite brother Prince 'Willi' had become King George I of Greece. He had been chosen for this position in curiously haphazard fashion. Years later the Princess gave her own version of this episode in a conversation with Randall Davidson, afterwards Archbishop of Canterbury.[30] According to her, one night at Marlborough House, shortly after her marriage, Palmerston and Lord John Russell asked Prince William if he would like to be King of Greece. The eighteen-year-old naval cadet answered jokingly that there was nothing he would like better, thinking to himself that if he were a king he would have no tiresome examinations to pass. The English Foreign Office consulted privately with the King of Denmark and, before anything official was said either to the boy or to his parents, he was formally nominated King and his consent made known in Europe.

The Princess of Wales was under no delusions as to her brother's new dignity. It seems that she had heard of the scheme before he did himself, and had always been against it. 'So William has become King of Greece,' she wrote to the Dowager Queen of Denmark on 9 June; 'I am very sad for that. God give him strength and patience, to stand up to what the future may bring.'[31] From her brother's election as King of Greece dated the Princess's preoccupation with Balkan politics. It cannot be pretended that she knew much about that complicated subject; her policy was the simple one, 'My brother', or later, 'my nephew, right or wrong'. England had guaranteed the new Greek constitution, England, with some assistance from France and Russia, had bolstered up Greek finances, England had in fact put the King on his throne, therefore, she argued, it was the plain duty of England to keep him there.

In November Prince William's father himself became a king. On the death of Frederick VII Prince Christian ascended the Danish throne as Christian IX. In December war broke out; German troops occupied Holstein which the Danes surrendered without a blow whilst preparing to fight their hardest to keep Schleswig. The Princess's cousin, the Duke of Augustenburg, outraged Danish feeling by coming out on the German side and having himself proclaimed Duke of a united Schleswig-Holstein.

As they were to do nearly every year until 1901, the Prince and Princess spent the anniversary of the Prince Consort's death at Windsor. In Queen Victoria's mind thankfulness for once mingled with her grief; 'we must be thankful that in Bertie's so improved and altered conduct and in his happy marriage with dear Alix who is a *most* noble, excellent, dear creature we have a realisation of what my Angel so ardently wished.'[32] Although the Queen was, of course, pro-German in sympathy this did not alter her affection for her Danish daughter-in-law. The Princess, however, could not control her feelings, hard though she tried to do so. For her the Christmas holiday at Osborne was not a happy time so that she was delighted to return to Frogmore House at Windsor and to the company of her motherly lady-in-waiting, Lady Macclesfield.

That winter the frost was intense; all day long on 6 January the lake at Frogmore was a gay scene, with a band playing and the ice crowded with skaters playing ice-hockey. In the evening the Princess gave a big children's party, a form of entertainment in which she delighted, thoroughly enjoying the games, the snapdragon, and the Christmas tree. Skating she always loved and although she was not so imprudent as to suggest skating herself, she was determined next day to drive to Virginia Water to watch the skaters there, disregarding some twinges of pain which were attacking her. The Prince of

Wales pooh-poohed Lady Macclesfield's fears and off the party drove to join in the fun, the Princess sitting on a sledge-chair on the ice. Not till dusk did they return to Frogmore. Almost immediately after their arrival home Lady Macclesfield, who had herself given birth to thirteen children, realised that the Princess's time had come and that the baby was about to be born two months too early. She sent in haste for the Windsor town doctor, none of the royal doctors being within reach, and she herself prepared to act as nurse. Nothing was ready, so that in the midst of all the other preparations she was obliged to go herself to Caleys, the local draper, to buy some yards of flannel. In the Royal Archives there is to be found a list headed 'Outfit Provided for His Royal Highness the Eldest Son of the Prince of Wales'. Seldom can a royal baby have had a more inadequate layette:

'2 yards of coarse flannel
6 yards of superfine flannel
1 sheet of wadding (lent by Mrs Knollys)
1 Basket (contents wanting)
1 superb lace christening robe.'[33]

The Prince of Wales behaved admirably, doing all he could to comfort and encourage his wife, whilst the Princess herself showed touching confidence in Lady Macclesfield – 'As long as I see your face I am happy' – seeming only alarmed for the safety of the child. All went well, and at nine o'clock a boy was born weighing only three and three-quarter pounds but strong and well. Nobody was present at the birth except the Prince, the doctor and Lady Macclesfield, who used her flannel petticoat as a receiving flannel. Lord Granville, however, chanced to be at hand and he was able to bear the customary testimony to the birth of a future heir to the throne.

When the excitement was over Lady Macclesfield drove everyone from the Princess's room, insisting on sleep and quiet. Peeping in a little later to make sure that all was well, she found that the Prince had quietly come back and that the two young parents were crying in each other's arms.

DENMARK AND PRUSSIA AT WAR

The premature baby throve, and so at first did his mother. When six of the most celebrated doctors in England, having arrived too late for the actual birth, marched into her room to hold a solemn consultation, she burst out laughing in their faces. Queen Victoria was delighted with her grandson and difficulty only arose over the choice of his name. Like many another grandparent the Queen felt strongly on this subject; in her opinion the only possible names were Albert Victor, after his paternal grandparents. Although the parents agreed with her they felt that the choice should rest with them. 'I felt rather annoyed,' the Prince of Wales wrote to his mother with a proper display of parental possessiveness, 'when Beatrice told Lady Macclesfield that you had settled what our little boy was to be called before I had spoken to you about it.'[1]

Princess Beatrice was then aged six, therefore perhaps to be excused this slight indiscretion.

The child was accordingly christened Albert Victor Christian Edward, but except by his grandmother, he was invariably called 'Eddy'. Queen Victoria attended the christening wearing 'my poor, sad dress', which, however, was 'much liked and thought *bien convenable*'. The occasion was not a very cheerful one. 'The poor baby roared all through the ceremony, which none of you did,' the Queen informed the Crown Princess; 'Alix looked very ill, thin and unhappy, she is sadly gone off'.[2] A chorale composed by the Prince Consort was sung to some singularly uninspiring verses written especially for the occasion. The birth of a child who would one day, if all went well, sit upon the throne of England, was heralded by an outburst of remarkably bad poetry. An unnamed curate produced an effusion which opened with the superb line, 'The night is riven by a new-born star', whilst Martin Tupper must of course publish a *Lyric of Congratulation* beginning, 'Song of the Patriot, awake! Prayer of the Christian, arise!' *Punch*'s contribution was more down to earth:

'O hush thee, my darling, thy Sire is a Prince
Whom Mama beheld skating not quite five hours since,
And Grandpapa Christian is off to the fray
With the Germans, who'd steal his nice Duchy away.

But slumber, my darling, the English are true,
And will help him for love of Mama and of you!
The Channel Fleet's coming, with powder and shot,
And the Germans must run, or they'll catch it all hot!'

But although the man in the street would have done almost anything 'for love of Mama', so great was the Princess's popularity, the politicians were certainly not sending the Channel Fleet to the aid of Grandpapa. As the spring of 1864 wore on it became perfectly clear that the Great Powers were not prepared to rescue Denmark from inevitable defeat. A week after the baby's birth Prussia sent an ultimatum to Denmark which the Danes rejected. Hostilities were renewed; the Danes were driven out of their positions on the Danewerk, the traditional frontier of their country, and by mid-February the whole of Schleswig was in German hands with the exception of the stronghold of Dybboel.

Anxiety for her own family and distress for Denmark's plight preyed upon the Princess's mind and retarded her recovery to full health. Before her marriage both she and her parents had been warned in no uncertain terms that she must abandon her Danish sympathies and become in political matters entirely an Englishwoman. Queen Louise now had the wisdom to remind her daughter where her duty lay. In a series of charming if ungrammatical letters to Lady Macclesfield, thanking her for her kindness and help, Queen Louise describes the baby's birth as 'the only real joy I have had since November' and adds, 'pardon, dear Madame, this very black letter in answer to your rosy dear letter but to write cheerful now must indeed be more than any sensible woman could do'. Nevertheless, she insists that her daughter must know that 'her duty is for those to whom she belongs now and which give her so many precious signs of love and sympathy'.[3]

Perhaps it was too much to expect that an emotional, warm-hearted young woman could so dissociate herself from the fate of her native land. Certainly the Princess made not the faintest pretence at impartiality. At an evening party on 10 March word went round that the Prussian diplomat, Bernstorff, had omitted to raise his glass to the toast of the King of Denmark, whereupon the Princess, exquisite in pink satin, conspicuously cut him dead for the rest of the evening. On 11 May Lucy Lyttelton saw her at a Court and noted that she was looking 'terribly thin and pale, in deep black' – she was in mourning for her maternal grandmother – 'must be wretched at the reverses of the Danes, who have just lost Dybboel.'[4]

On 11 March Queen Victoria wrote anxiously to King Leopold, who was then staying at Buckingham Palace, telling him that 'Alix's altered appearance is the observation of everyone'. She begged King Leopold to urge the Prince to take greater care of his wife – 'You must not mince the matter but speak strongly and frighten Bertie'[5] – and she enclosed a rough memorandum which clearly showed her anxiety over her daughter-in-law's health and her concern with the upbringing of her little grandson. In the last clause she insisted 'that Bertie should understand what a strong right I have to *interfere* in the management of the child or children; that he should never do anything about the child without consulting me'.[6] Although this was ominous of troubles to come, for the present Queen Victoria's chief concern was for the Princess. In July she was writing again to King Leopold, 'the young parents look very unwell and quite worn out by the *most* unhealthy life they lead'.[7] For the Prince and Princess the London Season of 1864 was even more gay, and therefore more strenuous, than the Season of 1863. They dined, they danced, they attended race-meetings, they entertained largely at Marlborough House, and night after night, when at last the Princess came to bed very late, it was only to lie awake weeping for the tragic happenings in Denmark.

The Prince of Wales was much moved by the sight of his wife's tears. Before his marriage he had been, if anything, pro-Prussian in sympathy; now he swung right round and came out openly on the side of the Danes. Never again was he to regard Prussia with anything but dislike and suspicion. His attitude towards Prussia was to have its effect upon European history, and although later it was to be much intensified by the intolerable behaviour of his nephew, Kaiser William II, it was an attitude which in origin dated from the time when he watched his wife grieving for the wrongs Prussia had inflicted on her native land. In February the Queen had described him as being 'frantic, thinking everyone wishes to crush Denmark'.[8] Wishing to be of some practical use, he offered to serve as a channel of communication between the King of Denmark and the British Government. When his offer was discreetly shelved he went so far as to put himself in touch with the leaders of the Parliamentary Opposition. 'That was the only occasion during his life,' writes Sir Philip Magnus, 'on which the Prince displayed any disposition to imitate former Princes of Wales by becoming entangled with the Parliamentary Opposition, and it frightened Queen Victoria.'[9] Where this major political issue was concerned his mother's wishes, his sister's interests, even his respect for his father's memory, counted for nothing when set against the influence of his wife.

The Princess's influence did in fact count for very much, not only with her husband but with the nation at large. 'Denmark and all that concerned it had suddenly come much to the fore owing to the immense popularity of the Princess of Wales',[10] writes George Villiers in his biography of Lord Clarendon. Queen Victoria deplored the fact that 'the feeling against Prussia has become *most violent* in England, and quite ungovernable'.[11] This anti-Prussian feeling was a new thing in

England and in this particular instance it was not entirely justified by the facts of the case. There were, as Queen Victoria had pointed out, wrongs on both sides; it was just as much an over-simplification of an immensely complicated issue to stigmatise Prussia as an aggressor as to glorify her as the champion of the German-speaking people in the Duchies. The English people would not have been so horrified at the not-unusual spectacle of a large nation bullying a small one had their idolised Princess of Wales not been a member of the small nation thus attacked. That perspicacious man, King Leopold, saw the situation clearly enough, and he realised too that the Queen's continued seclusion only served to increase the Princess's already phenomenal popularity. His letter on the subject is worth quoting at some length:

> 'I cannot help saying a few words about Bertie and Alix. You will recollect when first Albert spoke to me about Alix he said, "We take the Princess, but *not* her relations". That might have remained as he wished for years, without the death of our cousin of Denmark. That of a sudden gave us a *Danish** Princess, and the consequences of a Constitution which even the late King had *not* sanctioned. Our own *dreadful* loss put Bertie and Alix *forward*; he and his wife are *constantly before the public in* EVERY IMAGINABLE SHAPE *and* CHARACTER, *and fill entirely the public mind.*
>
> 'The English are very personal; to continue to love people they must see them, and even in part touch them: this shows itself by the wish to get something that belongs or belonged to them; it must be palpable. This state of affairs gives the young couple great influence on all classes, and is even calculated to influence the Cabinet, and to strengthen the Opposition, which would be quite powerless on that question without the strong popular feeling.
>
> 'Vicky little dreamt, in selecting a charming Princess, that she would become a source of difficulties for England, and perhaps the cause of a popular war against Prussia. I have

* He is presumably referring to the possibility that the family of Schleswig-Holstein-Sonderburg-Glücksburg might have taken the German side, as the Schleswig-Holstein-Augustenburg family did, had Prince Christian not been chosen King of Denmark.

no doubt the great majority in England would like a war with Prussia. . . .'[12]

King Leopold had miscalculated. The Princess's personal popularity could, and did, permanently alter the image which Prussia bore in English minds; it could not bring England into the war against Prussia. In July Denmark was forced to capitulate and to relinquish her sovereignty over the two Duchies of Schleswig and Holstein. King Christian IX had not been on the throne a year before he had lost more than half his kingdom.

In these circumstances the Princess was more than ever anxious to visit her old home and to bring what comfort she could to her parents. Queen Victoria, however, demurred, fearing that such a visit might have political repercussions. Throughout this troubled summer relations between mother-in-law and daughter-in-law had, not unnaturally, become very strained. In moments of depression the Queen even went so far as to regret the Danish marriage. In a letter to King Leopold she referred to Princess Marie of Leiningen, wife of her half-nephew Ernst, as 'quite like my own daughter, much more so than poor Alix, with whom I can never get more intimate, much as I like and love her. She comes completely from the enemy's camp in every way – Stockmar was right.'[13]

Because the Princess always took particular care not to set herself up in open opposition to her mother-in-law no one seems to have noticed how often, when their wishes clashed, it was she who in the end quietly won the victory. So it was now; when the British Government made no objection to the proposed visit the Queen gave permission, even allowing the baby Prince Albert Victor to accompany his parents, though stipulating that he must be sent back to her at Balmoral after the Danish visit, and not be taken on a further trip to Sweden, Germany, and possibly Russia. She was justifiably worried about the health of her baby grandson, whom she described as 'very backward and delicate-looking, though a dear good little thing', adding sadly, 'I can't help being anxious about it!'[14]

In September therefore the whole family set off for Denmark, where they were received with open arms, King Christian remarking that the day of their arrival was the first happy one he had known for a very long time. The Princess was rapturously greeted wherever she appeared and the Danes were delighted to find her husband strolling about the streets of Copenhagen with as little fuss and formality as the members of their own Royal Family. During this visit she took the opportunity to introduce him to Denmark's most famous citizen, Hans Andersen, whose stories had been the delight of her childhood.

Most of their stay was spent at the Castle of Fredensborg, where the talk was chiefly concerned with the engagement of the Princess's favourite sister, Princess Dagmar, to the Russian Czarevitch. The Princess was obviously delighted to be back with her own relations but the only member of the Danish Royal Family who was really congenial to her husband was the eldest son, the Crown Prince Frederick. The Prince of Wales's Danish sympathies were not strong enough to reconcile him to the boredom of life at the Danish Court; he was hard put to it to endure the uncomfortable rooms, the indifferent food with the inevitable currant jelly for dessert, and the tedious evenings occupied with nothing more exciting than an old-fashioned game of loo. He was greatly relieved when at last he could escape to Sweden, where the Swedish King's tastes were more in accordance with his own. From Stockholm he wrote to Prince Frederick about various Swedish beauties, 'Miss Hannah is very *comme-il-faut* and Miss Ida's songs charming', whilst Prince Frederick, visiting Stockholm a few months later, in his turn chaffed the Prince of Wales about 'the perfume shop we visited and that little very nice girl told us with sorrow of how much she hurted you in blowing the perfume in your eyes'.[15] Queen Victoria had ordered that in Stockholm the Prince and Princess must be entirely incognito, staying at an hotel, but the Prince defiantly accepted the Swedish King's invitation to stay at the Royal Palace, writing home to his mother that, 'the hotels are not good and I have not the intention of letting Alix be uncomfortably lodged if I can help it'. In spite of Miss Hannah, Miss Ida, and that little very nice girl in the perfume shop he was always mindful of his wife's interests; in this same letter he pointed out that when his sisters came to England they stayed for two or three months in their old home and complained that the brief fortnight which the Queen had allowed the Princess to spend in Denmark was certainly 'not a liberal allowance'.[16]

On their return Queen Victoria was less than pleased with the effect that their Scandinavian holiday had had upon her son and daughter-in-law. All that she heard confirmed her in her dislike of the Danish connection and especially of the influence of Queen Louise. 'I am sure the Queen had made Bertie do many things which he had promised he would not do',[17] she wrote to the Crown Princess, and again, still more emphatically, 'he is entirely in that most mischievous Queen's hands – Alix, good as she is, is not worth the price we have had to pay for her having such a family connection. I shall not readily let them go there again.'[18] Part of Queen Victoria's annoyance was due to the fact that on the journey home the Princess had refused to call upon the Queen of Prussia, 'which I think very injudicious'.[19]

Queen Victoria could write thus in moments of irritation but angry though she might be with the Princess's family she could never keep up a show of anger with the Princess herself. Her daughter-in-law's famous charm worked as certainly with her as with everyone else. She knew all too well that her son was anything but an ideal husband and in her inmost heart she was grateful to the Princess for continuing to love him in spite of much provocation. 'Alix is really a dear, excellent, right-minded soul whom one must dearly love and respect', she wrote to the Crown Princess on 19 November, when the Prince and Princess of Wales were paying her a visit at Windsor. 'I often think her lot is no easy one, but she is very fond of Bertie, though not blind.'[20] In the years that were to come the Princess would be more and more frequently forced to turn a deliberately blind eye towards her husband's behaviour, but her fondness for him was never to fail.

The Princess of Wales's affection for her husband is certain but how warm was that affection? Did her early girlish infatuation ever ripen and develop into mature love? These are unanswerable questions; it is nevertheless impossible to refrain from asking them. Lady Antrim, who lived much in Court circles and came to know the Princess very well in later life, believed that if she had loved the Prince as warmly as he loved her, he might have proved a more faithful husband. Driven perhaps by the instinct for self-preservation, very beautiful women are often a little cold, and the Princess may well have been one of these chilly beauties. She was certainly a woman who found her chief fulfilment in her children, and in spite of her husband's infidelities, what little evidence we have goes to show that she never contemplated taking a lover of her own. The pattern of her marriage was a common one in her day and a not unusual one even now, when the social code has altered fundamentally and a husband's infidelity is normally regarded as a perfectly adequate reason for breaking up a marriage. In the nineteenth century such a step would not merely have been frowned upon; it would have been impossible because of the state of the divorce laws. A wife's infidelity was a serious matter; the family, not the individual, was the basic social unit and family stability demanded that a man should be reasonably certain that his children were his own. Wives, however, put up with unfaithfulness in a husband much as they put up with meanness or bad temper or any of the other disagreeable qualities for which the law offers no redress. The Princess may or may not have been cold; her husband was certainly polygamous by nature and it is improbable that he would have remained strictly faithful to any wife, whatever her temperament. She made the best of the situation in which she found herself; her unfaithful husband remained devoted to her and she could always fall back on that fact for consolation. 'After all,' she is reputed to have remarked to a member of the Seymour family, 'he always loved me the best.'

For the present she had need of all the consolation and support she could find for the next few years were not to be easy ones. The real root of the trouble was her husband's enforced idleness, a state of affairs for which he was in no way to blame. He was not by nature lazy; he could not bear to be unoccupied, and thwarted in his desire to work he naturally filled his empty hours with play. He yachted, he hunted, he shot, he attended race-meetings, he frequented theatres and music-halls, he even made friends with the head of the London Fire Brigade, *Iolanthe*'s 'Captain Shaw, type of true love kept under', and he would often be seen at a big fire, lending a hand with the firemen. Above all, he gambled, though not so largely as gossip made out. Rumour, however, was none the less damaging because it was not entirely true, and colour was given to these exaggerated stories by the fact that he was known to be in financial difficulties. Where money matters were concerned the Princess was no sort of help to her husband but rather the reverse. She was totally lacking in financial sense; money meant as little to her as painting to the colour-blind or music to the tone-deaf. The root of the difficulty was not so much her extravagance as her generosity. She would give away any amount of money to anyone, and if remonstrated with she was all too apt to retaliate by doubling the amount of her original gift. Generosity is a charming characteristic but, carried to these extremes, it is also a very inconvenient one.

Neither the Princess's lack of money-sense nor her husband's gambling were the real cause of their financial troubles which were almost entirely due to the enormous expenditure incurred at Sandringham where a grandiose programme of improvement had been embarked on out of all proportion to the real value of the property. Without counting money spent on the estate the rebuilding of the house alone was reckoned to cost £80,000, so that it is not remarkable to find that every year from 1863 to 1867 the Prince's expenditure exceeded his income by at least £20,000. Sandringham being in no way suitable for a royal residence, the business of turning it into one was an undertaking necessarily involving astronomical expense. At the beginning of 1865 the old house was still standing because Humbert, the chosen architect, had not yet succeeded in producing a satisfactory design for a new one but the kitchen and servants' quarters were under reconstruction, a billiard room had been built and the old conservatory converted into an indoor bowling-alley.

The estate was in no better condition than the house and required a fortune to be spent on it. New farms were bought, old farms were repaired and made water-tight, although it was whispered that the Prince cared little for his tenants' comfort or the condition of their crops in comparison with the well-being of the pheasants and partridges in which the estate abounded. At Sandringham the game was preserved with a strictness which gave rise to talk even in a generation when landlords as a whole were fanatical on the subject of game-preservation, a strictness which made the Prince unpopular with some of his tenants. His unpopularity, however, never touched his wife. The most disgruntled farmer of them all, a certain Mrs Cresswell, author of a diatribe entitled *Eighteen Years on the Sandringham Estate, by 'the Lady Farmer'*, took care to exempt her from all strictures, even writing ecstatically, 'It never occurs to me that the Princess is a woman at all but some exquisite little being wafted straight from fairyland to say and do the kindest and prettiest things all her life and never, never grow ugly or old.'

At Sandringham in these early days hunting was almost as important as shooting. It was a sport which the Princess herself much enjoyed, greatly to the horror of Queen Victoria who at one time went so far as to forbid her to hunt at all, arguing that everyone was shocked by the spectacle of the Princess of Wales following the hounds. At first the Princess was much distressed by this prohibition but she had her own way of dealing with such difficulties. She yielded for a while, but before very long she was back in the saddle and out with the hounds again, and this time the Queen was wise enough to admit defeat and let the matter drop. When the Princess could not hunt she would drive herself to the meet; she was an excellent whip even if slightly reckless and given to driving much too fast.

Guests at Sandringham had two major causes for complaint, the cold Norfolk climate and the abominably late hours kept by their hosts. Whist and poker were the usual occupation in the evening, except on Sunday when convention demanded some such innocuous game as "General Post", and play would be kept up until two or three of a morning. The Prince was always downstairs at a reasonable hour next day but the Princess never appeared before eleven at the earliest. This fact, coupled with her gross unpunctuality, made the Queen suspect that her son's wife did not make his home altogether comfortable to him. Certainly the Princess had no great interest in domestic detail and as a housekeeper she was haphazard. As a hostess, however, she excelled; 'sat next to the Princess at dinner,' one guest of these early days recorded, 'most charming of all princesses.'

Among the guests invited to Sandringham this year of 1865 was Wally Paget. Her comment on the marriage which she herself had done so much to bring about was a slightly disquieting one:

> 'We went to Sandringham. I was told that some mischief had been made by a compatriot of the Princess's. Others said that the conscience of Madame von B., rather an intriguing person, was not quite clear of reproach on that point. The Prince has however, whatever his other faults may be, contrived by his unvarying kindness and thoughtfulness to keep the affection of the Princess and they have lived on cordial and harmonious terms. I noticed with some regret that the influence of the Duchess of X. was very much in the ascendant. Without fearing any positive harm I thought that so utterly matter-of-fact and *terre-à-terre* person could not be an ennobling element.'[21]

The identity of Madame von B. and the mischief-making Danish lady unfortunately remain unsolved but the Duchess of X can be no other than the German-born Duchess of Manchester. She was as clever as she was beautiful and she counted among her admirers no less than three Foreign Secretaries, Lord Clarendon, Lord Granville, and in later years, Lord Rosebery, whilst her liaison with Lord Hartington was common knowledge. On the death of her husband she married her lover who had by then succeded to the Dukedom of Devonshire, and as 'the Double Duchess' she continued to entertain and intrigue London Society until her death in 1911.

As might be expected, Queen Victoria disapproved of the Duchess of Manchester, who had for a short time been her Mistress of the Robes, chosen for the post by Lord Derby because of 'her exquisite taste in dress'. There was no hint of love in the friendship between the Duchess and the Prince of Wales and it was the Princess's liking for the lady rather than her husband's which most alarmed the Queen. 'Believe me, dearest child,' she admonished her daughter-in-law, 'the Duchess of Manchester *is not a fit companion for you*,'[22] and to Sir William Knollys she wrote firmly, 'It is the duty of the

Prince and Princess to let her feel that her conduct has obliged them to be distant towards her.'[23] Distant towards the Duchess they could not bring themselves to be; she was a frequent guest both at Marlborough House and at Sandringham while they in their turn were often to be found at the Manchesters' town house in Great Stanhope Street or at their country seat of Kimbolton.

The Queen objected to many of the Prince and Princess's other friends and in particular to Lord Carrington, Lord Wilton and the Duke and Duchess of Sutherland – 'he does not behave as a Duke ought' – whilst the Duchess was 'a foolish injudicious little woman'.[24] Queen Victoria carefully scrutinised their list of engagements and did her best to prevent their attendance at any which she thought unsuitable. Her son and daughter-in-law bore her interference with commendable patience and usually succeeded in finding some very good reason for going their own way.

In August a great family reunion took place at Coburg where the Queen unveiled a statue of the Prince Consort. It was not a happy gathering and only the Princess's tact and good humour made the occasion bearable for the Queen. Lady Geraldine, whose waspish pen made the worst of any piece of gossip, recorded that Mrs Hardinge, a Lady-in-Waiting, described the assembled royalties as constantly quarrelling and 'at fisty-cuffs', with the exception, of course, of '*our* dear little Princess'.[25] The year 1865 was indeed one of bickering and disagreement, the more so because now a question arose which was to divide the Royal Family into two opposing camps: the question of Princess Helena's engagement to Prince Christian of Schleswig-Holstein-Augustenburg.

The problem of finding a husband for Princess Helena had much exercised Queen Victoria's mind. Marriage had taken the two elder girls away from her to homes in Germany; understandably, the Queen longed to have one daughter always at hand. She had hoped that her daughter-in-law might have filled this need but as she wrote to Uncle Leopold on the subject, 'Alix I can't depend on as they are never with me for long and besides she knows *none* of my intimate affairs.' Princess Helena therefore must stay at home but not necessarily as a spinster. A plan to marry her to a Prince of

Oldenburg came to nothing; 'Either Lenchen must remain in single blessedness, which would be most unfortunate,' the Queen told King Leopold in the same letter, 'or we must find someone else.'[26] That someone else must be prepared, of course, to live in England and to subordinate his own claims on his wife's attention to those of his royal mother-in-law.

Even without this stipulation the problem of marrying off Princess Helena presented difficulties; as Countess Blücher wrote bluntly, 'She is wanting in *charm*.'[27] However, at last a possible husband was discovered in Prince Christian of Schleswig-Holstein-Augustenburg. Prince Christian was neither rich, handsome, young or amusing. A typical anecdote shows the nature of his conversational powers. In later life he was unfortunate enough to lose an eye in a shooting accident. When conversation flagged at a dinner-party, as happened so often when he was the host, he would bid the footman bring him a tray containing his collection of glass eyes, which he would exhibit to his embarrassed guests, explaining at great length the peculiarities of each one – 'and this one, you see, is blood-shot, I wear it when I have a cold.'

This was the man selected as bridegroom for a nineteen-year-old girl of considerable ability and intelligence. The Queen's second daughter, Princess Alice, believed that her sister's happiness was being sacrificed to her mother's convenience; the Crown Princess, on the other hand, sided with the Queen. On Princess Alice's side were her two brothers, the Prince of Wales and Prince Alfred, and also the Queen's cousin, the Duke of Cambridge. By far the loudest protests came from the Prince of Wales, urged on by his wife, who in this matter felt more strongly than any other member of the Royal Family. Because the proposed bridegroom had taken the enemy's side in the German-Danish war the Princess was not prepared to treat him as a friend, much less as a cousin and a brother. She regarded the match as a deliberate insult to her parents and to Denmark; worse still, she chose to see it as a personal reflection on herself, an indication that the Queen no longer loved and approved of her. 'What do you say to this charming marriage of Helena?' she wrote bitterly to Lady Macclesfield. 'I cannot say how painful and dreadful it will be to me.'[28]

The Queen affected to make light of this opposition, but secretly she was a little afraid of the reaction of her son and daughter-in-law. From Balmoral she wrote to King Leopold on 14 September 1865:

> 'I fear that when Bertie and Alix arrive the *hubbub* will commence but I will not allow it to do so. I had much to go through with *his* marriage, which was disliked by *all* our family.'[29]

At first both the Prince and the Princess had the tact to dissemble their feelings a little. 'Bertie and Alix, though naturally not liking it, have taken the announcement of Lenchen's matrimonial prospects much better than we could have expected,'[30] the Queen informed King Leopold with an almost audible sigh of relief. It was not long, however, before the Prince voiced his very determined objections; so strong was his opposition that he announced his intention of absenting himself from the wedding ceremony.

At this threat both the Crown Princess and Princess Alice took fright. Princess Alice had somewhat altered her opinion; she still believed that Princess Helena was being sacrificed to the Queen's convenience, but she now realised that the girl herself was a more or less willing victim. Princess Helena saw clearly enough that if she did not marry Prince Christian she would in all probability never marry at all; this was her one chance and she was prepared to grasp it. Hoping to prevent an open rupture in the family Princess Alice sent her brother a charming and affectionate letter in which she begged him to relent:

> 'Oh, darling Bertie, don't let you be the one who cannot sacrifice his *own feelings* for the welfare of Mother and Sister. Mamma knows and deeply regrets what you feel, but, nowhere would she find another, and as she almost broke with Papa's only brother and all her other relations and friends for you and Alix, saying never should political feelings stand between her and her son's happiness do you both dear ones repress your feelings for a Mother's sake and let not political feelings towards Alix's relations stand between you and your own sister's happiness.'[31]

The Crown Princess wrote in similar terms, assuring the Prince that this marriage was no sign of any change in the Queen's affection for his wife – 'You know Mamma loves Alix much; she must not take this marriage as a proof of the reverse, which it is not.'[32] Prince Alfred, whose views always carried weight with his brother, wrote in more down-to-earth strain: 'The engagement has taken place and we must put a good face on it. Of course the relationship is painful to you, but you must try to accept him for what he is worth personally, and don't look at him with a prejudiced eye for he is really a very good fellow though not handsome.'[33]

Other people too were anxious to avoid a public show of disapproval on the part of the Prince and the Princess. The Queen's Private Secretary, General Grey, wrote guardedly about 'the power which they possess, in the present disposition of the public mind, of making their opposition if not effectual at least annoying by enlisting on their side the sympathy of the people for the Princess.'[34] Knowing well enough the strength of the Princess's popularity, he feared that the nation would be on her side, not on that of the Queen, if there should be an open quarrel over what Lady Geraldine stigmatised as 'this *abominable, disgraceful* marriage' with 'a miserable starveling German Princeling'.[35]

Under such pressure from his own family the Prince withdrew his opposition, but the Princess could not bring herself to be so accommodating. 'I cannot tell you what I have suffered,' the Queen wrote to the Crown Princess just before Christmas; 'Bertie is most affectionate and kind but Alix is by no means what she ought to be. It will be long, if ever, before she regains my confidence.'[36]

THE PRINCESS'S ILLNESS

On 3 June 1865 the Princess gave birth to her second son, Prince George. The baby arrived a month early, although his uncle, Prince Alfred, had doubts on this point. 'Pray tell me, it was just at the right time, was it not?' he demanded of his brother. 'Mamma and everybody fancied it should only be in July but you told me to expect it just when it did happen. I am sure you said it was later on purpose.'[1] Whatever may be the truth about this baby's timing it is a fact that the Queen, who conceived it her duty to attend the confinements of her daughters and daughters-in-law, never succeeded in being present at the birth of any of the Princess's children, because they had an inconvenient habit of arriving long before she had been led to expect them. 'It seems that *it is not to be* that I am to be present at the birth of your children, which I am very sorry for,'[2] she wrote rather plaintively to her son.

The arrival of this child brought great joy to his other grandparents, the King and Queen of Denmark, saddened as they were by the death of Princess Dagmar's betrothed, the Czarevitch Nicholas. Queen Louise, who had no great command of the English language, wrote her son-in-law a charming, unstudied letter of congratulation, which shows very clearly the real nature of the woman whom Queen Victoria persisted in regarding as an unprincipled schemer:

'Well, my dear Children, you are the most extraordinary pair I know, and I feel so happy as if I were a new-born baby myself. Thank God. His blessing *is* on you, may you never forget how merciful and gracious Our Lord is to you. The burial* is Friday but I must not name it in this letter, you see I write on pink paper. I am dressed in colours for Freddy† and now your second son. How proud you must be, two boys, don't you grow more attached to Alix at every present thus brought to you in pain and anguish?'

The Queen then speaks of the child's early arrival. 'What will your dear Mama say? Will she not say it is all weakness in Alix?' Queen Louise herself is quite unperturbed. 'If the children are healthy they can have any other secret why they want daylight before their time. I only hope it is a good sign for their character to be *before* the time in any good impulse of their life and for every good and noble deed.'[3]

Queen Louise could find personal comfort in the birth of this second grandson but the political outlook for Denmark and her allies was bleak in the extreme. In June 1866 Prussia launched what Sir Philip Magnus describes as 'a coldly calculated aggressive war against Austria'. This action horrified Queen Victoria, who for once found herself at one with her daughter-in-law in dismay at Prussian aggression and dislike of the Prussian Chancellor, Bismarck. When Austria capitulated at the end of seven weeks' fighting, many of the Princess's relations who had taken the Austrian side found their territories annexed by Prussia and themselves deprived of their personal fortunes. But although Queen Victoria could sympathise a little with the Princess's anti-Prussian feelings she was none the less going through one of her periodic phases of disapproval of the Princess herself.

The upbringing of the two little boys was a source of contention – 'Alix and I never will or can be intimate; she shows me no confidence whatsoever especially about the children' –

* Funeral of the Czarevitch.

† It was the birthday of her eldest son, Crown Prince Frederick.

and so too was what Queen Victoria referred to as 'Alix's going on or at least going out so much in Society'. She declared that her daughter-in-law 'is grown a little grand' and become 'haughty and frivolous'; she even complained of 'a want of softness and warmth', an accusation so unfounded as to show more clearly than anything else how strained the situation had become.[4]

The Crown Princess was the recipient of most of these complaints and she was wise enough to know that irritation always melted away in the sunny warmth of the Princess's actual presence. On 9 November she wrote urging the Queen to see more of her daughter-in-law:

> 'I know Alix has the greatest wish to be now and then alone with you. She says she is not amusing, she knows and she fears she bores you, but she loves you so much, and it seems to be a little ambition of hers to be allowed to be alone with you sometimes. It was Bertie who told me this and it quite touched me. It would please them both so much if you would take her once for a drive or walk *alone* with you.'[5]

The Queen took this good advice, and at once peace was restored. 'Dear Alix arrived here yesterday with the tiny little boys,' she wrote from Windsor on 14 November. 'She is dear and good and gentle but looking very thin and pale. I was some time alone with her yesterday and shall take her out alone this afternoon.' The result of these *têtes-à-têtes* was all that the Crown Princess could have hoped. 'I have taken a nice walk and drive with dear Alix and nothing could be nicer or dearer than she is. I never saw a purer mind – it is quite charming to see her and hear her. She looks delicate. I do love her dearly.'[6]

Whilst the Princess was visiting the Queen at Windsor the Prince was at St Petersburg for the wedding of his sister-in-law to the Czarevitch Alexander, brother of her first betrothed. The union was to be a genuinely happy one. Princess Dagmar had specially begged for the Prince's presence because so few of her own Danish relations could afford the expense of attendance at a Russian Imperial marriage. Being once again pregnant the Princess of Wales had been forced to stay behind, and she confided to Princess Louise that the six weeks' absence of her '*beloved one*' seemed an endless time. A charming relationship as of an elder and a younger sister had sprung up between her and this favourite sister-in-law. The Princess addresses Princess Louise as 'my little pet' or 'my own dearest Louise', she bemoans the fact that Queen Victoria will never allow Princess Louise to stay either at Sandringham or Marlborough House, and she begs her to 'think sometimes of the sister who loves you'. In her turn, Princess Louise gives her sister-in-law little presents of china pugs, and confides to her all the tangled complications of young love.[7]

In St Petersburg the Prince was reported to be paying too much attention to various Russian beauties. When he returned to England he found his wife slightly ailing. On 15 February she complained of pains and chill; he nevertheless persisted in leaving London to attend a steeplechase and a dinner at Windsor. Three telegrams were sent after him but not till noon next day did he return, to find the Princess in agonising pain, suffering from a severe attack of rheumatic fever.

For some days anxiety was intense. On 20 February the Princess gave birth to a daughter. For the past five days she had suffered acute and constant pain in her leg and hip, and now she had to go through her confinement without relief from any anaesthetic, the doctors thinking it wiser not to administer chloroform, although as the Prince wrote pathetically, 'she wished for it very much'.[8]

The Queen was not allowed to see the patient until a week after the baby's birth. When at last she was admitted to the sickroom she was horrified to discover that the tone of her son's letters had been far too optimistic and that the Princess's condition was much worse than she had been led to believe. Although the Princess had weathered her confinement better than could have been expected neither the rheumatic pains nor the fever showed any signs of abatement; the doctors were of the opinion that at any moment the condition might become serious. One of the Queen's most attractive characteristics was her quick sympathy with any invalid; she said of herself that she always felt drawn to a sick-bed. Now she was all solicitude and kindness, sending flowers and presents, and frequently making a special journey up from Windsor to visit the Princess, whom she described as being 'in a most pitiable state'. On one occasion when particularly oppressed by pain and sleeplessness, 'she said so pitifully "Will it never get better?" and laid her dear, sweet, weary face on my shoulder'.[9]

Much as the Princess appreciated the Queen's affectionate attention she relied chiefly on Lady Macclesfield for motherly love and comfort. With 'dearest old Mac' she was completely at her ease; Lady Macclesfield herself wrote home to her husband telling him how 'the poor little darling liked to be petted and loved'. Only the Queen and Lady Macclesfield, who, it must be admitted, was something of a croaker, seem to have realised the serious nature of the illness. The doctors issued cheerful and quite unrealistic bulletins, whilst the Prince's apparent unconcern was a source of constant irritation – 'the Prince, childish as ever, does not see anything serious about it'. Queen Louise, that kindest of parents, failed to grasp how very ill her daughter really was. In reply to an anxious letter from Lady Macclesfield telling her how much the Princess longed to see her she wrote, 'Pray do not humour her too much in giving way to her sensibility but rather cheer her by advising her to overcome this feeling of depression', cold comfort indeed for her daughter, who could take no food because of the inflamed state of her mouth and throat, nor sleep without doses of the strongest opiates. The pain in the knee was so bad that sometimes Lady Macclesfield would find her 'crying most piteously – 'it almost makes me cry to hear her'.

The Prince's reaction to his wife's illness was not a helpful one. He might be full of anxiety but he was behaving in a manner calculated to give exactly the opposite impression. Night after night he would be out seeking his pleasures until the small hours, whilst his wife lay awake, consumed with anxiety till his return. 'The Princess had another bad night,' runs one passage in Lady Macclesfield's letters, '*chiefly* owing to the Prince promising to come in at 1 a.m. and keeping her in a perpetual fret, refusing to take her opiate for fear she should be asleep when he came! And he never came till 3 a.m.! The Duke of Cambridge is quite *furious* about it and I hear nothing but general indignation at his indifference to her and his devotion to his own amusements.' Both General Grey and Sir William Knollys echoed the Duke of Cambridge's opinion, stressing the damage done to the Prince's reputation by the talk and scandal to which his behaviour was giving rise.

Lady Macclesfield had reason, too, to complain of his thoughtlessness in other ways. For instance, when the Princess's paternal grandmother died early in March it was decided that the news must be broken to her with the greatest care. After a particularly trying day, when the doctors had been examining the Princess's knee, thus unavoidably causing her much pain and discomfort, Lady Macclesfield heard her crying inconsolably; the Prince had chosen this most unsuitable moment to tell her of her grandmother's death. 'This was very bad for her and might just as well have been left till the morning,' Lady Macclesfield commented with justifiable anger, 'he really is a *child* about such things and will not listen to advice.'

The Prince's childishness was the real explanation of his apparently heartless behaviour. For all his twenty-six years he was still very immature; and the young and immature tend to shut their eyes to anything which they find frightening or unpleasant. Just so did he try to shut his eyes to the frightening and unpleasant fact of his wife's illness. But the Prince was not only frightened; he was bored and boredom was the condition he could least tolerate. He genuinely loved his wife and so long as he could be with her he was reasonably happy; it is on record that he had his desk moved into her sick-room so that he could write his letters at her bedside. For long periods, however, when he was necessarily banished from her presence he found time hanging very heavily on his hands. He could not face long hours spent in the decorous company of Lady Macclesfield and Sir William Knollys, so he escaped to more congenial friends and pleasures elsewhere.

Letters from the Prince and from Lady Macclesfield, backed by one from Queen Victoria herself, had convinced Queen Louise that she had been mistaken in supposing that her daughter's illness was not serious, and on 18 March she arrived in England, King Christian following a few days later. On the 18th Knollys saw the Princess for the first time since the beginning of her illness. She was lying on her back, unable to move, but she was in brilliant spirits at the thought of seeing her mother. Her long hair was loose about her shoulders and the solemn Sir William recorded that 'the upper part of her figure would have formed a study for a painter'.[10]

The arrival of her father and mother gave the Princess intense pleasure but it did not produce any improvement in her condition. Lady Macclesfield described the King as being very soft-hearted and both parents as very indulgent, and for the first time she complained about the Princess herself – 'her obstinacy is enough to provoke a saint'.[11] Not till 20 April was there any real sign of improvement. Then at last the Princess was wheeled to the window to enjoy the sunny spring weather and to delight in the fresh green of the trees, which had been black and leafless when last she had seen them. On 10 May, still in bed but looking ravishingly pretty with a pink bow in her hair, she was wheeled in to attend the ceremony of her baby's christening. Later that same day the Prince left to attend the opening of the Paris Exhibition. Not all of his time in Paris was devoted to official functions; 'the accounts I subsequently had of this visit were very unsatisfactory,' Knollys recorded disapprovingly, 'supper after the opera with some of the female Paris notorieties, etc. etc.'[12]

All this while there had been grumblings and rumblings from the great British public, who felt that they were being kept too much in the dark about the illness of their beloved Princess of Wales. She was certainly far more popular than either her husband or her mother-in-law. When the Prince went to Ascot week he received 'a very flat reception as the Princess was not there but suffering at home'.[13] By the beginning of July the Princess was sufficiently recovered to be able to look forward to attending a military review; at the last moment, however, this was cancelled because of the news of the shooting of the Emperor Maximilian. 'I was extremely glad both for the sake of the Princess and of the Queen that the Review did not take place,' Knollys commented; 'the Princess would have received an ovation but it would have been at the expense of the Queen.'[14] The Princess was, in fact, hardly fit enough for such exertion; her leg was still completely stiff and apt to swell, giving her much pain. Not till 2 July did Queen Victoria at last find her sitting up in a wheeled chair, 'looking very lovely but still, *altered*'.[15]

The Queen's comment was sadly apt. This long illness

marked a turning-point in the Princess's life; she emerged from it in some ways a changed person. For the first time she had experienced acute and prolonged physical pain (her first two confinements had been exceptionally quick and easy); worse still, during this long trial her husband's love had not been strong enough to keep him by her side. The Princess's discretion was absolute; no one can tell if she knew of the St Petersburg beauties, the Paris notorieties, the 'fashionable female celebrities' whom Sir William Knollys had so unwillingly invited to luncheon with the Prince at Ascot, or of the episode which Sir Henry Ponsonby described as 'spooning with Lady Filmer'. Even if she had known of her husband's infidelities maybe she had not cared overmuch. Far harder to bear than discreet infidelity was his open neglect; now all London and all Paris knew that whilst his wife lay sick in Marlborough House the Prince had been amusing himself elsewhere.

Physically the Princess's illness meant that she was left with a completely stiff knee, forced to face the probability that she would be lame for life, a gloomy prospect for a young woman who delighted in dancing, riding, skating, gymnastics and all athletic activities. The Princess was, however, as yet unaware of the most serious disability resulting from her illness. From her mother she had inherited the disease known as otosclerosis, a form of deafness which can be brought on or accentuated by illness or by pregnancy. Now, following her attack of rheumatic fever and the birth of her third child, the Princess grew increasingly deaf.

Only those who have been deaf themselves can realise the full meaning of deafness, the isolation it imposes and the evil effects it can have upon the character. A deaf person is cut off not merely from his fellows but also from many arts and pleasures, from the theatre, for instance, and, tragically enough for the Princess, from all forms of music. The deaf find it difficult to learn a foreign language, or to follow those who speak with unfamiliar accents, difficult too to make friends with children, who are too shy to speak up, and with sick people who cannot speak up even if they would. The judgment of deaf people often goes astray because, unlike the blind, they do not develop exceptional powers of comprehension and perception, like psychical *antennae*, to take the place of the lost sense. The natural tendency is to help and sympathise with blindness, a handicap which is immediately apparent to strangers; but only the deaf really sympathise with the deaf. Almost inevitably when anyone fails to hear what is said the speaker repeats the remark in a loud impatient tone; the deaf person then retires yet further into his shell, more and more convinced that he is a nuisance to his fellow men, more and more prone to develop those two unattractive characteristics, misanthropy and self-pity.

That this description of a typical deaf person is so wide of the mark where the Princess is concerned is a measure of her triumphant success in overcoming her handicap. For a royal personage deafness is an even greater disability and embarrassment than was the stammer which afflicted the Princess's grandson, King George VI. Stammering can be at least partially cured but the operations which can now restore hearing to those suffering from otosclerosis were not known a century ago, whilst the only hearing-aid available for the Princess was a cumbersome and ineffectual ear-trumpet, which she was too vain to use. Clever though she was at disguising and circumventing her deafness, some of its drawbacks were unavoidable. In the first place, she tended to become too dependent on one or two chosen friends whose voices she could hear because they were familiar to her, and to let herself fall too much under their influence. Secondly, her deafness meant that she became intellectually stunted. The Princess learnt from people rather than from books; as her mother-in-law frequently complained, she was no reader. Even if she had possessed perfect hearing the Princess would never have been a clever, well-instructed woman but she need not have become a stupid one. 'Her cleverness has always been under-rated partly because of her deafness,' Lord Esher was to write; 'in point of fact she says more original things and has more unexpected ideas than any other member of the family.'[16] However unintellectual her own personal friends might be, by virtue of her position she was thrown much into the company of the most famous and brilliant characters of her generation; she was on intimate, friendly terms with Gladstone, Tennyson, Balfour, Rosebery, Asquith, to mention but a few names out of many. Had she been able to hear it is impossible but that she should have learnt something from the conversation going on all around her in such company.

The last and most serious effect of the Princess's deafness was the way in which it prevented her from sharing fully in her husband's life. She delighted in the social round hardly less than he did, and she frankly enjoyed her position as the acknowledged leader of fashionable society, but as her affliction closed in upon her she found herself taking less and less pleasure in such things. The effort involved was too great and the satisfaction to be gained by such an effort grew progressively less as her hearing decayed. As Sir Philip Magnus puts it, 'increasing deafness destroyed a large part of the Princess's ability to continue to share without exhaustion her husband's intense enjoyment of the society over which he reigned for half a century'.[17] Cut off by deafness from things both intellectual and social she tended more and more to make her home and her children the central interests of her life whilst for amusements she turned to dogs and horses and the undemanding pleasures of the countryside. The ties of affection which bound husband and wife together were never broken; she did not allow herself to become seriously estranged from the Prince but as the years went by she found herself increasingly cut off from the interests and amusements which made up the stuff of his daily life. Inevitably they spent more and more time away from one another, inevitably they drifted slightly apart. Taking into account both the Princess's deafness and the Prince's infidelity it is remarkable that the gap which widened between them never became impassable.

In the summer of 1867, however, all this was still in the future. Only slight signs of deafness had as yet appeared, the chief trouble being the rheumatic knee, which remained obstinately stiff. It was decided to try what a cure at a German spa could do. On 18 August the Prince and Princess started for Wiesbaden, accompanied by their three children, their complete household, and twenty-five servants. They sailed in the royal yacht *Osborne* as far as Dordrecht, where they spent Sunday. The sailors' 'sing-song' profaning the Sabbath evening shocked Sir William Knollys:

'The sailors of the Osborne had as usual been singing the two previous nights, and Lord Henry Lennox persuaded the Princess to ask for it again. As it was Sunday I suggested that it would not only scandalise Protestant Dordrecht but might be objectionable to the sailors themselves. I had heard the songs and knew that one was a very objectionable one to be sung before modest women. I was, however, overruled. I consoled myself in trusting that the Princess only half-heard the song and only half-understood its meaning, but the Princess seemed seriously annoyed with me for trying to get her away before this objectionable song was sung.'[18]

Although deafness may have had something to do with her determination to listen to this improper song, all her life the Princess could not refrain from gently teasing anyone who was pompous or a prude.

Next day the party transferred to a river steamer. A cabin had been specially built on deck so that the Princess could wheel herself about in her chair, and at first she enjoyed herself well enough, attempting to sketch the scenery of the river banks. Very soon, however, trouble arose. Her eye fell upon the Prussian flag fluttering at the stern. In vain was it pointed out to her that it flew there only because of international agreement and custom, in vain was her attention drawn to the Union Jack flying at the mizzen and her own Danish flag at the fore; her anger was not to be assuaged.

Queen Victoria had always been against this visit to Wiesbaden, dreading the proximity both of Rumpenheim and of the wicked town of Baden which the Prince Consort had stigmatised as 'a little Paris'. Events proved her right; the Prince, who insisted on attending the Baden race-meeting, wasted far too much time and money on betting and general extravagance. The Queen was to complain especially of the amount he had spent on gratifying the Princess's taste for jewellery, wondering what a woman could want with new pieces who already had more jewels than she could ever wear. (It is of course possible that not all the jewellery the Prince bought on this occasion found its way into the possession of his wife.)

However, in Queen Victoria's judgment her son's extravagant and riotous living was a very small evil compared with her daughter-in-law's bad behaviour towards the King of

Prussia. The Prince chanced to be away on 19 September when a telegram arrived from the King announcing his intention of calling on the Princess at Wiesbaden at any time convenient to her that evening or the following day. Knollys had no option but to take this unwelcome message direct to the Princess, who at once dictated a refusal so blunt that he refused to transcribe it. Thus the matter was left until the Prince's return in the evening. Finding that his wife was not to be persuaded to withdraw her refusal the Prince did his best to gloss over her rudeness by sending a tactful message saying that he himself would call upon the King but that she was not well enough to receive visitors. The Princess, however, proceeded to underline the all too plain meaning of her behaviour by travelling to Rumpenheim to be present at her grandfather's funeral. If she was well enough to attend a funeral she was well enough to receive a social call; it was clear that her refusal to see the King had been intended as a deliberate rebuff.

Upset by this insult to her father-in-law, the Crown Princess wrote to Princess Alice stigmatising the Princess of Wales's behaviour as 'neither wise nor kind' and begging Princess Alice to see the Prince and persuade him to make some sort of *amende honorable* to the King. The Prince needed no persuading; his problem was to persuade his wife. All her life she was to remain adamant in her hatred and contempt for Prussia; on this point she could not and would not compromise. In this *impasse* the Prince turned for support to one of the most improbable of allies, his mother-in-law. Queen Louise had very good cause to hate Prussia but as the Prince said to Knollys, 'she was so sensible that she would make her daughter do what was proper'.[19] The Prince and Knollys were actually in consultation with Queen Louise when a polite and conciliatory telegram arrived, tentatively suggesting a visit from the King. Queen Louise promised that if he were to come she would swallow her own feelings and be present at the meeting but she gave no help at all to Knollys and the Prince in their attempts to make her daughter agree to this idea. Arguments were useless; 'it was a question of feeling with the Princess,' Knollys recorded, 'and she would not listen to reason of any kind.'[20] At length, provoked beyond endurance but still unyielding, she rose to her feet and, leaning heavily upon her

Four generations—Queen Victoria, the Princess of Wales, the Duchess of York, and Prince Edward afterwards the Duke of Windsor, at the White Lodge, 1894

The Princess of Wales and Prince Albert, later King George VI, 1896

The Marquis de Soveral

A drawing of Mrs Keppel
by Ellis Roberts

A portrait of the Princess of Wales, 1894
by Sir Luke Fildes

Queen Alexandra with Princess Victoria and the Dowager Empress, at the Royal Air Force Pageant, Hendon, 1923

Sir John Fisher
a photograph by Queen Alexandra

Queen Alexandra with her camera, 1913

Sir Dighton Probyn

Miss Charlotte Knollys

Queen Alexandra in coronation robes

stick, hobbled with some dignity from the room.

At this point the Prince asserted his authority and without consulting his wife, he sent the King a telegram inviting him to call. The Princess continued to fight a rearguard action, constantly altering her plans, in the hope that the King might lose patience and cancel the whole arrangement, but in the end she had to admit defeat. On the day before the proposed visit Knollys thought it best to keep at a prudent distance from the Princess who was the more angry because the King's visit had meant the departure of all her own relations. Forgetful of her promise, Queen Louise had started packing the moment she heard the news and had left hastily for Rumpenheim, taking with her the young Princess Thyra and the King of Greece. The next morning Knollys was sitting alone in the drawing-room awaiting the arrival of the Prince of Wales with their unwelcome guest, when the door opened and the Princess limped in, her face very white. Commenting on her pallor Knollys expressed a fear that she had caught cold. 'Maybe I *am* pale,' came the reply, 'but it is not from cold but from anger at being obliged to see the King of Prussia. And what I mind most is that it is in consequence of those two old women, the Prince of Wales's sisters, interfering, or I should not have been obliged to do so.'[21]

In spite of this outburst she behaved civilly enough to the King, who let it be known that he had been very satisfied with the manner in which he had been received. Nevertheless, the Princess's attitude understandably angered Queen Victoria. In a letter to the Crown Princess, she praised her daughter-in-law for being 'unspoilt and simple', but added, 'If only she understood her duties better! That makes me terribly anxious. This behaviour about the King makes me extremely angry.'[22] To the Prime Minister, Lord Derby, she expressed the same apprehension:

> 'The Queen trusts that Lord Derby will take an opportunity of expressing *both* to the Prince and Princess of Wales the *importance* of *not* letting any private feelings interfere with what are their public duties. Unfortunately the Princess of Wales has *never* understood her *duties of this nature*, thinking it her *duty* to follow Danish and Hessian advice. It

is a great source of grief and anxiety to the Queen for the future.'[23]

Although the Princess's general health had improved at Wiesbaden her stiff knee showed little signs of yielding to treatment. It must be admitted she was less inclined to persevere with quite unavailing efforts to cure her lameness than to teach herself, with high-spirited courage, ways and means of circumventing her disability. By November 1867 she was already walking fairly well with two sticks. The Princess with a stiff leg was a more graceful mover than most women with the full use of their limbs; she did not walk so much as glide over the ground, and soon Society ladies were copying 'the Alexandra limp'. Although she was not as 'diminutive' as some writers have described her the Princess was certainly a small woman, but she was also a very strong one. Her muscular control was remarkable; she would pick up her friend, Lady Augustus Hervey, carry her round the room on outstretched arms, and laughing, fling her on the sofa. Now she refused to allow her lameness to hinder her physical activity; she skated and danced as beautifully as ever, and she continued to ride, moving the pommel to the other side of her saddle in order to accommodate her stiff leg. On one point the Princess was determined: no physical disability was going to hinder her from accompanying her husband on an official visit to Ireland which was scheduled to take place in April 1868. She had good reason for wishing that the Prince should not go to Ireland without her. The year 1867 had been overshadowed by the activities of Irish Fenian agitators and during the autumn it had even been thought necessary to take security precautions at Sandringham. Although the only suspicious person to be discovered turned out to be a harmless tradesman, who fancied himself in love with the Princess and who was in the habit of writing her passionate love-letters, the danger was none the less a real one and there was genuine anxiety over the Prince's safety in Ireland.

In spite of the possible dangers the Government decided that the visit should take place. Disraeli at least was on the Princess's side in wishing that she should accompany her husband, pleading her cause with the Queen with typical gallantry: 'Is it not worth Your Majesty's gracious consideration whether the good might not be doubled if His Royal Highness were accompanied by the Princess? Would it not add to the grace, and even the gaiety, of the event?'[24]

Queen Victoria, however, remained unconvinced. She was always critical of what she described as 'rushing about', continuing to hope against hope that some day her son and daughter-in-law would settle down to a quiet domestic life interrupted as seldom as possible by any visits, official or otherwise. On this occasion she had a particular objection to 'rushing about' because the Princess was again pregnant. The Princess herself, however, felt it would be far more trying for the nerves of an expectant mother to sit at home worrying over the possible danger to her husband rather than to face the fatigues of an official visit and, as usual, she was gently determined to have her own way. The letter which she wrote to the Queen begging for permission to accompany the Prince is both ingenuous and eloquent, though almost wholly lacking in punctuation:

> 'I have a sort of *very* strong wish and feeling, if I may say so, to go with my Bertie this time to Ireland, and as three medical men don't see any objection I feel I [would] much rather go (although I must say it won't be very amusing for me) than be left behind in a state of fever about him the whole time which I don't think can be very good for me now and as I really feel so well and my leg is so much stronger I feel I can as well go to balls etc there than here and as for the journey I don't really much mind that. Besides I know Lady Abercorn so well and she wrote me such a nice letter. I really think and have a sort of conviction that it will do me no harm and therefore have almost made up my mind to go with my Bertie. In these times now I think one gets to feel more anxious about those one loves most in the world and it makes me always feel anxious when we are obliged to be separated for a while but in this case I confess I almost shudder to think of the possibility of his going alone, and I should feel DREADFULLY disappointed if anything really were to prevent my going with him. I feel like a sort of call and wish to go.

Please excuse this long explanation but I wished myself to tell you my feelings and wish about it and I hope dearest Mama that you will understand me. All of this I have not told my Bertie as I did not like to say anything about my private feelings for him but to you dear Mama who know what I mean I could not help opening my heart to.'[25]

Faced with such a plea the Queen could only relent and give permission, turning a discreetly blind eye to the equally discreet hint – 'I have almost made up my mind to go with my Bertie' – that were permission refused the Princess would go without it. On 15 April the Prince and Princess landed at Kingstown; what *The Times* described as 'the Danish Conquest of Ireland' had begun.

The Princess needed all her courage and pertinacity to face the strenuous ordeal of this Irish visit. She had only just learnt to walk again without the aid of two sticks and she was several months pregnant. In this condition she was to be one of the two central personages in a series of public functions, stared at by thousands of people, all quick to mark any sign of lameness, any thickening in a figure so justly famous for its slimness. Added to these more serious difficulties she started for Ireland suffering from that prosaic and disfiguring complaint, a bad cold in the head. To quote *The Times* again, this time at its most sententious, 'It is fortunate that the Princess is able to gratify the eyes of the people without inconvenience.' Perhaps *The Times* did not realise how very much inconvenience this gratification did in fact involve.

Political troubles as well as physical disabilities stood in the way of the success of the Irish visit; that spring of 1868 the Irish crowds were in no mood to applaud English royalty. But although the Irish are a people with a notoriously tenacious and bitter political memory they are also a people possessed of a delightful capacity to put aside political rancour for a while if someone or something chances to take their fancy. And, of all men, an Irishman is the first to capitulate to a woman of charm, beauty, and courage. Disraeli was right; had the Prince of Wales gone to Ireland without his wife the occasion would have lacked just those qualities of gaiety and grace which appeal especially to the Irish temperament. It was the Princess rather than the Prince whom the Irish took to their hearts; at the great military review at Phoenix Park a voice was heard shouting from the middle of the vast crowd, 'We'll never let her leave us, and if she's here the Prince will have to stay too.'

It was not only on such enjoyable occasions as a State Ball that the Princess charmed everybody by her evident pleasure and interest; at a long and dull university function she listened with rapt attention and apparent enjoyment to a Latin speech which must have been entirely incomprehensible to her. Together with the Prince she visited schools, police barracks, orphanages and Roman Catholic colleges, she attended official luncheons and dinners, and she spent a rainy day at Powerscourt admiring the waterfalls. After reading the details of such an exhausting programme it is a relief to come upon Sir William Knollys's assurance to Queen Victoria that 'the Princess of Wales has returned to London without being in the least the worse for her visit to Ireland – rather the contrary.'[26] Perhaps the prettiest of all the tributes paid to the Princess during her Irish visit was a poem appearing in *Aunt Judy's Magazine*, a paper edited by Mrs Gatty and her daughter Mrs Ewing, both of them well-known writers of books for children. The last verse ran thus:

> 'Hurrah! her little feet have trod
> For the first time on Irish sod.
> Oh, flags and blossoms, wave and nod
> To welcome such a traveller!
> Hurrah! she comes to Erin's isle;
> Our very hearts she did beguile;
> And treason vanished at her smile,
> And we would give our lives for her.'

As Lady Abercorn wrote, the success of the Irish visit had 'exceeded even the fondest hopes'. The enthusiasm it had aroused might possibly have developed into a more permanent sentiment had it not been for Queen Victoria's obstinacy and lack of imagination. The Princess had learnt from experience how much the Irish enjoyed the presence of royalty, and she went so far as to hint tactfully that the Queen ought to pay

Ireland a personal visit. 'I think the Irish people very loyal, she had written to Queen Victoria from Dublin; 'wherever we have been, they have never forgotten "their Queen", one always heard "Three cheers for the Queen", or "Let the Queen live here amongst us for some months!" '[27] Both Disraeli and, later, Gladstone wished the Prince of Wales to have a permanent residence in Ireland, and to live there for a month or two every year. The Princess warmly welcomed this plan. She had never cared much for the Scottish holidays so dear to Queen Victoria and now in her lame state she found the prospect even less attractive – 'I don't *entre nous soit dit*, exactly think the Highlands the most suitable place for a stiff leg,'[28] she confided to Princess Louise. Lady Geraldine reported a conversation at a tea-party on 30 April: 'We got some talk with her about her visit to Ireland, with which she is charmed! Quite delighted! So charmed with the people, the fun, enthusiasm, warmth! So filled with admiration for the country, "far more beautiful than Scotland", she said. *She* would be charmed to have an Irish Balmoral!'[29]

The Princess would seem to have been exactly the person to fit happily into an Irish background, with her spontaneous gaiety, her informality, her lack of logic, her love of horses, and, be it said, her want of method and her hopeless and incurable unpunctuality. She would have found herself perfectly at home in that country where the clock has no significance. As a Dane too, she was better equipped than the average English person to sympathise with the outlook of a small, defeated nation, brooding bitterly over its wrongs.

The dream was a pretty one but it was not to be. The Princess of Wales and the Irish people were to have no chance of becoming better acquainted because Queen Victoria firmly vetoed the idea of an Irish residence for the Prince and Princess. All that the Princess could do to show the friendly Irish populace that she had not forgotten them was to appear at Ascot in the same outfit that she had worn at Punchestown Races, a green dress of Irish poplin trimmed with Irish lace, with Irish shamrocks in her white bonnet. This gesture cost her something; one of her female relations remarked rather cattily, 'Dear Alix was looking a little less than her very best.'

Chapter seven

THE GORGEOUS EAST

The house at Sandringham was now being rebuilt; it was therefore proposed that the Prince and Princess should spend the winter of 1868–9 on a tour of Egypt, travelling there by way of Denmark, Berlin and Vienna. The months following the Irish visit had not been happy ones for the Princess. Stories about her husband's love affairs were circulating freely; Lady Geraldine complained of 'his troop of fine ladies', and more explicit gossip linked his name with that of the actress, Hortense Schneider. The Princess was delighted to escape from England for a while and she was particularly pleased at the prospect of taking her children to visit their Danish grandparents. Only the baby Princess Victoria, born on 6 July, 1868, was to be left behind; the Princess was determined to take little Princess Louise, who had been named after her Danish grandmother, and was therefore that grandmother's special child. On 28 October the Princess wrote to Queen Victoria begging, with her usual tact and courtesy, for permission so to do:

> 'I have been wanting to write to you for some time but I put it off till I had spoken to the doctors and obtained their

permission for the children to undertake the journey. I asked Dr Farre and Mr Paget to write to Sir William Jenner and to give him their opinion about the three eldest children. Thank God, I can say with a clear conscience that I think our little Louise is now quite strong and healthy enough to undertake the journey with us to Denmark, and Mr Paget, who has seen her more often than the other doctors this year and by experience has observed how well she stands up to the change of climate, assured me that it would be good for her health and thought it would do her no harm. I must say, that as I am now convinced that she is strong and well, I do *not* want to be parted from the little thing, especially as later on, we *must* be separated from them all for so long. I would prefer to *give up* the trip rather than leave the little darling behind. *You* will understand this best, my angel mother and therefore I speak so openly to you. It would affect me in the same way as yourself, dearest Mama, if you had to be parted from your little Beatrice. If the doctors decide that she can undertake the journey and if she is well at that moment I would consider it a *blessing* from *Heaven* for the past hard trial and pain, and I would be *grateful* to *God* if we obtained such happiness. I need not tell you, dear Mama, how delighted I am, after nearly *five* years, to return to my paternal home and to show them our three eldest children. Oh, what a joy! But it would *break my heart* if I could not take the three children and daily I pray to God that *nothing* should arise which would hinder this long hoped-for happiness.

Forgive me, dear Mama, that I have written to you at such length about my joys and anxieties. You are *always* so kind to me and understand my thoughts and feelings so well, that I could not omit doing so.'[1]

Queen Victoria very reluctantly agreed that the two boys might go, but she remained adamant on the subject of the little girl, arguing that it was extremely selfish of the Princess to risk the health, maybe even the life, of so young a child to gratify her own foolish whim. Cut to the quick by this accusation, the Princess dissolved into tears. The Prince of Wales may not have been a faithful husband but he was a very loyal one in the sense that he would allow no one, not even his mother, to criticise his wife. The letter which he now wrote was calculated to make even Queen Victoria think twice:

> 'I regret very much that you should still oppose our wishes but as you throw responsibility entirely on Alix if we take Louise, I naturally shall share it and have not the slightest hesitation or fear in doing so. Alix has made herself nearly quite ill with the worry about this but what she felt most are the words which you have used concerning her. Ever since she has been your daughter-in-law she has tried to meet your wishes in every way and you have never said an unkind word to her or of her. You can therefore imagine how hurt and pained she has been by your accusing her of being "very selfish" and "unreasonable", in fact, risking her own child's life. None of us are perfect – she may have her faults – but she certainly is not selfish – and her whole life is wrapt up in her children – and it seems hard that because she wishes (with a natural mother's pride) to take her eldest children with her to her parents' home every difficulty should be thrown in her way, and enough to mar the prospect of her journey, and when Vicky and Alice come here nearly every year with their children (and I maintain that ours are quite as strong as theirs) it seems rather inconsistent not to accord to the one what is accorded to the others.'[2]

On receiving this letter the Queen agreed that the little Princess Louise might go, but she continued to raise objections about the composition of the suite which was to accompany the Prince and Princess. Oddly enough, Queen Victoria raised no objection to one name appearing on the list as 'extra equerry', that of Oliver Montagu, an officer in the Blues and younger son of Lord Sandwich. His brother Edward, a close friend of the Prince, wrote after his first meeting with the Princess, 'I think her as near perfection as a mortal can be.'[3] Oliver Montagu would have echoed that sentiment. As a friend once wrote of him, 'his devotion to the Princess was proof of a loyal friendship as well as of a romantic and chivalrous devotion to a beautiful woman'.[4] Louisa, Lady Antrim was a young girl just 'come out' in London Society at the time when the friendship between the Princess and Oliver Montagu was most in evidence. Her considered opinion, written many years later, deserves attention:

> 'The Princess of Wales floated through the little ballroom world like a vision from fairyland. She went out a great deal, and chief among her cavaliers was Oliver Montagu. Her husband by this time was living in a very fast set, indulging in many flirtations. It is surprising that, young and lovely as she was, the Princess never gave any real occasion for scandal. I think it must have been due to Oliver Montagu's care for her. He shielded her in every way, not least from his own great love, and managed to defeat gossip. Oliver Montagu was looked upon with awe by the young as he sauntered into a ballroom, regardless of anything but his beautiful Princess, who as a matter of course always danced the first after-supper waltz with him. But she remained marvellously circumspect.'[5]

And if the Princess was circumspect she was also virtuous. There is no doubt that Oliver Montagu loved her – of her own emotions there is much less evidence – but equally there is no doubt that he was not her lover. She was the Princess of Wales, she had been strictly and religiously brought up, and she was not a character who could easily over-step the conventions. The Prince referred to Oliver Montagu as one of 'those wicked boys' and Oliver's own brother complained of 'the sort of rollicking life he leads' in the company of 'a noisy sporting lot of people'.[6] But, like the Princess, Oliver Montagu was religious; the two of them would discuss religion together. It is not altogether surprising that their affair remained a platonic one, but it is very surprising that Society should have accepted it as such and that gossip should have been practically silent on the subject. The Queen herself, though disapproving of Oliver Montagu's friendship with her son, never gave the slightest hint that she thought it unwise that he should be so much in the company of her daughter-in-law.

Such idealistic love affairs were, however, much more common in nineteenth-century England than they are today. The

Victorians believed that love could exist quite independently of sex, especially if the object of that love was in some way set apart from common humanity by rank or beauty or any other transcendent quality. Although the Princess of Wales and Oliver Montagu were oddly cast for the roles of Dante and Beatrice, few or none doubted that their love affair remained on that plane. The presence of this young man, so gay, so devoted, so attentive to her every wish, was to add to the Princess's pleasure in the journey which now lay before her.

The Prince and Princess were to go first to Paris, joining their children in Denmark in time for Christmas. This was the Princess's first visit to Paris and it was a most successful one. Queen Victoria had previously vetoed a suggested visit to the Emperor Napoleon III at Compiègne. Apparently when the French Court was resident in Paris the standard of behaviour was comparatively respectable but, as the Queen put it, 'the proceedings at Compiègne and Fontainebleau made it undesirable that the Prince and Princess should visit either of these places'.[7] King Leopold was of the same opinion – 'that court is not calculated for Alix'.[8] Now, however, the Emperor and Empress were all kindness and attention, giving a dinner party and a ball in honour of their guests, at which, in spite of the presence of the beautiful Empress, 'there was no lady in the room who in appearance came half-way up to the Princess of Wales'.[9]

'You ask me if I like Paris,' the Princess wrote to Princess Louise. 'Yes, I was *delighted* with it and with all I saw, and went about all day long and to a great many shops, which was most amusing. Our visit to Compiègne went off beautifully and I was much taken with the lovely Empress.' Since Princess Louise's love affairs were not going smoothly her sister-in-law proceeded to give her warm sympathy combined with some surprisingly sensible advice:

> 'My thoughts have been a great deal with you, my sweet Louise, and I have been wondering how things have gone on and hope they have not been again teasing you dear, like the last day I saw you when you looked quite worn and sad!! Pray don't let yourself be guided by so many!!! but better go straight about that kind of thing to your Mama. I am

sure she would not thus misunderstand you, and she surely would give you the best advice, and don't ever believe she would think first of herself in such a case as this!!! Those who tell you that give you the worst advice and don't either do any good by it but harm. So pray Darling, follow my advice, and listen to a sister who, God knows, means well and loves you very much.'[10]

After a family Christmas spent at Fredensborg came a tearful parting from the three children, who were to travel back to England from Hamburg whilst their parents went on to Berlin. Here the Princess met Bismarck for the first time and here too, not altogether surprisingly, she suffered some rudeness from the Prussian Queen. King William, however, admitted to finding her charming.

After a journey of twenty-four hours with the thermometer registering twelve degrees of frost, the Princess stepped out of the train at Vienna looking exquisitely fresh, to be greeted by the Emperor Francis Joseph and a galaxy of princes, archdukes and ambassadors. This was not at all the quiet welcome which the Prince and Princess had expected but they soon discovered how impossible it was for any royal personages to pay an 'unofficial' visit to Vienna. Court mourning had caused the abandonment of some functions but even so formal dinners and parties followed each other in an endless stream. By custom a visit had to be paid to every member of the Imperial Family resident in Vienna; as there were at that time twenty-seven archdukes living in or near the city, not to mention smaller fry, this in itself was a considerable undertaking. More to the Princess's taste were the skating parties, the ballet performances, a concert at which Johann Strauss conducted his own waltzes and a tour of the Imperial stables housing the five hundred horses which were the special interest of the Empress Elizabeth. On this journey the Princess met for the first time the two Empresses, Eugénie and Elizabeth, who were her friendly rivals for the palm of beauty. With the intellectual and melancholic Elizabeth she had very little in common beyond a love of horses and a feminine taste for beautiful clothes; on one occasion the Empress was heard to remark that of all European royalties only the Princess and herself really knew how to dress. As far as looks were concerned only one fault could be found with these two beautiful women; both Empress and Princess were too thin for nineteenth-century taste.

During this Austrian visit the grace and gaiety of the English royal couple stood out in favourable contrast to the stiffness of the Imperial Court. They were not sorry to escape from this formality to the freedom of life on board the frigate H.M.S. *Ariadne,* which took them from Trieste to Alexandria. Once they had landed in Egypt life took on a magical glow. The first sight of the East is an unforgettable experience for any Westerner. Some people are repulsed, others feel an attraction which, though they may never return in person, yet draws them back over and over again in memory. So it was with the Princess. The East which she now saw for the first time was not the tamed and Westernised East of today, but the authentic land of the *Arabian Nights.* Everything was new and strange to her, the scenery, the architecture, the people, their habits, speech, dress, religion, even their food. She, who had known so many royal residences, had never seen one in the least resembling the Ezbekieh Palace at Cairo put at their disposition by the Khedive. Indoors were magnificent oriental carpets and hangings, bedsteads of solid silver, fountains playing in the rooms, and an enormous *salon* one hundred and forty feet long, whilst outdoors in the grounds were troups of acrobats and a travelling menagerie. She revelled in these romantic surroundings without troubling herself about the lack of European comforts which her husband found slightly disconcerting. The Prince, however, was enjoying himself greatly. He already knew something of Egypt, having visited the country before his marriage, and he delighted in acting as guide to so enthusiastic a sightseer as his wife. One of the sights they saw was the departure of the pilgrims for Mecca, another, where the Princess of course went alone, the inside of the Khedive's harem.

On 6 February the party started up the Nile in a fleet of steamers, barges and *dahabiahs.* Wisely, the Prince had entrusted the arrangements for this trip to 'Baker of the Nile', the explorer Sir Samuel Baker, a choice which had much displeased Queen Victoria. 'Sir Samuel Baker's principles are *not* good,' she had written in alarm, 'I regret that he should be associated for any length of time with you and dear Alix.'[11] Whatever his principles may have been Sir Samuel proved an excellent organiser and an agreeable travelling companion. The Prince and Princess travelled in a *dahabiah* named *Alexandra* specially fitted up for them under his supervision – 'And very well he has succeeded,' the Prince commented. Behind the royal party, in another fleet of boats, came the party of the Duke of Sutherland. The two parties would combine for sight-seeing expeditions ashore, when the Princess rode on a white donkey or walked tirelessly, regardless of her lame leg. Everyone dressed just as they pleased and behaved with complete informality; 'habited in what he or she deemed the climate required the cavalcade was as grotesque as it was amusing.'[12]

The chief objects of interest were, of course, the ruins of ancient Egypt, but time was also found for visits to such places as a sugar-factory, the palace at Beni Hassan, and a school where the pupils, when asked to point to Lake Nyanza on the map, located it first in China and then at the South Pole, much to the amusement of Sir Samuel Baker, the discoverer of that lake. The party remained several days at Luxor, visiting Thebes and the Colossi and going on a moonlight expedition to Karnak where champagne was drunk whilst fireworks soared above the temple columns.

As usual, the Prince's chief amusement was sport. The little Princes, Eddy and George, had written to their parents expressing the hope that they would not be devoured by *Crokkydiles*; the Prince now succeeded in shooting one of these animals. The trophies which the Princess in her turn collected to be brought home were living ones. In a characteristic access of pity she carried off a small Nubian orphan whom she attached to the party as a kind of mascot. When he arrived in England he was baptised in the little church at Sandringham, the Prince and Princess standing as godparents. Unfortunately his Christian teaching failed to impress upon him the desirability of keeping his hands from picking and stealing. Nothing was safe from his thieving fingers; on one occasion he even made bold to steal the Prince's own gun and added to his offence by breaking it. The Princess's other trophy, which was also to find a home at Sandringham, proved far less troublesome than young Ali Achmet. This large black ram, which she had reprieved from the butcher's knife because it was tame enough to eat out of her hand, lived on board one of the boats, an object of great interest to the crew, who garlanded it with flowers in honour of its royal mistress.

Day after day glided by as the procession of boats made its slow way upstream to Wadi Halfa, which was to be the turning-point. The members of the party were young and cheerful; they had escaped from the formality of Court life to the enchantment of a land where time flows by as effortlessly as the Nile water. Relaxed and at ease, the Prince was at his most agreeable whilst Oliver Montagu was always at hand, amusing, helpful and devoted. No wonder that one night, sitting on deck and looking up at the star-studded velvet of an eastern sky, the Princess declared that she had never before known such happiness.

Back again in Cairo there was more sightseeing to be done; 'Alix is much struck with the Pyramids but disappointed with the Sphinx,'[13] the Prince wrote to his mother. The Princess paid a farewell visit to the ladies of the harem, who amused themselves by painting her eyes and eyebrows in oriental fashion and sending her back in yashmak and burnous to mystify her husband. From Cairo the party visited the unfinished Suez Canal before sailing to Constantinople, where they were entertained by the Sultan, Abdul Aziz. The Princess's style of beauty appealed very much to Turkish taste; 'the Princess of Wales is a gift of cream and honey sent specially by Allah for the good of the English people',[14] declared one enthusiastic *pasha*. The Prince and Princess took particular pleasure in shopping incognito in the bazaars where they mingled with the crowds, passing themselves off as 'Mr and Mrs Williams'.

After a tour of the Crimean battlefields came ten days in Athens and Corfu. This was perhaps the most delightful time of all for the Princess since it gave her an opportunity to see her brother 'Willi', now King of Greece, and to meet his Russian wife, Queen Olga, and their baby son Prince Constantine or 'Tino', whose stormy career was to be of great concern to her in after years. The tour was to end as it had begun with a few days in Paris, where the Princess planned to do some shopping. 'Pray, dear children,' Queen Victoria wrote in some alarm, 'let it be your earnest desire not to vie in dear Alix's dressing with the fine London Ladies, but rather to be *as different as possible by great simplicity*, which is more elegant.'[15] The Queen need not have feared that her daughter-in-law would ever adopt an extravagant or *outré* style of dress. In the many photographic groups in which she appears the Princess invariably stands out as the best-dressed woman because of the severe simplicity of her style. In an age when fashion and the arts generally were remarkable for a profusion of ornament and detail she relied, as a good architect does, almost entirely upon perfection of line. Some of her Paris dresses are still in existence, a delight to the eye and exquisite in cut and material.

On 12 May 1869 Lady Geraldine noted that she had visited the Royal Academy and there seen 'the Prince of Wales, who with the Princess only arrived from their six-month tour in the East two or three hours earlier!!! and moreover have a Court Concert before them tonight!!!' Lady Geraldine might have been even more lavish of exclamation marks had she known that the Princess was once again pregnant. As a week-end retreat during the coming Season she and the Prince planned to use the Duke of Devonshire's famous Palladian villa at Chiswick. 'There is great fear,' Queen Victoria warned them, 'lest you should have gay parties at Chiswick instead of going there to pass the Sunday, a day which is rightly considered one of rest, quietly for your repose with your dear children.'[16]

Queen Victoria may have disapproved of Chiswick, but she disapproved still more strongly of Rumpenheim, where the Prince and Princess went visiting as soon as the Season was over. Lady Geraldine chanced to be staying there at the same time, and on 3 August she noted in her diary, 'The Prince of Wales has disfigured himself by cutting off *all* his whiskers and beard, leaving nothing but a slight moustache and very small Imperial; it is more unbecoming to him than language can express! He is positively frightful so!!' Three days later comes the ominous entry, 'A commission has been ordered to investigate and report if Harriet Mordaunt is truly mad.'

Harriet Mordaunt was reasonably well known to the

Princess. As a childhood acquaintance of the Prince's she was on sufficiently familiar terms to be invited to informal parties such as small dances at Abergeldie. After the birth of her first child this young woman – she was only twenty-one – confessed to her husband that she had committed adultery with 'Lord Cole, Sir Frederick Johnstone, the Prince of Wales and others'. The ensuing scandal was immense. Although rumours first reached the Prince and Princess in the spring of 1869 whilst they were still on their travels, the resulting case did not come up for trial till February of the following year. Throughout the affair Sir Charles Mordaunt behaved with great bitterness towards the Prince and although he did not actually cite him among the co-respondents he threatened to subpoena him to appear as a witness.

'Dear Alix has entirely taken the same view in the matter that I have and quite sees that it is an absolute necessity for me to appear in court, should I be called,'[17] the Prince wrote to Queen Victoria; and again, 'Alix has been informed by me of everything concerning this unfortunate case'.[18] The public had cast the Princess for the role of much injured wife. This was a part she steadfastly refused to play, nor would she withdraw, or allow her husband to withdraw, for a while from public life. Whilst the case was actually in progress she continued with her full programme of social engagements, driving in the Park, going twice to the theatre, dining out at private houses, even giving a large dinner-party at Marlborough House which was attended by several members of the Cabinet. It is pleasant to learn that at this trying time husband and wife found opportunity to relax together in a carefree manner, 'spending several hours daily skating upon the ice of the private water of the Toxophilite Gardens, Regent's Park'.[19]

After many delays and postponements the Prince was called on 23 February as a witness on Lady Mordaunt's side, not on that of her husband. He acquitted himself admirably; when the final question was put – 'Has there ever been any improper familiarity or criminal act between yourself and Lady Mordaunt?' – to be answered by an emphatic 'Never!', there was a sudden burst of applause. That very evening the Prince and Princess had a long-standing engagement to dinner with the Gladstones. The Princess was looking her loveliest and she worked hard to make the evening a success, but she could not always command her countenance; 'the Princess looked lovely but *very* sad when she was not exerting herself,'[20] wrote Mrs Gladstone's niece, Lucy, now married to Lord Frederick Cavendish.

If husband and wife had to dine out anywhere on this particular night it was as well it should be with the kind and friendly Gladstones. Although the Prince had left the court cleared of the imputation of adultery with Harriet Mordaunt the feeling against him ran very high. Never since the reign of George IV had royalty been so unpopular. Queen Victoria's determined seclusion had not endeared her to her people; as the *Observer* put it in a leading article on the Mordaunt Case 'there are not wanting those among the opponents of the monarchical system who, failing to sympathise with the domestic sorrow of Her Majesty, have ceased to regard royalty with that veneration and enthusiasm which they have hitherto shown.'[21] In fact, the only really popular member of the Royal Family was the Princess. She was warmly cheered when she appeared in a box at the theatre but the cheers turned to hisses when her husband joined her.

Queen Victoria proved to be surprisingly forgiving and sympathetic towards her son. The Prince and Princess visited her the day after he had appeared in court; perhaps intentionally, for the next month or so the Princess saw more of her mother-in-law than usual, often driving or walking with her alone. Nevertheless, the Queen blamed the wife as well as the husband for the bad company they kept. 'They lead far too frivolous a life,' she wrote to the Princess Royal on 2 March, 'and are far too intimate with people – with a small set of not the best and wisest people who consider being fast the right thing.'[22] However, in a letter written in reply to one from Queen Louise of Denmark rejoicing that 'our beloved Bertie has been able to vindicate himself publicly with a good conscience',[23] she praised the Princess with special warmth: 'She has behaved so beautifully, so splendidly, but it was a hard trial for her; she is so simple, so honorable, and, as we say, so right-minded, but I must often wish for better company for her.'[24]

Chapter eight

A TIME OF TROUBLE

On every hand it was agreed that the Princess had behaved splendidly over the Mordaunt scandal, but it was also agreed that she had been badly hurt by that affair. The Prince had been foolish enough to write letters to a very attractive woman and to pay calls on her in private; although he had cleared himself of the charge of adultery all the world now knew that he was anything but an ideally faithful husband. To say that she could put up with private infidelity but that she could not bear public scandal is not to call the Princess a hypocrite; in the peculiar circumstances in which she and her husband had to live their married life it was essential that no obvious cracks should appear in the façade they must present to the world. The Prince had been unfaithful time and time again, but on this occasion, when he had not in fact been unfaithful at all, he had exposed his wife to open shame and embarrassment.

Sir Philip Magnus goes so far as to suggest that when the Princess left for her usual summer holiday in Denmark she intended to stay there for a long time, perhaps indefinitely – 'The Princess of Wales, who had been deeply hurt by the Mordaunt trial, was in Copenhagen on a visit which was expected to last for a considerable time.'[1] The facts do not bear out this supposition. The Mordaunt trial was over by the end of February; the Princess did not leave England till July, the date when she might normally be expected to set off on her Danish holiday. She took the three elder children with her but left behind little Princess Victoria and the baby Princess Maud (born 26 November 1869), giving strict instructions that the baby's diet was to remain unaltered till her return. No devoted mother, such as the Princess certainly was, would ever have left these instructions about an eight-months-old baby had she herself intended to be away for a very prolonged period. Nor does the Prince of Wales's behaviour suggest that any serious rift existed between husband and wife; he insisted on accompanying the Princess to Denmark and he begged the Queen to allow him to remain there for at least a week or ten days, a favour which was not granted. In the event the Princess's stay in Denmark turned out to be a very short one. On 15 July the Franco-Prussian War broke out; in these circumstances it was thought advisable that she should return to England immediately.

Angry though the Princess may have been with her husband she had no intention of quarrelling seriously with 'my naughty little man', as she described him in a letter she wrote to Princess Louise, congratulating her on her engagement to Lord Lorne. The Princess wrote rather coldly since neither she nor the Prince approved of this match, which in fact proved a most unhappy one, but she softened a little towards the end of her letter – 'you know, my pet, in me you will always find a true friend, whatever may happen.'[2] Personal feelings about Princess Louise's engagement combined with political differences over the Franco-Prussian War to drive a slight rift between the Queen and the Princess. 'Unity in the family is of great importance,' the Queen wrote sadly to the Crown Princess. 'Alix is not clever and her feelings are so anti-German and yet so little really English that she is no help – good, dear and kind as she is and much as I love her.'[3]

This autumn of 1870 the Prince and Princess's great interest was the re-opening of Sandringham House, now almost entirely rebuilt. The new house was very much a home and not a palace. The original eighteenth-century building had vanished and in its place was a red-brick, Victorian-Tudor mansion planned for comfort rather than for grandeur. Opulent it certainly was but not magnificent. Because he had worked for the Prince Consort at Osborne and had collaborated with Grüner in designing the mausoleum at Frogmore, the Prince of Wales had chosen Humbert rather than a better-known architect such as Salvin. The result was a solidly built house in Salvin's manner but lacking in just that touch of distinction which marks most of Salvin's work. Bay windows to let in plenty of light and air were the main features of the design. Although the house was a large one, inside the accommodation was inadequate; Prince Eddy and Prince George, for instance, slept in bedrooms the size of the average Victorian bathroom. The main rooms, however, were spacious and comfortable, furnished almost entirely with contemporary furniture, some of it 'built-in'. Except for the trophies and curios which the Prince brought home from his journeys the pictures and ornaments were also, for the most part, of the same date as the house; there were no ancestral portraits and almost no 'antiques'. Perhaps for this reason Sandringham had none of the atmosphere of an English country house; the Prince of Wales liked to think of himself as an old-fashioned Norfolk squire but his home was the typical home of a nineteenth-century industrial magnate.

The Princess, whose taste in dress was exquisitely simple, in house decoration preferred a cluttered cosiness. Ornaments were everywhere, varying from exquisite trifles by Fabergé – he was to make tiny models of all the Sandringham animals, including even the farmyard turkeys – to objects of no value whatsoever except a sentimental one. In the great hall a ferocious-looking stuffed baboon held out a tray in which visitors could drop their cards. This hall or 'saloon' was the chief meeting-place, a fine high room comfortably furnished with desks, a piano, and tables supplied with books and newspapers, a fitting centre for a house where everything was large and handsome. Only the drawing-room preserved a feeling of formality and protocol. In the dining-room hung the set of Goya tapestries which were Sandringham's great artistic treasure. Much of the life of the house centred round the billiard-room and the bowling-alley, one end of this alley being furnished in semi-oriental style, complete with hookahs, to form an oddly amusing smoking-room.

In the Princess's upstairs sitting-room the stucco decorations were copied from those she had so much admired in her room in old Sandringham House. Her bedroom was fantastically crowded with photographs, holy pictures, little crosses and mementoes of every sort and kind. By her bedside she always kept a small replica of Thorwaldsen's statue of Christ; over her bed, in the angle of the curtains draping the bed-head, the carved head of a cherub hung above a large crucifix.

This was the house which the Princess was to love and to live in for the rest of her life. There were now five children in the Sandringham nurseries. The Princess of Wales was once again pregnant, a pregnancy which was affecting her as none of her previous ones had done. She tired quickly and became easily depressed but she insisted on leading a normal, busy life, accompanying her husband everywhere, fearful perhaps as to what he might be doing were she not at his side. On 6 April 1871 she gave birth prematurely to her third son.

At Sandringham nothing was ready; as on the occasion of Prince Eddy's birth there was no nurse, no baby-clothes and only the local doctor in attendance. Although all went well and easily for the mother, the frail little baby, hastily christened Alexander John Charles Albert, but known in the family as John, only lived for twenty-four hours.

The loss of a baby must be a tragedy to any mother. The Princess's bitter grief was only to be expected; what was more surprising was the Prince of Wales's reaction. The lady-in-waiting, Mrs Stonor, described him with 'the tears rolling down his cheeks',[4] insisting on putting the child's body into the coffin himself and carefully arranging the white satin pall and the piles of white flowers. From her bedroom window the Princess watched her husband walking in the short funeral procession hand-in-hand with the two little Princes, Eddy and George, solemn in grey kilts, *crêpe* scarves and black gloves. On hearing the news, Queen Victoria had kindly offered to come at once, an offer which the Prince gently refused, pointing out that his wife must have complete rest and quiet. The Princess herself added the pretty rider that she would wish the Queen's first visit to Sandringham to be on an occasion of joy, not sorrow.

Throughout her life the loss of this little child was to be often in the Princess's mind. On 6 April 1882, the eleventh anniversary of the child's birth, she wrote to Prince George, 'it is sad to think that nothing remains on earth to remind us of him but his little grave'.[5] Now, in her sadness and depression, she went through agonies of self-reproach, believing herself to be responsible for her baby's death because she had not taken sufficient care during the months preceding its birth. No modern doctor would hold her to blame. Over-exertion and fatigue can perhaps cause a miscarriage but not a premature birth; in all probability the Princess's babies were born before their time because she suffered from a hormone deficiency. Queen Victoria agreed with the Princess's opinion, but being wise enough to blame the father rather than the mother, she asked her friend and adviser, Dean Wellesley, to speak to her son on this subject. The Prince duly promised to take better care of his wife, remarking, however, that 'she [Alix] is naturally very active in mind and body and I am sure a sedentary life would not suit her'.[6] Matters therefore went on much the same as before the birth and death of little Prince John but for one significant change; although the Princess was as yet only twenty-six, from now onwards there were to be no more children.

The usual summer routine was varied this year by a visit to Ober-Ammergau for the Passion Play. The Prince and Princess were so anxious to preserve their incognito that they did not reserve seats; they even asked their friends not to raise their hats or bow when passing them in the street. One of those friends, Lady Battersea, described the Princess as looking particularly bewitching in a Tyrolean hat. Both husband and wife were deeply moved by the play and by a conversation they had afterwards with the actor who played the Christus. The Princess is reputed to have given him a ring in memory of the occasion whilst the Prince declared that he had never been so much impressed with anyone in his life. From Ober-Ammergau they travelled to Jugenheim; whilst the Princess remained there with a large party of Hessian relations the Prince went alone to Homburg, where his gambling activities gave rise to some scandal. However, a sudden turn of fate was soon to silence all adverse criticism. At the end of October the Prince and Princess went on a visit to Lord Londesborough's house near Scarborough. Several people who had been at this house-party, including two servants, were afterwards taken seriously ill; and on 23 November it was announced that the Prince of Wales was suffering from an attack of typhoid fever.

Many accounts of this illness can be read in old newspapers and in standard histories and biographies; the best description, however, of the Princess's reactions and the part she played is to be found in the unpublished letters of her dear friend and lady-in-waiting, Lady Macclesfield, who wrote almost every day to her husband describing the ups and downs of the patient's condition and the behaviour of the relations who came flocking to his sick-bed. Princess Alice chanced to be at Sandringham and she naturally stayed on to nurse her brother, just as ten years previously she had nursed her father. Lady Macclesfield's opinion of Princess Alice varied considerably. At first she was delighted to have her help and practical experience in illness; however, if Princess Alice was efficient she was also domineering and very soon Lady Macclesfield was complaining of her manner towards her sister-in-law – 'We are all furious at seeing our Princess *sat upon* and spoken of as if she had not sense enough to act for herself.' Over the vital question of a doctor the Princess had indeed acted for herself. On her own responsibility she sent for Doctor Gull and put him in charge of the case although, at the Queen's suggestion, she agreed also to have Sir William Jenner, 'reckoned first-rate for fevers' according to Lady Macclesfield, 'though a mean time-server and a dismal croaker'. The Princess was bent on doing all she could for her husband, though her deafness was a sad draw-back in a sick-room. She would only go out to take some fresh air if absolutely compelled to do so by the doctors or Lady Macclesfield, and at night she lay down, but not to sleep, in a dressing-room opening out of her husband's bedroom. On occasions, however, the doctors absolutely insisted that she should leave the patient, for the sake of her own peace of mind. 'I believe his ravings have been very dreadful,' Lady Macclesfield wrote on

29 November, 'and that for *that* cause she was kept out of his room one day, all sorts of revelations and names of people mentioned.' Face to face with death the Prince was sadly remorseful and penitent; on one occasion, when half wandering, he told the Princess that he was sure she would desert him now because of his past neglect. He addressed her as 'my good boy' and when she told him that she was his wife, he replied sadly, 'that was once but is no more; you have broken your vows.'[7]

On 29 November Queen Victoria arrived, sent for personally by the Princess of Wales against Princess Alice's judgment. Only a few months ago the Princess had expressed a wish that the Queen's first visit to Sandringham should be an occasion for rejoicing; now the two women greeted each other with tears. Prince Alfred was already in the house; the eighteen-year-old invalid, Prince Leopold, had begged to come too but had been refused – 'Prince Leopold, poor boy, is so dreadfully anxious to come here as he thinks he could comfort "dear Alix", whom he idolises.' The day after the Queen's arrival the patient showed symptoms alarmingly reminiscent of his father's fatal illness; now, for the first time, the Princess broke down, 'almost distracted with grief and alarm'. She quickly recovered herself – 'the dear Princess behaves admirably, she does not disguise the truth from herself but her self-control and composure are perfect, she never thinks of herself, and is as gentle and considerate to everyone as ever.' Lady Macclesfield was particularly touched one night to find on her blotting-book a little note in the Princess's handwriting, 'Goodnight, my dear little Mac, thank God the Prince seems a little more easy tonight.'

The Princess's birthday, 1 December, passed unmarked by any celebration. The day afterwards her husband, returning to consciousness, asked if it were her birthday. 'What a shame not to have told me!' he exclaimed, on being told that the anniversary was already past. In the middle of all her cares and anxiety the Princess did not forget Lady Macclesfield's own birthday on 3 December, but presented her with a photograph and a crystal watch.

Cheered by the patient's return to consciousness and by other hopeful signs the Queen had left Sandringham on

1 December. Everything seemed to be going well; on 7 December the Princess and Princess Alice actually dared to go out together for a drive over the snow in a sledge drawn by two grey ponies. In his apparent convalescence the patient was more than ever dependent upon his wife, which made Lady Macclesfield the more anxious that they should be given the opportunity to be alone together for a while:

> 'But how Princess Alice is to be rooted out it is not easy to see. I shall have a great deal to tell you on that subject. Suffice it is to say for the moment that she is the most awful story-teller I have ever encountered, meddling, jealous, and mischief-making. For a short time she is everything that is charming, but the less one knows of her the better.'

The Prince's recovery, however, was only temporary. 'Imagine our consternation this morning at hearing that the fever had all lighted up and was beginning all over again, as bad as ever or worse!' Lady Macclesfield wrote on 7 December. Later in the day she added the note, 'Worse and worse, the doctors say that if he does not rally within the next hour a very few more must see the end. The Princess has telegraphed that herself to her parents. She keeps up heroically.' The Queen rushed back to Sandringham with every available member of the Royal Family, the young Princes Leopold and Arthur, Princess Louise, Princess Beatrice, even Princess Alice's husband, Prince Louis of Hesse. The Princess of Wales telegraphed for her brother Crown Prince Frederick who was unable to come; she was glad, however, to have one member of her own family with her in the person of the Duke of Cambridge. The house was crammed so full that Princess Louise and Princess Beatrice were obliged to sleep in one bed. The Queen was 'charming, so tender and quiet' and the Princes Arthur and Leopold, '*very* nice, so amiable and anxious about their brother'. On the whole, however, the presence of 'this extraordinary family' was a hindrance rather than a help – 'it is quite impossible to keep a house quiet as long as it is swarming with people and really the way in which they all squabble and wrangle and abuse each other destroys one's peace'. Deadly tired and looking like a ghost, the Princess still remained calm. Almost all the time she was at her husband's bed-side, and when she crept away to fall asleep from sheer exhaustion it was almost impossible to rouse her, so greatly had the strain increased her deafness. For days the Prince hung between life and death. Even now Queen Victoria, with commendable fortitude, persisted in taking her daily walk in the grounds, regardless of slush and snow; the Princess refused to leave the house except in the evening when, if her husband could spare her, she would slip out unseen in the gathering dusk to pray in the little church in the park. On Sunday, 10 December prayers were offered there, as in churches throughout the country, for the Prince's recovery. Before the service began, a note from the Princess was handed to the parson: 'My husband being, thank God, somewhat better, I must leave, I fear, before the service is concluded that I may watch by his bedside. Could you not say a few words in prayer in the early part of the service so that I may join with you in prayer for my husband before I return to him?'[8]

Although that short letter was intended to be kept entirely private somehow its contents reached the press, and its publication awoke more sympathy for the Princess than did any other episode in the course of her husband's illness. Nobody could accuse poor Princess Alice of levity or lack of thought, but her very different attitude still further enraged Lady Macclesfield: 'Talking of Providence Princess Alice burst out, "*Providence*, there is no Providence, no nothing, and I can't think how anyone can talk such rubbish." Imagine having to struggle through all this without any trust in God to support one! Our dear Princess does believe and pray and she finds comfort in so doing.'

The Princess had need of all the comfort she could get. At one point, when the doctors told her that her presence excited their patient too much, she crawled into his room on her hands and knees so that he would not see her. The watchers sitting about in hall and library waiting anxiously for news were filled with superstitious dread at the approach of the ill-omened day, 14 December, anniversary of the Prince Consort's death. On the 13th the Queen recorded in her journal that the

Prince had suffered the worst attack yet: 'Only Alix and one of the nurses were there, and the doctors were at once hastily summoned. But the dreadful moment had passed. Poor Alix was in the greatest alarm and despair, and I supported her as best I could. Alice and I said to one another in tears, "There can be no hope."'

That very evening, however, the doctors reported slight signs of improvement; the next day, on the much-dreaded anniversary, they issued a cheering bulletin, 'His Royal Highness has slept quietly through the night and there is some abatement of the gravity of the symptoms.' The Prince was conscious again; against all probability he was not going to die but to recover. That evening his wife and his mother had tea alone together, rejoicing over the good news, and the Princess took this occasion to tell the Queen how glad she was that the change for the better should have come on that particular day so that thankfulness for present mercies might soften remembrance of past grief.

'My time has been entirely devoted and belongs in fact to my darling husband who thank God is really getting on wonderfully,' the Princess wrote on 31 January. 'Dearest Lady Mac, you who were here at that awful time and shared my agonies and suffering so truly, you will understand me when I say that it all seems to me now like a most terrific awful dream and hardly can I now understand how I ever could have lived through it and survived it. Thank God, that is of the past, and the Lord's name must ever be praised, Who was merciful to me and gave me back my all but lost darling. This quiet time we two have spent here together now has been the happiest days of my life, my full reward after all my sorrow and despair. It has been our second honeymoon and we are both so happy to be left alone by ourselves.'[9]

To Princess Louise she wrote in similar strain: 'Oh dearest Louise, you who knew what I suffered and saw my utter despair and misery – you would hardly know me now in my happiness. We are *never* apart and are enjoying our second honeymoon. *Never, never* can I thank God enough for all His mercy when He listened to my prayers and gave me back my life's happiness.'[10]

The Prince and Princess spent Christmas together at Sandringham, the children remaining at Osborne, where they had gone at the beginning of their father's illness. The Princess sent them charming letters and cards for Christmas, her letter to little Prince Eddy perhaps being worth quoting in full, if only because it is one of her very few surviving letters to this eldest son:

'My own darling little Eddy,
Mama sends a thousand thanks for all the very nice little letters, and is so glad to hear from Mr Dalton that Eddy is a good little boy. Mama is so glad dear little Eddy has been going on praying God for dear Papa's recovery and the Almighty God has *heard* our prayers, and darling Papa is going to be quite well again and very soon we hope you may all come home again to see dear Papa once more! Mama is so glad her little Chicks will spend a happy and merry Christmas with dear Grandmama, and Mama sends you each a little Christmas card with many good wishes for Christmas and the New Year, which I hope will begin brightly and happily for all of us, and that my little Eddy will try and become a very good obedient boy. Remember me kindly to Mr Dalton with many thanks for all his letters, kiss Grandma's hand, and give my love to Uncle Leo and Aunt Beatrice.

Ever your loving
Mama Alix.'[11]

As soon as the Prince was fit to travel they joined the children at Osborne. During her stay there what time she could spare from her family and husband the Princess spent riding with her young brother-in-law, Prince Arthur, and playing piano duets with Prince Leopold, who wrote to Princess Louise, 'Alix is looking very well and more *lovely*, I might say more angelic, than ever.'[12]

A thanksgiving service for the Prince's recovery was to be held in St Paul's Cathedral, a plan much disliked by Queen Victoria. In this the Princess agreed with her – 'It seems to me to be making too much of *an outward show* of the most sacred and solemn feelings of one's heart.' She had, nevertheless, an instinctive feeling that the people at large would expect such a service to be held, and she persuaded the Queen to withdraw her opposition, pleading that 'the whole nation has taken such a *public* share in our sorrow, it has been so entirely *one* with us in our grief, that it may perhaps feel that it has a kind of *claim* to join with us now in a public and universal thanksgiving.'[13] So on 27 February the Princess, exquisite in blue velvet and sables, drove with the Queen and the Prince to St Paul's through streets lined with dense crowds. The boos and hisses of a year back were now forgotten; the people cheered the Queen because at last she was showing herself to her loyal subjects, they cheered the Prince of Wales because all criticism of his behaviour was forgotten in relief at his all but miraculous recovery, but they cheered the Princess for herself alone. As the Mayor of Windsor had remarked at an official reception a few days previously, 'With reference to the Princess you will permit me to say she is a universal favourite.'

LIFE AT SANDRINGHAM

Compared with the eventful years of the Princess's early married life the eighteen seventies and eighties appear a relatively quiet period. Not that the halcyon second honeymoon atmosphere lasted for very long; it was as short-lived as the Prince's sick-bed resolutions of amendment. By 1873 he and his brother Prince Alfred were again causing scandal; their behaviour shocked even the young Lord Rosebery, who was certainly no prude, having been sent down from Oxford for running a horse in the Derby (unfortunately the animal came in last).

Meanwhile the centre of the Princess's life was slowly shifting from Marlborough House and her husband to Sandringham and her children. Discipline was not a great feature of life in the Sandringham nurseries and schoolroom. Remembering his own over-disciplined childhood the Prince was perhaps inclined to go too far in the opposite direction; 'if children are too strictly or perhaps, too severely treated,' he once wrote to the Queen, 'they get shy and only fear those whom they ought to love.'[1] That sentence, together with one from another letter, 'I think a child is always best looked after under its mother's eye,'[2] gives the clue to the system, or lack of system, followed by the Prince and Princess in the upbringing of their children. On two points, however, the Princess was adamant. She would allow no quarrelling in the family; 'Above all *don't ever quarrel* with your brother,'[3] she admonished Prince George, and again, 'Mind that you in particular do not quarrel with or irritate your brother.'[4] The second point was well put by Queen Victoria in a letter to the Crown Princess. After criticising the Princess of Wales's neglectful attitude towards her children's education she wrote, 'One thing, however, she does insist on, and that is great simplicity and an absence of all pride, and in that respect she has my fullest support.'[5]

Although the Prince was devoted to his family his need for constant distraction made it impossible for him to live quietly alone with them for more than a very short time. His wife fully recognised this fact; she understood that their home must not only be a quiet sanctuary designed for the upbringing of children but also a place suitable for the entertainment of those gay, 'fast' friends whose company he found so entertaining. To combine the simple home atmosphere in which she herself had lived as a child, and which she naturally desired for her own children, with the social whirl and glitter in which her husband delighted would have been a task beyond the powers of most women; she, however, being an illogical woman, saw nothing odd in the combination of incompatible elements and somehow at Sandringham she achieved the impossible. Perhaps she succeeded because she enjoyed both sides of her life so much; in the days when there were small babies in the nursery she had been equally happy to slip on a flannel apron and bath one of the children or to dress up in full evening dress with jewels and tiara and entertain a party resplendent with the smartest of guests. As a special treat, if she liked the smart guests well enough, next day she might invite them to help bath the baby.

Not only the babies but the older children also were more in evidence than was usual in Victorian households. They were encouraged to mix freely with their parents' guests, too freely, indeed, for the comfort of some of these guests, who were inclined to echo the verdict which Queen Victoria in a moment of exasperation once passed on her two grandsons, then aged eight and seven, 'They are such ill-bred, ill-trained children I can't fancy them at all.'[6] She described them as being 'wild as hawks', that exact phrase being echoed by Lady Geraldine who went so far as to write, 'the boys were past all management'.[7] Lady Geraldine described the three Princesses, Louise, Victoria and Maud, as 'rampaging little girls', but Princess Victoria, who was usually known as 'Toria', she reported as being '*very* sharp, quick, merry and amusing'.[8] Queen Victoria, however, found this particular child exceedingly naughty.

To the Princess the members of the household and even the domestic servants counted almost as members of her own family. In 1874 she was much grieved by the death of the Prince's equerry, Major Grey. In one of the very few of her letters to her husband which have escaped destruction she describes how she visited the dying man, who had begged earnestly to be allowed to see her – 'I should like so much to see her once more, I promise I won't speak, I only want to take her by the hand' – and how she waited for hour after hour in an adjoining room until at last when she was told that he was dead, 'I was *ashamed* that I could no longer control myself and sobbed aloud'. She ends her letter with the heartfelt exclamation, 'Thank God over and over again that you were spared to me!'[9] 'Dear sweet excellent Alix looked so distressed and shaken by all the heart-rending scenes they had witnessed,' Queen Victoria wrote to the Princess Royal after Major Grey's death; 'she is so simple, so good, so truly pious and so full of sympathy for others'.[10] When her maid, Mrs Louisa Jones, lay dying the Princess was by her bedside for the whole of the last two days, writing afterwards, 'my poor dear Louisa, she died in my arms'.[10]

Nearest and dearest of all the members of the household were the two who first joined the service of the Prince and Princess in the early seventies. Dighton Probyn, a dashing young officer who had won the Victoria Cross during the Indian Mutiny, was appointed equerry to the Prince in 1872; a year later Sir William Knollys's daughter, Charlotte, became the Princess's Woman-of-the-Bedchamber. These two were to be her faithful friends and servants for life. Dighton Probyn openly proclaimed his worship of 'the Blessed Lady', the name by which he always referred to the Princess, and served her with an unselfish devotion which could give no cause for scandal. After his wife's death he was always believed to be on the verge of matrimony with Charlotte Knollys, who was deeply attached to him. One Christmas he gave her an unusual present in the shape of a bathroom fitted up for her at Sandringham, with mirrors all round the walls so that she could see herself from every possible angle, an idea which greatly delighted Charlotte, who was an exceptionally ugly woman. Dighton Probyn had an odd taste in bathrooms; his own, which still survives at Sandringham, is equipped with three basins labelled 'Head and Face only', 'Hands', 'Teeth'.

Dighton Probyn was a charming, simple character who agreed admirably with everyone; not so Charlotte Knollys. She was the bugbear of officials such as the Captain of the Royal Yacht, and the Royal Family referred to her somewhat ruefully as 'the inevitable Charlotte'. She had an ever-growing influence over the Princess, to whom she soon became quite indispensable, and she gave herself entirely to the Princess's service, seldom taking as much as a day's holiday. The Princess repaid her with equal devotion and nursed her through several illnesses. In 1877, for instance, when Charlotte fell ill of typhoid at Abergeldie, the Princess stayed on to nurse her at great inconvenience both to herself and to the Prince, refusing to go south until her patient was fit enough to travel.

The Prince's illness had marked a turning point in the relations between the Queen and the Princess. Their shared anxiety had brought the two together as never before; from now onwards the Queen had little but good to say of her daughter-in-law. On 10 March 1873 she noted in her *Journal* that it was the anniversary of the Prince's wedding, 'a day which I am ever thankful for as it gave me such a dear sweet daughter as darling Alix'; she was to make some such comment almost every year either on the wedding anniversary or on the Princess's birthday. Apart from the disputes which invariably arose whenever the Princess wished to take her children to Denmark the only serious difference between them concerned church-going. The Queen began by complaining that her son and daughter-in-law were too irregular in their attendance. In later years this complaint could never have been made against either of them; the Prince's young niece,

Princess Alice, was considerably surprised by the only piece of advice her uncle gave her on her marriage – 'Wherever you may be, always remember to go to Church on Sunday.'[12] Now they duly promised to reform, a reformation which took the unwelcome shape of attendance at the highest of all high churches, All Saints, Margaret Street. Not surprisingly, the Queen was horrified and, as so often, she sought the help and advice of Dean Wellesley. He tactfully pointed out that he believed the real cause of the trouble to be the Princess's deafness which made the dull, inaudible service at the Chapel Royal a real penance to her – 'not hearing, she hates and is wearied beyond anything by the service there'. The Dean suggested that 'some Protestant Church in London, where the Princess of Wales could hear, ought to be found for her, and seats be got there.'[13] In the end the Princess compromised by attending the Chapel Royal with her husband on Sunday morning and going to Evensong and an occasional weekday service at All Saints with Charlotte Knollys. Although careful not to obtrude her views, the Princess remained very much of the High Church school, and in 1884 she even went so far as to attend that new-fangled service, the Three Hours' Devotion on Good Friday, although she confessed to finding it 'rather too much of a good thing'.[14]

All Saints, Margaret Street was a church famous for its music, which was part of its attraction for the Princess, who did not allow her deafness to interfere with her musical interests. Music was a great feature of life at Sandringham where guests might be expected to play duets with the Princess or even struggle with a Schumann concerto arranged for two pianos. 'The pace set was terrific,' wrote Lady Randolph Churchill, 'and I was rather glad that there was no audience.'[15] Although conventional, the Princess's musical taste was more serious than might have been expected. In the seventies the revival of interest in Bach had barely reached England; she, however, attended and much appreciated the performances of his works given at St Anne's Church, Soho, being present at *The Christmas Oratorio* as early as 1873. She was much interested in the London Bach Choir, which counted Gladstone among its first members, and she helped to find a suitable hall for its concerts. Both the Prince and the Princess actively supported Lady de Grey's efforts to revive opera at Covent Garden, the Princess being rapt in admiration of Wagner whilst her husband much preferred Offenbach. When the famous singer, Melba, first appeared at Covent Garden she was a failure; hearing that the Princess of Wales had much admired her voice and was very anxious to hear her again, she decided to attempt another London season which, of course, proved triumphantly successful. The Princess frequently attended the concerts given in London by the famous Hallé Orchestra from Manchester and all her life she kept in touch with Sir Charles Hallé's second wife, the violinist, 'my beloved Madame Neruda', trying her best to help the more struggling members of Madame Neruda's family. The interest which both the Prince and the Princess took in the Royal College of Music went much farther than the formal patronage which royalty usually extend to any deserving institution; on more than one occasion they arranged that the students should give a private concert at Marlborough House, so that they could judge for themselves the standard of individual talent and performance. Well might Sir Henry Ponsonby remark, 'I must say Marlborough House is working the Royal College of Music violently.'[16]

In spite of all this concern with musical matters it must be admitted that the Princess's interest in music was neither particularly well-informed nor was it what would today be called 'highbrow'. She was nothing of an intellectual; 'the melancholy thing is that neither he (the Prince of Wales) nor the darling Princess ever care to open a book',[17] lamented Lady Frederick Cavendish, unconsciously echoing a complaint frequently made by Queen Victoria. When other people opened a book in her presence the result could be surprising. At her first meeting with Tennyson she politely asked him to read aloud the famous *Ode of Welcome* which he had written for her wedding. Halfway through, the situation struck them both as unbearably funny; the book fell on the floor and Princess and poet went into fits of uncontrollable laughter.

This sense of fun – it can hardly be described as a full-blown sense of humour – went hand in hand with a liking, in which her husband shared, for practical jokes and for rough-and-tumble horse-play. In their letters she and her son Prince

George would recall with sentimental pleasure the way in which they had squirted each other with soda-water syphons during the Christmas festivities at Sandringham. The Princess could squirt and be squirted and yet keep her dignity. Lady Frederick Cavendish described how at Chatsworth 'our Queen of Hearts' played at 'pockets', 'whisking round the table like any dragonfly, punishing the table when she missed, and finally breaking her mace across Lady Cowper's back with a sudden little whack. Likewise at bedtime, high jinks with all the ladies in the corridors, and yet through it all one had a sense of perfect womanly dignity and a certainty that one could never go an inch too far with her. She can gather up her beautiful bright stateliness at any moment.'[18]

This cheerful informal spirit was characteristic of Sandringham parties. 'It is very jolly here indeed,' wrote Oliver Montagu's brother Victor, 'very unstiff and only a certain amount of etiquette, very quiet and gentlemanlike altogether.'[19] 'Very jolly' was the epithet he also applied to his hostess although he complained that her deafness made conversation difficult. There would be sport of all kinds to entertain the guests, hunting as well as shooting, and in very hard weather, games of ice-hockey, and skating on the lake, a sport in which the Princess delighted in spite of her lame leg. She was more interested than ever in horses and when wishing to buy or sell she would consult Henry Chaplin, one of her husband's more intimate friends and a famous judge of horseflesh. To dogs she was almost ludicrously devoted, first pugs and later 'Japanese spaniels' and pekinese being her favourite breeds. She also cherished a liking for parrots – a white cockatoo lived permanently in the hall at Sandringham – although even she admitted to feeling daunted when a friend presented her with no less than forty of these birds.

As a matter of course the Princess was always in London for the summer 'Season', where of necessity life was a little more formal than at Sandringham, although there was a notable lack of stiffness about the smart friends of the Prince and the Princess, known collectively as 'the Marlborough House set'. The Season of 1873 was made particularly delightful for the Princess by a visit from her favourite sister 'Minny', now the Grand Duchess Marie Fedorovna, with her husband the

Czarevitch Alexander, whose nickname in the family circle was 'Sacha'. The two sisters delighted Society by their frequent appearances dressed exactly alike, in blue and white foulard of a morning in Hyde Park, or in exquisite evening dress at parties when the Grand Duchess's jewels were a sight in themselves. As long ago in their childhood the Grand Duchess was judged the livelier of the two but the Princess the more beautiful; 'the sisters set each other off,' wrote Lady Antrim, 'and became the centre of a glittering crowd wherever they went'.[20] Wonderful parties were given in honour of the Russian visitors, one of the most magnificent being a ball in the huge conservatory at the Horticultural Gardens. As the guests danced to Strauss waltzes played by Hungarian bands in red and blue uniforms the ladies' dresses rippled like a sea of colour between the palms. Even this splendid entertainment paled in comparison with a superb fancy-dress ball given the next year, 1874, at Marlborough House, at which the Prince appeared dressed as Charles I and the Princess as a Venetian lady in a ruby red frock with a small jewelled cap on her hair.

When the London Season ended the Prince and Princess would be off on holiday, the one usually to some German spa, the other to her family home in Denmark. Husband and wife seldom went abroad together except on official occasions, such as their visit to Russia in 1874 to attend the wedding of Prince Alfred to the Czar's daughter, the Grand Duchess Marie. On this visit the Princess alarmed and astonished the more timid ladies-in-waiting by venturing on a switch-back or *montagne russe*; she seems to have had a lasting taste for this fairground amusement, since a much later photograph shows her as an old lady whizzing down a 'scenic railway' with Dighton Probyn in attendance complete with top hat. In a charming letter to little Prince Eddy she describes how 'Aunt Minny and Mama drive in sledges every day and skate too; and then we are driven down some steep icebergs on little chairs and seats which is most amusing.'[21] The Princess seldom went to France, and of her husband's many French friends she was familiar only with a half-English couple, the Standishes. Helen Standish was so like the Princess as to be sometimes mistaken for her, the more easily because she affected the same mannerisms and style of dress. Lord Esher describes how, at a *bal masqué* held one summer's evening at Strawberry Hill, 'the Princess and Mrs Standish, dominoed alike, led the baffled dancers into endless confusion, with Lady Waldegrave sitting, like some overblown autumn rose, on a triangular gothic throne.'[22]

The Princess could seldom escape from the necessity of paying an autumn visit to Scotland, although she was frankly bored at Abergeldie and the Prince distressed by the state of affairs at Balmoral, where John Brown reigned supreme. On one occasion the Queen went so far as to tell the Princess that she was sorry to hear from Brown that the ghillies' ball at Abergeldie had not been a good one, a comment which naturally gave rise to some annoyance. The Princess in her turn caused what Ponsonby described as 'unpleasantness' at Balmoral by her inveterate unpunctuality. From Balmoral Ponsonby wrote enviously of the warmth and comfort of Abergeldie, 'so different to this cold empty house we shiver in here', and, unlike John Brown, described the ghillies' ball there as the greatest success, 'everything so cheerful and lively, the Wales going round and speaking to all the servants, everyone enjoying themselves except Princess Beatrice who sat like a frump all night but I believe, poor girl, she had the strictest orders only to dance with her brothers.'[23]

During the winter of 1874–5 the Prince was busy with tentative arrangements for a visit to India planned for the following year. He kept these schemes a secret from his wife as he did not intend to take her with him. When at last the Princess discovered what was afoot she was extremely indignant. To India she would go and nobody should stop her; when reminded of her duty towards her five children she replied, 'The husband comes first.' Leaving aside the fact that her husband was not at all anxious to have her company it must be admitted that her determination to go was not wholly inspired by disinterested love of him and solicitude for his welfare; she had so much delighted in her Egyptian travels that she hankered after another and more extended visit to the romantic East. India caught her imagination; she could not bear to think that she was to be deprived of this chance to see its splendours. But she was not to have her wish. In vain did she personally petition Disraeli to intervene; her only real ally was Gladstone, who regretted very much that she should not go, deploring the long separation between husband and wife. In the end the combination of the Queen and the Prince of Wales was too strong for the Princess, who was forced to admit defeat. Never did she forget or forgive this thwarting of her wishes. 'I do still envy you dreadfully having been there and seen it all when I was not allowed to go when I wished it so very, very much,'[24] she wrote to her son on his return from India more than thirty years later. A visit to 'that most beautiful and fairylike country'[25] became the unfulfilled ambition of her life, a dream to which she referred over and over again.

The Prince was due to leave England on 11 October 1875. The Princess was miserable at the prospect; just before her husband's departure she went with him to see their old friend Dean Stanley, who noted that she was looking 'inexpressibly sad'. When the actual moment for parting arrived the Prince was as much upset as she was and for two or three weeks afterwards he appeared 'tremendously low', not at all 'up to his usual form'.[26]

The Princess consoled herself by having her parents to stay, an arrangement which gave rise to some friction. Queen Victoria refused to invite either the Princess or her father and mother to the christening of the Duke of Edinburgh's child, on the grounds that their presence would make too much of a crowd, 'certainly an odd way of looking at it in Windsor Castle', Ponsonby commented. Later she insisted that the Princess should visit her at Osborne, leaving King Christian and Queen Louise behind in London, an action which made it all too clear that she had no wish to entertain 'the Denmarks'. 'Of course the Princess of Wales sees this,' Ponsonby wrote, 'and will talk about it and if it gets about that the Queen is unkind to her when she is so very popular there will be a row.'[27]

The Queen's disapproval of 'the Denmarks' ' English visit was as nothing compared with her disapproval of the Princess's plan to return with them to Denmark and to spend the winter in her old home. Of all the many rows over Danish visits this one of 1875 was the biggest and best. Even Disraeli was dragged into the quarrel, writing ruefully to the Prince that his stay at Windsor had been a painful time because of 'the unfortunate subject' of the Danish visit. The Queen had reluctantly agreed that the Princess might go, and, still more reluctantly, that she might take her children with her, returning, however, in time for the State Opening of Parliament in February. Contrary to her usual custom, on this occasion the Queen planned to open Parliament in person and in the absence of the Prince of Wales she considered it essential that his wife should accompany her. The Princess was furious at this curtailment of her stay in Denmark, including the unfortunate Disraeli in her anger. He had taken the opinion of the Lord Chancellor, Lord Derby, and Lord Salisbury, and when all these notabilities agreed with the Queen's view he had no option but to insist that the Princess should return. 'I have the painful duty to communicate this opinion to Her Royal Highness,' he wrote to the Prince; 'I fear very much that she will misunderstand my motives and conduct.'[28]

Queen Victoria too was writing to her son on the subject, replying to a letter in which he had argued that his wife's return was unnecessary:

> 'As regards dear Alix's return I have written always in the same strain, and now the whole is over, but I *cannot* be *silent* upon the *one* point of it which, I must say, pains and hurts me, which is yours and dear Alix's treating my reasons for wishing her to return as an *act of unkindness on my part*, and this applies generally to the *so often* repeated *long* visits abroad. It is the very reverse; if I did *not* love you both as I do, or if I did not feel that what I thought and knew to be right on public grounds [*sic*] I would never insist upon what unfortunately dear Alix *never* does view in the *right light*. Dear Papa said to me once when he refused something which I wished very much, the refusal of which annoyed me but the justice of which I fully admitted afterwards and told him so: – "I love you far too much to let you do what would do you harm", and so it is on this occasion with dear Alix. *Her not returning* and being with me on *this* occasion, when *you* were abroad, would have been misunderstood and have done her harm. Your Father in-law quite understood this but not so the Queen and I felt it my duty to write in answer

to her letter fully to explain what the *real duties* are and how little people here are accustomed to see Princes and Princesses belonging to England by marriage absenting themselves so often and for so long.'[29]

Back the Princess had to come to take her place on the Woolsack, the traditional seat of the Royal Princesses at the Opening of Parliament. All these comparatively unimportant disagreements were, however, soon forgotten in the emergence of a serious scandal. The Prince had persuaded his friend, Lord Aylesford to accompany him to India: now, on 20 February 1876, Aylesford received a letter from his wife announcing, somewhat prematurely, her intention of eloping with another one of the Prince's friends, Lord Blandford, himself a married man.

In his biography of Edward VII Sir Philip Magnus has given a very full account of the Aylesford affair. The Prince was deeply involved because a few years previously he had had a flirtation with Lady Aylesford which was probably an innocent one but, innocent or not, he had written her some very imprudent letters. Lord Blandford's brother, Lord Randolph Churchill, persuaded the lovers not to elope; Lord Aylesford, however, refused to reconsider his decision to seek a divorce, a decision in which he had the support of the Prince of Wales. Disappointed in her hope that her old admirer might intervene in her favour, Lady Aylesford gave her packet of incriminating letters to Lord Randolph, asking him to use them as a weapon to force the Prince to use his influence to persuade Lord Aylesford not to take divorce proceedings.

As the Prince was in India Lord Randolph could not confront him face to face; instead he deliberately sought to involve the Princess in the affair. She had, of course, already heard of Lady Aylesford's conduct and so had Queen Victoria, who had written several times to her son mentioning the subject, but neither of them knew that the Prince's own reputation was threatened by this scandal. Lord Randolph now enlisted the help of Lord Alington, a kindly individual whose pity for Lady Aylesford overcame his better judgment, and together with Lady Aylesford, the two men called one afternoon at Marlborough House, sending up a message to ask if the Princess of Wales would receive them for a few minutes. The Princess now made the type of mistake that the deaf know all too well; mishearing the names as 'Lady Ailesbury' she at once agreed to see the waiting caller. She was naturally very upset when Lady Aylesford entered with Lord Randolph Churchill and Lord Alington and still more so when Lord Randolph explained their errand. He told her of the existence of the packet of letters and assured her that if they were published her husband 'would never sit upon the Throne of England'.[30] It was for her, therefore, to persuade the Prince, who would certainly be subpoenaed in any divorce action, to do his best to prevent Lord Aylesford from bringing any such proceedings.

Having thus made the position brutally clear, Lord Randolph and his friends departed, leaving the Princess in deep distress. Feeling the need of consulting someone older and more experienced than herself she sent for Sir William Knollys and was in the middle of pouring out the whole story to him when by some mischance the Duchess of Teck* was announced. She would not refuse to see her cousin, but not even to such a near and dear relative could she tell the whole story and reveal the scandal threatening her husband's good name, yet some reason she must give for her all-too-apparent agitation. Thinking quickly, she poured out a tale of woe which was wholly true yet not the whole truth. She explained the way in which her deafness had misled her into receiving Lady Aylesford and her fear of what gossip might say if once it got abroad that she had received a woman of such doubtful reputation. What was the wisest thing to be done in such circumstances?

The Duchess's answer was prompt and to the point: 'Order your carriage at once, go straight to the Queen and tell her exactly what has happened. She will understand and entirely excuse you from any indiscretion. It will be in the Court Circular that you were with the Queen today and any comment will be silenced.'

Knollys at once perceived that this was excellent advice. By far the best course for the Princess was to go at once to the Queen and to tell her everything that had happened that after-

* In 1866, Princess Mary Adelaide had married the Duke of Teck, son of Duke Alexander of Würtemburg by a morganatic marriage to Countess Rhèdey.

noon, so very much more than even Princess Mary Adelaide knew. 'Her Royal Highness is giving very good advice,' he urged; 'pray follow it at once.' And so the Princess did, with exactly the result that Knollys had expected.[31] The Queen at once absolved the Prince of anything worse than gross indiscretion; her anger was entirely directed against those who had sought to involve his wife in this nasty business. Writing for the Queen, Lady Ely informed Disraeli that 'the Queen felt so sorry the Princess of Wales's name should be mixed up in all this, she being so young'[32] – the Princess was in fact thirty-one and not inexperienced in the wicked ways of the world – whilst to the Prince the Queen herself wrote, 'her dear name should never have been mixed up with such people'.[33]

Meanwhile, the Prince wrote 'a very dear letter' to his wife begging her on his return to meet him '*first* and *alone*'.[34] Accordingly on 11 May she went out by herself to board the *Serapis* off the Needles whilst the rest of the family waited at Portsmouth. That evening, after an official drive through London to Marlborough House, husband and wife appeared together in their box at Covent Garden with their two young sons, Prince Eddy and Prince George. Queen Victoria had disapproved of this plan, thinking that they should have remained quietly at home on their first evening together. The Prince and the Princess judged otherwise; although the world at large knew little or nothing about the Aylesford scandal, London drawing-rooms were humming with gossip and it was to London Society that they must show themselves as a happy and united couple. The loud applause which greeted them as they stepped to the front of their box at the beginning and end of every act warmed the Princess's heart and proved to her that on this occasion at least she and her husband had acted with excellent judgment.

The Aylesford affair in the end petered out without doing much harm to anyone except the principals involved in this sordid drama. Lord Aylesford forebore to divorce his wife, separating from her privately, Lady Blandford behaving likewise towards her husband. Lord Alington, who much regretted the part he had played, wrote offering 'a humble apology to the Princess of Wales' for his 'fearful mistake'[35] and received full forgiveness; within eighteen months his name appeared among the guests invited to a Sandringham house-party. Not so Lord Randolph Churchill; although he too apologised to the Princess he refused to apologise to her husband. 'If I have been guilty of the slightest disrespect to H.R.H. the Princess of Wales by approaching her on so painful a subject I most unreservedly offer H.R.H. the Princess my most humble and sincere apologies,' he wrote to Lord Hardwicke, adding the unequivocal phrase, 'this is the only apology which circumstances warrant my offering.'[36] Ultimately Lord Randolph was induced to sign a formal apology, but nevertheless, for many years the Prince refused either to see or to speak to him.

Chapter ten

HUSBAND AND SONS

The Princess was delighted to have her husband home again after his long absence and she had by now learnt to accept him on his own terms. She appeared to be very little affected by the Aylesford scandal, although the hurt may have gone deeper than people imagined because on 23 August Lady Geraldine noted 'At seven came the Princess of Wales, looking lovely and outwardly unchanged, but so changed in *Herzlichkeit* and affection!! *la vie est triste!*' In the course of the next few years much occurred to which the Princess thought it best to shut her eyes. The Prince was fascinated in turn by a Miss Chamberlayne, an American debutante whom the Princess rudely nicknamed 'Miss Chamberpots', by the great actress Sarah Bernhardt, and by the most famous of all professional beauties, Lillie Langtry.

In the early spring of 1877 the Princess's health broke down; ordered away on holiday, she chose to go to Greece to stay with her favourite brother, King George. The Princess was no archaeologist and she might well have echoed the comment of her son Prince George after a visit to the ruins of Mycenae, 'They are no doubt very fine but I am afraid I don't take much interest in old stones.'[1] On this occasion she visited the Acropolis and reported that she had enjoyed it immensely; most of her time, however, was spent sketching, roller-skating or playing with her young nieces and nephews. On her return she found Lillie Langtry's name in everyone's mouth and her photograph in all the shop windows; this unknown young woman from Jersey, with only one evening dress in her wardrobe, had taken exclusive London Society by storm. The Prince had met her for the first time on 24 May, whilst his wife was still away in Greece. Although he had had so many previous affairs Lillie Langtry was as it were his first 'official' mistress. The liaison was openly recognised, the more easily because the Princess was wise enough to accept the situation, entertaining Lillie Langtry at Marlborough House, and showing her much personal kindness. In her autobiography Lillie recounts how she was suddenly taken ill one evening at Marlborough House:

> 'The Princess, so kind and compassionate always, immediately told me to hurry home to bed, which I thankfully did. Half an hour later the Household Physician, Francis Laking, was ushered into my room, having been sent by command of the Princess of Wales to see me and report to her on my condition. By the next afternoon I was feeling better, and was lying on the sofa about tea-time, when the butler suddenly announced Her Royal Highness. The honour of the unexpected visit brought me at once to my feet ill though I felt, but the Princess insisted on my lying down again, whilst she herself made tea, chatting kindly and graciously. She always used a specially manufactured violet scent, and I recall exclaiming on the delicious perfume and her solicitous answer that she feared possibly it was too strong for me.'[2]

This pretty picture may well be the product of Lillie's imagination; it is nevertheless true that the Princess displayed great sweetness and kindness towards her husband's mistresses. Such an approach may not have been entirely dictated by Christian charity; it was certainly the wisest course open to her and one which earned her substantial dividends of respect and admiration both from her husband and from the ladies concerned. She was, however, a person who had a genuine horror of jealousy in any shape or form, believing, as she told her sister-in-law, Princess Louise, that 'jealousy is the bottom of all mischief and misfortune in this world'.[3] She herself built her life on that principle; her home remained a happy place because she refused to allow any particle of jealousy to corrode her relationship with her openly unfaithful but very loving husband.

In spite of this generous attitude on the Princess's part towards the end of the seventies stories of an estrangement between husband and wife were circulating freely in London. Sir William Jenner noticed 'an undefined feeling against him', which Ponsonby put down to the belief that he was not treating the Princess fairly; 'as she is most popular the remotest supposition of this nature creates indignation against him'.[4] In fact it was the Prince himself who made the situation tolerable to his wife by treating her with unvarying consideration and courtesy and by making very sure that other people did likewise. It also must have given her some secret satisfaction to realise that as far as looks were concerned she could outshine all her husband's mistresses; even Lillie Langtry's exquisite prettiness – she is described as having 'a Grecian profile' but all the photographs show her with a definitely snub nose – seemed almost commonplace beside the Princess's classic beauty.

The Princess does not seem to have contemplated revenging herself for her husband's infidelity by indulging in even the mildest flirtation. There may possibly, however, be some significance in an enigmatic letter which Oliver Montagu wrote to his father just when the affair between the Prince and Lillie Langtry was at its height. After referring to himself as 'the cock child' he writes: 'Outwardly he is a noisy crowing brute but if everyone knew what his inward feelings are and what he had to go through inwardly they would not envy him his existence. I know not nor have I read of anyone put into the unfortunate position that I have been and yet, thank God, to have got through the worst without much damage to others.'[5]

Although, of course, this letter may refer to some other and unknown trouble because of its date it is at least permissible to read it as a reference to Oliver Montagu's relationship with the Princess.

The curious decision of Providence which decrees that man should be on the whole a polygamous and woman a monogamous animal could have no more clear illustration than the case of the Prince and the Princess of Wales. The Prince was unable to live without women, and plenty of them; he was equally unable to live without the comforts of a happy home and a loving wife. The Princess, on the contrary, was a maternal character who by nature turned for compensation not to a lover but to her children. In 1877 Prince Eddy was thirteen, Prince George twelve, Princess Louise ten, Princess Victoria nine and Princess Maud eight. This youngest child had a reputation for bravery and was in consequence nicknamed 'Harry' after her father's friend, 'the little Admiral' Harry Keppel, a man famed for his courage. Seldom can there have been a more devoted family; the unkind might even have called them a mutual admiration society. The children rarely left home except to stay with their Danish grandparents or with Queen Victoria. These latter visits they regarded as something of a penance; the Princess describes how on one occasion when the little girls were leaving for Balmoral, 'they all cried floods and little Harry declared at the last minute "I won't go", with a stamp of her foot.'[6]

The year 1877 was to see the first break in this united family circle. The two boys were now to go as naval cadets to the training-ship *Britannia*. Devoted though they were to one another the brothers were very different in character. The younger, Prince George, whom Lady Geraldine truthfully described as 'a jolly little pickle',[7] was by far the more lively and intelligent of the two. He was, in fact, a very normal little boy, high-spirited, dutiful and with his fair share of brain; Prince Eddy, on the contrary, was apathetic, backward, lacking in 'manliness and self-reliance', an almost impossible subject for education. His gentleness and rather lackadaisical good nature endeared him to his mother and sisters, but his slowness irritated his father – 'I hear the Prince of Wales snubbed Prince Eddy uncommonly', Ponsonby noted.

The Princess herself was in Athens at the time when her two

sons were preparing to take their entrance examination for the *Britannia*. She wrote to the boys to tell them how much she was thinking about them at this anxious moment: 'My spirit will be with you and you will hear a little voice whispering in your ears to encourage my dearest boys and implore them to do their utmost. I cannot tell you how I shall be looking out tomorrow for the telegram which is to tell me the result of the day.'[8]

To the boys' tutor, John Neale Dalton, later Canon Dalton of Windsor, she wrote a kind and sensible letter thanking him 'for all the devotion you have shown to our boys and for the unending trouble and interest you have taken in their education.' She then went on to stress various points which she considered particularly important in the boys' upbringing: 'One thing I must ask you, especially now I am away, to pay great attention to their being obedient and obeying the moment they are told. Also let them be civil to everybody, high and low, and not get grand now they are by themselves, and please take particular care they are not toadied by the keepers or any of those around them.'[9]

The Princess's letters to Dalton show her in a slightly unusual light. Full of good sense, comparatively free of exclamation marks, and written in a more legible hand than the rest of her correspondence, they prove that she took a keen and surprisingly realistic interest in her sons' education. For instance, when the boys first went to *Britannia* they were discovered to be unexpectedly far behind their classmates in their standard of work. This she sensibly attributed to the fact that 'they never in any study were accustomed to work together, which would have prepared them for class work'. She begged Dalton to impress upon the boys that 'they are doing discredit both to themselves and to us', and she ended with the wise comment, 'I cannot help thinking that under these circumstances it is most unadvisable that they should have all these extra treats and excitements which you always used to tell me at home disturbed their minds for the next day.'[10]

In another letter she warned him that the boys 'are perpetually quarrelling and using strong language to each other' and she asked him also to do his best to put a stop to their inquisitiveness which was making them a positive nuisance –

'they always break into everybody's conversation and it becomes impossible to speak to anyone before them.' On one point she begs him to be particularly careful; 'politics of any kind, home or foreign, should be as much as possible kept from them' for the sensible reason that although the boys were too young to have any reasoned opinion on the subject, any opinion they might happen to express 'later on and in their position will stick to them for life'. Above all, 'our boys should take a *broad* view of everything and they should not be influenced by party spirit either in politics or religion'.[11]

In the summer of 1877 Prince Eddy fell ill with the dreaded typhoid fever, but he recovered in time to accompany his brother to Dartmouth for their first term on board the *Britannia*. As all mothers do when their children first go away to school, the Princess grieved sadly at her sons' departure, writing to Queen Victoria, 'It was a great wrench – but must be got through – I trust to God that all may go well with them – and that their first step in the world by themselves won't be a too difficult or hard one – poor little boys, they cried so bitterly.'[12] She feared with only too much reason that they would be suffering badly from homesickness. 'I am sure you must often feel as poor Walter did at first, at St Winifred's,' she wrote to Prince George; 'do you remember that charming book I was reading to you before you left?' Reading aloud was one of the Princess's favourite occupations with her children, the books chosen being usually of the standard of *St Winifred's or The World of School*, though later on she might sometimes rise as high as Tennyson. 'I hate to go past your dear rooms,' this letter continues, 'where I have so often tucked up my dear boys for the night. Have you got to like your hammocks now and do you sleep well?'[13]

From now onwards the Princess's letters to her son Prince George become of major importance in any study of her life and character. Of her five children this son was probably the most congenial, whilst he in his turn was entirely devoted to his gay and beautiful 'Motherdear', the children's invariable name for the Princess. Her letters to him are of an extraordinarily affectionate nature. It would be all too easy to deduce from them that her love for him was an abnormal emotion which served her as compensation both for her husband's infidelity and also for the disappointment she must have felt when it became increasingly clear that her elder son was both backward and dissolute. Too much, however, must not be read into these letters. In the first place there are no other letters in existence with which to compare them. Had her letters to Prince Eddy not been destroyed it would have been possible to know whether in fact this outpouring of emotion was something unusual or whether it was merely her normal manner of writing to her sons. Again, although no one could possibly regard the future King George V as an abnormally emotional character, his letters to his mother are quite as emotional as hers to him. If their expressions of mutual devotion appear rather too uninhibited to a psychologically-conscious posterity it must be remembered that life in the family circle at Sandringham and Marlborough House was almost entirely without inhibition; joy was unconfined and tears were not regarded as being in the least shameful. It is fair enough, nevertheless, to say that the relationship between mother and son was an unusually close one and that the love they bore to one another was a delight and a support to them both.

How close the relationship was their letters make very clear. Prince George habitually read aloud to his mother during the ritual of hair-brushing, which was then part of every woman's day, and in the evening he would say his prayers with her just as if he were still a little child. From her he learnt the simple direct religious faith and practice that was to characterise him throughout life, daily Bible-reading, regular attendance at church and at Communion. The Princess seems to have impressed on both her sons the importance of careful attention to their religious duties; when Prince Eddy is a grown man of twenty-six he rather surprisingly writes to his brother, 'I wonder if Motherdear has thought of the Communion for us on Sunday for that is the only thing that could bring me back before Tuesday.'[14]

There could be no greater contrast than the one between the letters which the Princess wrote to her son Prince George, and those which Queen Victoria wrote to her own children. Impossible to imagine the Queen writing of herself, 'What a bad old Motherdear not to write and you were quite right to say "naughty, naughty"!'[15] Even in her letters to her children Queen Victoria never forgets that she is Queen of England; the reader of these letters to Prince George is seldom, if ever, aware of the fact that their writer is the Princess of Wales.

Although written as early as the seventies and eighties these letters are Edwardian rather than Victorian in tone; to read them is not to be reminded of Victorian mammas in fact or in fiction but of Barrie's Mrs Darling. Here is more than a little of *Peter Pan*, the embarrassing whimsy, the undoubted charm, the understanding of children, the curious horror of growing-up. This time, however, it is not the boy who refuses to grow up, but the mother who will not allow him to do so. The Princess's great hope was that 'I shall always find my little Georgie quite the same and unchanged in every respect', words which she wrote to him when he was already nineteen.[16] Six year later, when he was a full-blown naval officer commanding a first-class gunboat, she ended a letter to him 'with a great big kiss for your lovely little face'.[17] Perhaps the oddest feature of this very odd situation is the fact that Prince George himself never seems to have resented his mother's attitude or to have found it in any way embarrassing or ridiculous. On the contrary he seems to have regarded it as perfectly natural for he writes back to her in the same strain. 'I wonder who will have that sweet little room of mine,' he writes as a grown man, 'you must go and see it sometimes and imagine that your Georgie dear is living in it,'[18] and he begs her to 'think sometimes of your poor boy so far away but always your most devoted and loving little Georgie.'[19]

Not only the Princess's sons but also her daughters had a childhood prolonged far beyond the usual term; Princess Louise, for instance, celebrated her nineteenth birthday with a children's party. Her mother, in fact, never properly realised that everyone of necessity grew up. Years later she caused some embarrassment to one of her nieces, a girl in her twenties, by sending her presents suitable for a child of ten. On one occasion this elegant young woman, who was nearly six foot tall, received a parcel with a verbal message delivered by a footman, 'To darling little Patsy from her silly old Aunt Alix'. This niece said of her aunt, whom she dearly loved and admired, 'Being with her, you suddenly had the sensation that in every way time stood still.'

Life at Sandringham as pictured in these letters would seem to be domestic and respectable enough in all conscience, but it did not appear so to Queen Victoria. On the occasion of the Duke of Connaught's* engagement to Princess Louise of Prussia the Queen wrote to his Comptroller, Sir Howard Elphinstone, 'It will be *most essential* that Arthur does not *consult* the Prince of Wales as to his plans in any way, or take the House at Sandringham with its very irregular hours and way of living as an example.' In the same letter she makes her disapproval of the Prince and Princess's way of life perfectly clear. After pointing out how much the parents of the young Prussian Princess 'rely on the Queen for help, guidance, and advice', she writes:

> 'The Queen was told the same thing about the Princess of Wales but she never could do anything. The Prince of Wales never left her quiet a moment and she was dragged about everywhere to the despair of the parents and in spite of any remonstrance from the Queen. When there was an idea of Princess Thyra for Prince Arthur the Queen of Denmark said she never could consent to a similar life for her to that of the Princess of Wales.'

The Queen then states her conviction that this way of life had caused the premature birth of five out of six of the Princess of Wales's children and the death of her last baby, adding for good measure that 'the result of all the fatigues and excitement' also included the Prince's attack of typhoid, the Princess's rheumatic fever, and the recent breakdown in health which had been the reason for her holiday in Greece. It was not, however, the physical health of her son and daughter-in-law that most worried the Queen: 'Besides this side of the question there is also the moral side. The Prince and Princess of Wales go far too much into Society, do not keep up the right tone, are not looked up to, living far too intimately with everyone irrespective of character and position. Arthur has also too many friends and ac-

* In May 1874 Prince Arthur was created Duke of Connaught.

quaintances. Alfred had, and it is a bad thing for Princes.'[20]

Naturally enough, Queen Victoria could not understand that by their open-handed hospitality her son and daughter-in-law were helping to restore the popularity of the Royal Family, which had been so badly damaged by her own retirement into seclusion, whilst by their warm friendliness and easy, intimate behaviour they were creating the new and less formal conception of royalty which would be essential if the monarchical system were to survive into the coming age.

The Princess naturally had been in favour of the plan mentioned in Queen Victoria's letter to marry Prince Arthur to the Princess's own sister, Princess Thyra of Denmark; in any case, she was unlikely to favour the idea of this Prussian marriage. It was therefore understandable that Prince Arthur's bride, whom the Queen described as young, shy and 'not a beauty', should be a little alarmed by her lovely sister-in-law, who could not be expected to approve of her on any count. The Princess, however, did her best to reassure her, apparently with some success. 'I am so glad you have got over your fright of me,' she wrote to the young Duchess of Connaught a year after the marriage, 'as I noticed you used to consider me a most formidable personage only to be approached with fear and trembling but now we know one another I hope we shall be good friends.'[21]

When this letter was written the Princess may have been the more disposed to look kindly on her new sister-in-law because by now her own sister was happily married. The match had been very much of the Princess's own making. As long ago as 1872 Princess Thyra had been staying in Rome with the Prince and Princess of Wales, where she met Prince Ernst August, then Crown Prince of Hanover, and in spite of his quite phenomenal plainness fell deeply in love with him. Although Prince Ernst was equally in love with her various difficulties kept the two apart for many years. Dread of offending all-powerful Prussia made the Danish Government oppose the match. At the end of the Austro-Prussian War Prussia had annexed the whole of Hanover; the Prussian authorities, and Bismarck in particular, now looked with disfavour upon a marriage between a Danish Princess and a

Hanoverian Prince who could be regarded as a possible rallying-point for anti-Prussian opinion. Added to this difficulty was the fact that as suggested in Queen Victoria's letter to Sir Howard Elphinstone, Princess Thyra had been half-promised already as a bride for Prince Arthur. This second obstacle mattered most to the Princess of Wales, who cared nothing at all for Prussian feelings; once the difficulty over Prince Arthur was satisfactorily settled she set herself to forward the match by all means in her power. Plans were made for an informal meeting between the lovers to take place in Denmark in the autumn of 1874, whilst the Princess of Wales was staying there with her parents. The Duke of Nassau, whose son had once been considered as a possible husband for Princess Thyra, wrote to Prince Ernst that 'the moment is very favourable, as Alix is there, with whom you are closely acquainted from Rome, and through whom an informal meeting would be made much easier.' Nothing, however, came of this meeting; Prussian pressure against the marriage grew stronger and yet stronger, so that for the present it was thought wisest to allow the matter to drop.

In 1878 Prince Ernst's father died, having previously appointed Queen Victoria as his executor in the matter of his considerable private fortune which had been confiscated by the Prussian Government. His son now assumed the title of Duke of Cumberland because although he was *de jure* King of Hanover, that title was no longer officially recognised. He refused, however, to abandon his claim to the Hanoverian throne, although Queen Victoria maintained she could not help him recover his confiscated fortune unless and until he did so. The dispute between them became very acrimonious. Just as the quarrel was at its height Prince Ernst's sisters were surprised to receive a letter from the Princess of Wales begging them to help her in her efforts to bring about a marriage between their brother and Princess Thyra. The letter is written from Marlborough House and dated 9 September 1878:

> 'My parents and Thyra are at the moment with us and I have informed them of the conversation we had, which *pleased* them *all*, and it is *Thyra's* wish to see dear Ernst

once more. But how could this be arranged? for unfortunately the recent complications make it *somewhat awkward* for *all* of us and, as you dear ones *know*, the *pressure* of the *robber* makes itself felt at home in our dear Denmark as well!!! Nevertheless she wishes so much to see dear Ernst. Would not a little journey incognito to Frankfurt be possible? We are leaving today, our parents, Thyra, and myself, for Rumpenheim. I am staying only one week, the rest three. A word from you would reach me there! and we could come to Frankfurt secretly! Unfortunately I must close now in a hurry as I am leaving in a few minutes.'

Although he was very much in love with Princess Thyra, Prince Ernst now took fright, imagining that he saw behind this innocent letter the formidable figure of Queen Victoria. He feared that acquiescence in her demands was to be made the price of Princess Thyra's hand; he therefore excused himself from the proposed meeting at Frankfurt and wrote to the Princess of Wales asking for a full explanation. She replied in typically incoherent but determined manner:

'I cannot express sufficiently how happy your dear letter made me. Everything which you say in it I understand completely. *We* can appreciate your fine feelings of duty and for just that reason it is *so desirable* that we should see and talk with each other again. Things can be spoken much more easily than written and my dear sister wishes this too so much. You have understood my letter completely, but nonetheless dear Ernst, she wishes to see you now and *we* believe that with time your *difficult situation* of the *present moment* will become easier. At least "time will have smoothed it over" and the world will have settled down again! – *Everything!* Your coming here etc. etc. can at all events be kept *secret*! So if you came incognito just for a few hours to Frankfurt no one need know anything of it and we could talk about so much. How well I understand your divided feelings in the matter and you see, dear Ernst, that I have not left you waiting long for my answer. Unfortunately Papa has already left but Mama is completely in agreement with everything which I have written to you, and my Bertie who is in Scotland at the moment and who spoke to you about this matter, will certainly also share our views.'[22]

To Frankfurt Prince Ernst accordingly went where in a very few hours all misunderstandings were resolved and everything decided. The Princess was delighted by the success of her scheming; the Prince of Wales too rejoiced over the marriage, in this matter, as so often, agreeing with his wife rather than his mother. The Princess took it upon herself to break the unwelcome news to Queen Victoria, who behaved with a good grace, merely remarking to the Crown Princess that the bride and bridegroom would be 'a very plain couple, though very amiable and good'.[23] The world at large refused to believe that Princess Thyra could be genuinely in love with so unglamorous a suitor, and wits described the match as '*un mariage de raison sans raison*'.[24] On the whole, however, the Princess had reason to be pleased with the result of her efforts to secure her sister's happiness; in spite of many troubles, not least among them being the grinding monotony of Princess Thyra's life at Gmunden, Queen Victoria could truthfully write several years later, 'she adores Ernst and he her'.[25]

The Princess's joy over her sister's engagement was soon overshadowed by a family tragedy. In November 1878, diphtheria broke out at Darmstadt among the family of Princess Alice of Hesse. One little girl, Princess May, died on 16 November; a week later Princess Alice herself was taken ill. This year the Prince and Princess of Wales went as usual to Windsor to attend the annual memorial service for the Prince Consort. On the morning of 14 December, the actual anniversary of his death, the Princess was standing half-dressed in her bedroom when the door suddenly opened. Queen Victoria came in and took her in her arms; a telegram had just arrived saying that Princess Alice was dead. 'I wish I had died instead of her,' the Princess exclaimed in deepest distress. During the sad days which followed Queen Victoria learnt to love her daughter-in-law as never before and to turn to her more and more for support and comfort. 'Dear Alix gave me a lovely onyx locket which had been intended for poor dear Alice for Christmas, to put little May's hair into', the Queen wrote in her journal on 13 December. When she attended the service held in her private chapel at the same hour as the funeral at Darmstadt it was upon her daughter-in-law's arm that she leaned. That evening the two sat alone together reading the letter which Princess Alice herself had written home telling of her children's illness. 'Dear Alix has been a real devoted sympathising daughter to me,' the Queen noted; from now onwards her daughter-in-law's place in her heart was unshakably secure.

In her turn the Princess cherished a real affection for the Queen, which shines clearly enough through the artless phraseology of her letters. For instance, after one visit paid by the Princess to Windsor, Queen Victoria must have been touched and perhaps a little surprised to receive a warm and grateful 'bread-and-butter' letter wishing her 'a few days' perfect rest and peace away from all the *bother* of your *country* and *family*!!!'[24]

Chapter eleven

RUSSIAN INVOLVEMENTS

The years from 1876 to 1878 had seen one of the Princess's rare excursions into politics. With the outbreak of the Russo-Turkish war she was posed with a pretty problem of divided loyalties. At one time it appeared inevitable that England would enter the war on the side of Turkey. Although the Prince of Wales was strongly pro-Turk the Princess inclined towards the other side, influenced less by the link with Russia through her sister, the Grand Duchess Marie Fedorovna, than by her connection with Greece, where Turkey was the hereditary enemy.

Although Greece had taken no direct part in the war, the Congress of Berlin, held in the summer of 1878, 'invited the Porte to rectify the Greek Frontier and . . . an article of the Treaty reserved to the Powers the right of offering their mediation to facilitate this settlement.'[1] Disraeli, who had been created Earl of Beaconsfield in August 1876, claimed that he had fought to gain this much for Greece simply because of his devotion to the Princess: 'I did something yesterday for Greece. It was very difficult but it is by no means to be despised. It was all done for Her Royal Highness's sake. I thought of Marlborough House all the time.'[2]

Her Royal Highness, however, was less than pleased with the result of his efforts. As might have been expected, the great Powers did nothing whatsoever; Greece had to wait three years before she received any portion of the territory indicated as due to her under this settlement and the rest she never received at all.

During her stay in Athens in the spring of 1877 the Princess had had much talk with her brother about the political problems in Greece and the difficulties of his own position as King of that country. She returned home more than ever convinced that England was in honour bound to concern herself with the affairs of Greece and that if it were not for English apathy the other great Powers would be prepared to see justice done. In November 1878 she summoned up her courage and tackled Queen Victoria herself on this subject:

> 'I am still terribly worried about my poor brother's affairs which seem to be getting more serious every day and if the promises made to Greece by the great Powers are not speedily fulfilled *all must be up*.
>
> It is but too clear that England is the only country which has it in its power to make Turkey do what she ought, and she now again is the *only* one who seems disinclined to carry out what all the others are trying their utmost to bring about! I could tell you lots about this, and how *everything* which Willy a year ago *predicted* has already come true to the very letter, and if we don't look sharp about the *Greek Question* we are sure to be the greatest loser in the end. After all, my brother living on the spot, and if I may say so, having a very clear head, is better able to form a correct opinion as to the future of the whole Eastern policy than anyone who merely judges from hearsay. It is a thousand pities Lord Beaconsfield does not see this, while there is yet time, and English interests are so vitally concerned. Willy writes most despondently and as things are now going on, they are gradually being absorbed in the Slav element, (which means Russia) and you will have seen this is already taking place in Macedonia and Bulgaria, and *they* don't allow the grass to grow under their feet. It is indeed a most despairing business, and my poor brother is already

threatened from *all* sides, both from within and from without – and forgive me for saying, it is a *shame* that we, who put him there, are now the *only* ones who almost prevent the other Powers helping him by forcing Turkey to carry out the decrees of the Congress.

We shall have no right for the future to complain of Russia's not fulfilling the articles of the Congress if *we* who have Turkey in our power, do not insist on her doing the same. – We were ready enough to take our share, and to let Austria have hers, – and why, may I ask, is poor Greece who after all, had the greatest right on her side, to be the only one, who is the loser in this affair, simply because she followed England's advice to be *patient.*

Excuse me, dearest Mama, for worrying you with all this, but the fact is that I am really distressed about my poor brother's position, that I feel I must make *one* more appeal to you on his behalf, and on that of his Country, before it is *too late*!'[3]

For all its naivety of expression this letter is an intelligent enough summary of the Eastern Question as seen from the Greek point of view. Queen Victoria was rabidly anti-Russian; her daughter-in-law therefore made a shrewd appeal to her feelings by pointing out that to favour the Slav element in the Balkans at the expense of Greece was merely to play straight into the hands of Russia. She was wise also to stress the point that unless England saw to it that Turkey fulfilled her Treaty obligations she could not insist on Russia doing likewise.

In her dislike of Russia and support of Turkey the Queen was of course influenced by her devotion to Beaconsfield. The Princess herself was more in sympathy with Gladstone, whose pamphlet on the Bulgarian Atrocities had aroused strong anti-Turkish feeling throughout the country. When he became Prime Minister in April 1880 he at once reversed his predecessor's policy, putting pressure on Turkey to agree to a frontier revision that would result in part of Thessaly becoming Greek territory. On 20 March 1881 the Princess wrote to Mrs Gladstone enclosing with her letter a jewelled pencil-case in the shape of an axe: 'I must ask you to give the dear "people's William" this little axe in remembrance of all the trees he has cut down, and of all the questions he has been *axed* but mind you tell him not to use it in cutting down any more of the Greek Frontiers! I trust you to keep him in mind of this.'[4]

Both the Prince of Wales and the Princess felt a real personal affection for the Gladstones, whom they invariably treated with a warm and respectful kindness which did something to make up for Queen Victoria's unconcealed dislike. In November 1880 the Gladstones spent a happy weekend at Sandringham. Mrs Gladstone particularly remarked on 'the wish to make their guests happy and the absence of much form or ceremony'; and, describing how the whole party went to church on Sunday morning, she commented on 'the interest the Royal pair take in the clergy and services'. As she was undressing on the last night of the visit there came a tap at her door; in peeped the Princess, 'offering in fun to help me and in the end tucking me up in bed'.[5]

Whilst the Princess was preoccupied with the political problems of her brother, the King of Greece, at home she was worried and distressed by the personal problems arising out of the peculiar temperament of her elder son, Prince Eddy. Prince George did well in *Britannia*; his brother conspicuously not so. In December 1878 there was even talk of removing him altogether, his standard of intelligence being too low to make it possible for him to compete with the average naval cadet. The Princess was much distressed by this suggestion, writing to Dalton on 11 December to give him her opinion on the subject:

'I must write you one line to say how *dreadfully* distressed I am with all the different reports about poor Eddy's progress; it is indeed to be regretted and deeply deplored that he should have got on so little this term – and in fact according to Lord Ramsay's account the Britannia has been a complete failure as far as he is concerned! and he as good as advised us to remove him from there!

Now I am sure this would be a great mistake and I am sure you will agree with me that nothing could be worse for him in every way than to be *educated at home alone* this time without even his brother! But whatever is done must be most carefully weighed before anything definite is settled.'[6]

It was decided that Prince Eddy should remain on at Dartmouth till the end of his time, when of course the same problem arose but in even more acute form. What was to be done with a boy who was all but abnormally backward but who was nevertheless in the direct succession to the British throne? Prince George was to adopt the Navy as a profession; it was therefore natural that on leaving *Britannia* he should go on a cruise like any other midshipman. After much heart-searching it was decided that his brother should accompany him. To continue with a naval training that could be of no possible use to him in after-life might not seem the best way of arousing Prince Eddy's dormant interest in intellectual matters. However, both his parents realised that the most hopeful trait in Prince Eddy's character was his devotion to his brother and for this reason they were determined that the two boys must not as yet be parted from each other.

The decision was a hard one for the Princess. She disliked nothing so much as parting from any of her children, even for a short time; 'I hate letting any of you out of my sight even for a week',[7] she wrote in May of this same year 1879. Now she had to face a separation from both her sons which was to last longer than two years. Before starting on their main voyage, which was to take them as far afield as Australia, China and Japan, the two Princes sailed in September 1879 on a seven-months' cruise to the West Indies. The Princess was so downcast by this parting with her sons that in a laudable effort to cheer her drooping spirits the Prince decided to abandon his usual holiday at a German spa and to accompany her on a visit to Denmark. For him this was a genuine sacrifice as nothing bored him more profoundly than a stay at Bernstorff or Fredensborg. On this occasion the Prince of Wales's fellow guest was his brother-in-law, the Czarevitch. Only a year previously England and Russia had been on the verge of war and although that catastrophe had been averted, trouble over Afghanistan had recently added a further complication to an already strained and dangerous situation. In these circumstances the meeting between the heirs to the English and the Russian thrones was not without its piquant side. The position was bound to be an embarrassing one, even for the members of their households, as indeed Dighton Probyn found it. The Princess, however, refused to be disconcerted; she was devoted to her brother-in-law and she remained convinced that in his heart of hearts he really liked the English. Dighton Probyn, however, looking on at the interplay of affection, patriotism and self-interest, believed that the Czarevitch's liking was not for the English as a nation but for his attractive English sister-in-law.

The Czarevitch was perfectly happy to spend his holidays in the quiet family circle at Bernstorff. His enormous, bear-like figure completely dwarfed the short and corpulent Prince of Wales, with whom he had very few tastes in common. The Prince was thankful to return to Sandringham, but the Princess found the house sadly empty without the two boys; 'every evening I expect to see you coming in after tea,' she wrote to Prince George, 'and every morning on awaking I can *almost* fancy your two little voices squeaking into my ear but instead it is only the two white kittens which the sisters are putting on my pillow.'[8] The boys' return home in the summer of 1880 was overshadowed by the prospect of a still longer parting. To her credit the Princess made no attempt to oppose the plan for a two-year cruise or to keep her sons nearer to her. The parting with 'my poor *little* boys' – they were aged sixteen and fifteen – was an extremely tearful occasion, Prince George in particular weeping copiously. For all his manliness he was still young for his years and it was a very homesick child who scribbled a last goodbye in a shaky, unformed hand: 'So *Goodbye once more my darling Motherdear* please give darling Papa and sisters my very best love and kisses and much love to dear Uncle Hans.* *So goodbye darling Motherdear, dearest Papa and sisters.*'[9]

Whilst the boys were away on this cruise on board H.M.S. *Bacchante*, the Princess wrote more or less regularly to Prince George and presumably also to Prince Eddy; unfortunately

* Prince Hans of Denmark, the Princess's uncle. A worthy man: to this day, if anyone tells a story and leaves out the point, the Danes call it 'A Prince Hans Story'.

all the correspondence between her and her elder son has been destroyed. Her letters to Prince George may be sentimental but they are also gay, warm-hearted and completely unaffected. Prince George himself described his mother's style exactly when he wrote to her, 'You say your letter is stupid: it is not, darling Motherdear, it is dear and charming and you write just as if you were talking.'[10] The Princess had a great addiction to what some Italian grammars describe as 'the endearing diminutive'; anything she particularly loves she invariably describes as 'little'. The effect is often embarrassingly mawkish, but at times it can have a certain artless charm, as when she writes, 'I am longing to hear from my little sprat',[11] or again, 'How I miss you and long to see your dear little turn-up snout again!'[12]

In these letters there is much talk of hunting and horses – 'the dear little Indian pony came all the way upstairs into my dressing-room and walked down again like a Christian'[13] – also news of various relations, including 'the Tecks'. Those two loving cousins, the Princess of Wales and the Duchess of Teck, had hoped that in their turn their children would become friends. In nursery days little Princess Victoria Mary, known as May, would be invited to Marlborough House to play with Prince George on his birthday; but, as so often happens, the children themselves refused to coalesce. 'The Wales cousins are coming; let's put the best toys away before they get broken' was the cry in the Teck nurseries. As they grew older, Prince Eddy and Prince George had little in common with the more sophisticated Teck boys whilst serious-minded, clever Princess May found herself shy and bored in the company of the three Wales Princesses. A further barrier was the attitude of the Princess of Wales herself. The Tecks knew well enough that although Queen Victoria always regarded them as full-blown royalty – after all, the Duchess of Teck was grand-daughter to King George III – for 'Aunt Alix', who had never outgrown her Continental prejudice about such matters, they were not, and never could be, quite of the inner circle because of the Duke of Teck's morganatic descent. The Princess was, however, very fond of the whole family and deeply interested in their doings; in May 1881, for instance, when sending Prince George 'a photograph of myself in all my grandeur going to the Drawing-Room', she adds, 'May has grown quite a tall lady since you were away, with her hair done up and long petticoats, nearly as tall as I am.'[14]

As well as writing to the boys themselves the Princess kept up a correspondence with Dalton, who was accompanying them on this voyage. Her letters to him are proof of the serious interest she took in her sons' upbringing and education. She enquires into their studies, she thanks Dalton 'for giving so much time and trouble to prepare them for Confirmation' and hopes that 'they fully realise the sacredness of the step they are about to take'.[15] She comments on 'all those little failings [which] tell so much against them', deploring 'that *horrid* habit of always squabbling', and hoping that Eddy is becoming less absent-minded and George 'not too full of himself'.[16] In the middle of her preoccupation with her own sons she does not forget to ask Dalton to enquire about a boy aboard the *Bacchante* whose old grandmother had written to her in some distress – 'he has evidently always been a very good boy and helped to support his grandparents who during his absence have been obliged to go into the Union.'[17]

The most important family event during the years of the boys' absence was the accession of 'Uncle Sacha' to the Russian throne in the most tragic of circumstances. On 1 March 1881 the world was shocked by the news of the assassination of the Czar Alexander II. Thus suddenly and brutally the Czarevitch found himself raised to the most elevated, and probably the most undesirable, position in Christendom. The dangers which surrounded him and his wife were only too obvious; from the moment she heard of the bomb outrage which had killed Alexander II the Princess of Wales went in terror for 'darling little Minny's' life. Her alarm was only too well-founded. Alexander II had been a ruler of pronounced liberal sympathies who had won the title of 'Liberator' by his action in freeing the serfs. If the Liberator himself was regarded as fair game for assassins the position of his successor was indeed a dangerous one. With that passion for shutting the stable door after the horse has been stolen which is so characteristic of security forces, the Russian police now enforced such stringent precautions that the new Czar was practically a prisoner in his own palace. His life was believed to be in imminent danger, a danger fully shared by his wife, who seldom if ever left his side.

Their marriage had been a singularly happy one. It was said of Alexander III, as the Czarevitch had now become, that there were two things he never wished to break, the peace of Europe and the Seventh Commandment. 'The new Emperor is a very stay-at-home kind of person, devoted to his wife and children, fond of music, and has hitherto surrounded himself with a small circle of very insignificant persons,' the British Ambassador, Lord Dufferin, wrote to Queen Victoria; 'there is still very little known about him, probably because there is very little to know.'[18] In 1881 there was more to know about Alexander than there had been in 1866, the year when he had married Princess Dagmar, now the Empress Marie Fedorovna. With great tact and perseverance she had encouraged him to make good some of the enormous gaps in his education, persuading him to read serious books, to take an interest in charitable schemes, to patronise the arts. She was always at his side to help and encourage him, but she did not interfere in politics, concentrating instead on the representational duties of their position, at which it must be admitted that her husband was extraordinarily inept. Even after she had done something to improve his uncouth manners he remained shy and awkward in company; she, on the contrary, frankly enjoyed occasions when she could appear wearing beautiful clothes and fabulous jewels, and she performed her social functions with the same grace and charm that characterised her sister the Princess of Wales. Whatever may have been true in later years, at this time the new Czarina was beloved by everybody, her evident popularity giving great delight to her devoted husband.

Popularity, however, was no real shield against the dangers which beset the Empress. So real did these dangers appear that in England there was a considerable outcry when Queen Victoria allowed both the Prince and Princess of Wales to attend the funeral of the murdered Czar. The Queen, however, sympathised deeply with the Princess's wish to be with her sister at this crisis, and refused to rescind her permission.

The actual departure for Russia was lightened by a tragicomic incident. The Princess found it almost as hard to part from her dogs as to part from her children. On this occasion a particularly beloved animal called Joss was allowed to accompany her as far as Victoria Station. Joss strongly objected to being left behind and just as the train started, whilst the Princess still leant out of the window waving goodbye, he slipped his collar and started in pursuit. The horrified crowd on the platform watched him chase the train down the line until both train and dog were lost in outer darkness. Still preserved among the solemn documents in the Royal Archives is a telegram in which young Princess Louise assures her grandmother, the Queen, that Joss had been recovered safe and sound next morning.

When the Princess emerged from the royal train after her long journey Lord Dufferin found her looking 'so pretty and as if she had just come out of a band-box'. The St Petersburg in which she found herself was very different from the gay city she had known on her previous visit. Everyone was in mourning; little black sleighs glided over the frozen Neva, black streamers flew from the tram-cars, the very lamp-posts were shrouded in *crêpe*. The Princess found the Empress looking thin and ill, her memory haunted by the sight of her father-in-law's mangled body as he had been carried back to the Winter Palace, blown half to pieces but still alive. For security reasons she and her husband had not moved into this vast palace, where the Prince and Princess were themselves staying, but remained in their old home of the Anitchoff Palace. Here the two sisters spent every moment they could together, the Empress finding support and comfort in her sister's company. Hundreds of men and women were engaged in digging a trench round the Anitchoff to frustrate any laying of mines; meanwhile, the Emperor was so closely guarded that for exercise he could only take a walk round a small, snow-covered garden no bigger than a back-yard. Once a day he was allowed to leave his palace in order to attend a service held beside the coffin of the murdered Czar in the fortress church of St Peter and St Paul. According to Russian custom the dead man's face was left exposed to be kissed by all of his relatives, a ceremony which they found a terrible ordeal; not only had the features been damaged by the bomb but decay had definitely set in before the actual funeral took place.

When this last service was over the members of the Prince and Princess's suite breathed a sigh of relief for there had been rumours of mines laid beneath the church and torpedoes embedded in the ice of the frozen river.

During these painful days the Princess had delighted everyone with her friendliness and astonished them by her beauty, which was well set off by her little Marie Stuart mourning cap and long black veil. The funeral over, the assembled royalties left Russia as quickly as possible. The Princess, however, was determined to stay although her husband, who was obliged to return to England, was naturally reluctant to leave her behind. However, she pleaded with him so persuasively that in the end he even went so far as to take her side when Queen Victoria quite rightly objected to the idea of the Princess of Wales remaining for so long exposed to the obvious danger of assassination. As usual, the Princess had things her own way. 'Never mind, dearest Mama,' she wrote to the Queen in almost airy strain towards the end of her visit, 'I have nearly come to the end now and through this my poor sister has had a few moments' more happiness. It really was very kind in my Bertie to let me stop but he knew how much our hearts were set on it – and after all it would have mattered much less if anything had happened to me than to him.'[19]

The sombre gloom of this Russian visit was not without its moment of light relief. The Prince of Wales had been commanded by Queen Victoria to invest the new Czar with the Order of the Garter. In his book of reminiscences Lord Frederick Hamilton gives an account of this ceremony:

> 'The Insignia, the star, the ribbon, the collar, the sword, and the actual garter itself are all carried on separate long narrow cushions of red velvet heavily trimmed with gold bullion. No one was to be present except the new Emperor and Empress, the Princess of Wales, the Grand Master and Grand Mistress of the Russian Court, the members of the British Embassy, and the Prince of Wales and his staff. The ceremony was to take place in the Anitchoff Palace. We all marched into the Throne Room, the Prince of Wales leading the way with five members of his staff carrying the insignia on the traditional narrow velvet cushions. We made, I

thought, a very dignified and effective entrance. As we entered the Throne Room a perfectly audible feminine voice cried out in English, "Oh! my dear! Do look at them! They look exactly like a row of wet-nurses carrying babies!" Nothing will induce me to say from whom this remark proceeded. The two sisters, Empress and Princess of Wales, looked at one another for a moment and then exploded with laughter.'[20]

When describing the investiture to Queen Victoria, Lord Dufferin rather naturally omitted this episode; perhaps, however, it was in his mind when he wrote, 'the quaint and novel features of the ceremony were an agreeable change from the gloomy preoccupations and the funeral services of the last fortnight.'[21]

Not until August 1882 was the Princess to have the pleasure of welcoming her sons home after their long voyage. Almost immediately they were sent off again to spend six months in Lausanne in a fruitless endeavour to make them fluent in the French language. In answer to Queen Victoria's complaint that her grandsons could speak no foreign language properly except Danish it should be pointed out that the fault lay with the boys themselves, not with their parents, who made strenuous efforts to have them taught both French and German. The Prince was a remarkably good linguist, a gift which unfortunately his sons did not inherit. In a laudable effort to arouse their interest in a language which they found very distasteful Dalton encouraged the boys to read some of Dumas' exciting stories. This earned him an unexpectedly solemn reproof from the Princess: 'Though I have no doubt that Dumas' novels are very interesting still I cannot help thinking that *Novels* are not useful reading and do the boys no good. In French literature there are so many useful and most entertaining books in the shape of memoirs and historical works which would be far better for them. Lamartine's *Girondins* for instance is most interesting.'[22]

Although neither boy made much progress in the French language, Prince George, as usual, far outstripped his brother. On 11 March 1883 the Princess wrote to Dalton in real distress about Prince Eddy, now aged nineteen. It is typical of her that in the middle of all her own anxiety about her son she does not forget the tutor's hurt and disappointed feelings:

'Although you kindly beg me not to distress myself about the contents of your last letter I cannot, I confess, help being very much grieved by the unsatisfactory account you are unfortunately obliged to give me of Eddy! It is indeed a bitter disappointment that instead of steadily improving as we hoped he had begun to do during the first half of his stay at Lausanne he should have relapsed into his old habits of indolence and inattention. It does indeed seem strange that at his age he does not yet see the great importance of exerting himself to the utmost, and lets his precious time slip by which can never be recalled.

But what pains me more than all this is his *seeming* ingratitude towards you, who, although you have always taken so humble and unselfish a view of your own services, have really devoted the best years of your life for his welfare and have thought no trouble too great as long as it could conduce to the good of the boys. Believe me, although I can so well understand how disheartening it appears to you at this moment, that Eddy is *not* so insensible as you think to all the good and devotion he owes to you and that all the trouble you take is only *for his own sake and as a true friend* towards him. At any rate I feel sure he will some day appreciate at its proper value all the sacrifices you have made on his behalf.'[23]

Devoted as the Princess was to her elder son she was only too well aware of his shortcomings and she made no attempt to hide them either from herself or from other people; as she wrote this same year of 1883 in another letter to Dalton, 'we are neither of us blind to his faults'.[24]

Queen Victoria's favourite Highland servant, John Brown, died on 29 March 1883, an event which yet once again plunged the Queen into deepest sadness. The Princess was too kind-hearted to think evil of the dead or to withhold sympathy from the living because their grief might seem foolish or misplaced. On 21 April the Queen wrote from Osborne to her daughter, the Crown Princess, in a state of profound depression, adding, however, 'Dear Alix has been here for two nights and nothing could exceed her tender sympathy and complete understanding of all I feel and suffer.'[25] Even in these melancholy circumstances the Princess could not entirely restrain her sense of the ridiculous; 'met the Queen and the Princess of Wales driving together in silence,' Ponsonby reported, 'H.R.H. made a peculiar smile at us as if to say that it was not lively.' According to Ponsonby the Princess's presence acted as a real tonic to the Queen – 'the Princess's visit stirred up H.M. and did her a deal of good as she is busy on dozens of things now.'[26]

The Princess was always grateful to Queen Victoria for the unfailing love and understanding she gave to the problem-child, Prince Eddy. He had charming manners; as Lord Napier had written after a visit to Gibraltar, 'he does the right things as a young gentleman in a quiet way'.[27] This characteristic endeared him to his grandmother; it should also be remembered that when he visited Balmoral this summer of 1883 to be invested with the Garter, Ponsonby, who was not one to flatter or over-praise royalty, thought quite well of him – 'he is pleasing, talks well, and will be popular when he gets more at his ease.' Ponsonby, however, touched the real difficulty when he noticed that 'he cannot apply himself for a length of time', and he also mentioned a handicap which although unremarked by most people, may well have accounted for some of Prince Eddy's slowness, 'I perceive he is a little deaf.'[28]

After Prince Eddy's visit to Balmoral his mother wrote the Queen a letter in which she touched very discreetly on her own chief difficulty in the upbringing of her sons, the discrepancy between the standards which she would wish them to adopt and the way of life pursued by their father:

> 'I am delighted to see Eddy looking so well and having enjoyed his visit to you in Scotland so much. I am so glad you seem to have understood his disposition, which is really an excellent one, and he is a very good boy at heart though perhaps he is a little slow and dawdly which I always attribute to his having grown so fast. I am delighted you gave him such good advice and the very points you mention are those which I always try to impress upon him, and I am

particularly glad you did not allude to any of the other subjects you intended speaking about, such as races, clubs, etc. as he really has no inclination that way and it might only have put them into his head beside placing his father in rather an awkward position.'[29]

The two brothers were now to be parted for the first time, Prince Eddy going up to Cambridge and Prince George being appointed to H.M.S. *Canada* of the West Indies and North American Squadron. As always, the parting from her beloved 'Georgie' was peculiarly painful to the Princess. On 12 June 'Thursday Night, 12.30' she wrote her son an ingenuous but essentially wise letter of goodbye, which clearly illustrates the emotional relationship, intense but curiously simple, existing between mother and son:

'My own darling little Georgie,

I have only just left you going to bed, after having given you my last kiss and having heard you say your prayers. I need hardly say what I feel – and what we both feel at this sad hour of parting – It will be harder for you this time to have to go quite by yourself – without Eddy, Mr Dalton, or Fuller* – but remember darling that when all others are far away God is always there – and He will never forsake you – but bring you safe back to all of us who love you so –

I need hardly say my darling little Georgie *how* much I shall always miss you – now we have been so much together and you were such a dear little boy not at all spoilt and so nice and affectionate to old Motherdear – Remain just as you are – but strive to get on in all that is good – and keep out of temptation as much as you can – don't let anyone lead you astray – Remember to take the Sacrament about every quarter which will give you fresh strength to do what is right – and also never forget either your morning or your evening Prayer – We must all try and console ourselves by thinking how quickly the year will pass and what delight it will be to meet once more. . . . And now darling Georgie I must say Goodnight and Goodbye as I am so sleepy my eyes will hardly keep awake and it is nearly two – So goodbye

* The Princes' valet.

and God bless you and keep you safe and sound till we meet again and watch over you wherever you are –

Goodbye, goodbye, Georgie dear

Ever your most loving affectionate old Motherdear.'[30]

At the end of the summer came the usual family holiday in Denmark where the Princess was delighted to meet her sister and her brother-in-law with their children. To the Czar and Czarina this time was a welcome change after the oppressive atmosphere in Russia, where their lives were over-shadowed by the constant threat of assassination. For this reason the parting at the end of the holiday was a particularly tearful one, even by the standards of the Danish Royal Family, who were never given to repressing their feeling on such occasions. The Princess described to Prince George 'that *awful* moment of tearing ourselves away from one another, not knowing *where* and *how* our next meeting may be. Poor little Minny, I can see her now, standing on the top of the steps in utter despair, her eyes streaming over with tears, and trying to hold me as long as she could. Poor Sacha too felt the parting very much and cried dreadfully.'[31]

On her return to England the Princess wrote to her son describing days out hunting and house-parties at Sandringham, where the guests had included 'Old Christian' – she had never become quite reconciled to this brother-in-law – 'who did nothing but *eat* and shoot other people's pheasants'.[32] Another party, consisting chiefly of 'distinguished foreigners, French and German, whom I had never seen before and who had never set eyes on each other', turned out to be that rare thing at Sandringham, a failure – 'somehow or other they did not pull together'.[33] Such occasions do not sound very amusing, but the Princess must have been in a particularly cheerful mood, for on New Year's Eve she could write 'certainly 1883 was one of the happiest years of my life'. 'Goodbye, dear little George,' the letter continues, 'keep well, always do your duty, fear God and love me, ever your old loving Motherdear.'[34]

JUBILEE AND SILVER WEDDING

On 1 December 1884 the Princess of Wales celebrated her fortieth birthday. Although she appeared young and beautiful as ever, she had in fact reached middle-age. Life at Sandringham and at 'dear old bright comfortable Marlborough House' seemed to be settling into a routine; with anyone as lively and as unpredictable as the Princess it could never settle into a rut. Queen Victoria continued to refuse her son any share in the work of the monarchy so that inevitably his activities were social rather than political. Surprisingly enough, however, in 1884 the Prince and Princess found themselves accused by the Tories of taking part in a Reform demonstration. Prompted not so much by reforming zeal as by idle curiosity they decided to watch a great procession which was to march through London in support of the new Reform Bill. The organisers of the demonstration had been warned that the Prince and Princess would be watching from Lord Carrington's house, opposite the Horse Guards. As the procession drew level with Carrington House the bands changed their tune from the *Marseillaise* to *God Save the Queen* whilst roars of applause greeted the appearance of the Prince and Princess on the balcony. After standing for an hour and a half acknowledging the rapturous greetings of the crowd the Princess turned faint

The Princesses Louise and Victoria of Wales, November 1871

Prince Albert Victor (Eddy), June 1879

Sandringham House

The Princess of Wales's private sitting-room in Marlborough House

Bernstorff, the summer home of the Danish Royal Family

Princess Louise, Princess Victoria, and Princess Maud, with their grandmother, Queen Louise of Denmark, 1882

The Princess of Wales and Prince George, *c.* 1875

Queen Victoria at Abergeldie, 1889
photographed by the Princess of Wales

(*From the left*) Prince Waldemar, Crown Prince Frederick of Denmark, Princess Louise (later Queen Louise of Denmark), the Empress Marie, the Emperor Alexander III, Queen Louise (seated), Queen Olga of Greece, King George I of Greece, the Princess of Wales, King Christian IX

Oliver Montagu
a caricature by Pellegrini

Julie Stonor at Sandringham House

The Princess of Wales as a Doctor of Music, Trinity College, Dublin, 1885

and slipped back into the house. The Prince without his wife was not what the people wanted; the yells and howls of disappointment were so vociferous that she agreed to return, and propped up on a great pile of sofa cushions she continued to wave and smile until the last of the procession had passed by. Even then the crowd outside the house was so great that Lord Carrington had to ask for room to be made for the royal carriage. Of their own accord the people then formed a lane so that the Princess and her daughters could drive slowly across the parade ground, 'receiving an ovation which did one's heart good'. The radical demonstration, which the Tories regarded as a portent of red revolution, had in fact turned into 'a regular triumph for the Royal Family', an earnest of the welcome which the Queen herself would receive when at last she should decide to emerge from her seclusion and show herself again to her people.[1]

A very different reception awaited the Prince and Princess next year in Ireland. The Princess, who had been for so long the object of a nation's love and adulation, was now, for a few brief but very uncomfortable hours, to find herself the object of a nation's hatred. With her husband and her elder son she landed at Kingstown on 18 April 1885. At first all went reasonably well; the Prince's equerry, Arthur Ellis, told Queen Victoria that the reception had been a good one, with only a few boos and hisses to be heard, and that 'Prince Albert Victor's unaffected good manners are much remarked upon'.[2] In Dublin the most memorable moment came when the Princess was made a Doctor of Music at Trinity College; 'anything prettier than the Princess of Wales in her gown (white with red sleeves) has never been seen in Dublin or in any other city of the world',[3] wrote the devoted Dighton Probyn. The Princess herself wrote that the ceremony had made her feel 'such a fool', but she also remarked gleefully that her husband had been made a mere Doctor of Law, 'not such a grand one as me!!!'[4]

'I don't think any Irishman here would do us any harm,' she wrote in this same letter to Prince George; 'they are all very nice and friendly.' She was soon to discover her mistake. At Mallow, where a near-riot broke out half an hour before the royal train was due to arrive, the military had to be called in to help the police clear the station. Worse, however, was to come. In spite of a reassuring letter which the Viceroy, Lord Spencer, had written to Queen Victoria, everyone was uneasy as to the kind of reception the Prince and Princess might receive in Cork. On a fine, bright morning they drove into the city, to be greeted with a storm of hoots, hisses and boos. Insults of every kind were screamed at them and an occasional onion thrown into their carriage. The few polite loyalist cheers were drowned by counter-cheers for the nationalist leader, Parnell; 'no Prince but Parnell, no Prince but Parnell' was the reiterated cry. In spite of the temper of the people the Prince of Wales refused to cut short the arranged programme. On he drove, his wife at his side, both of them calm and smiling, through a mob brandishing black flags and black handkerchiefs and yelling abuse. 'Never were there so many dirty, ill-looking countenances gathered together,' Arthur Ellis wrote afterwards, 'it was like a bad dream.'[5] Although the quay where the royal party was to embark was occupied only by well-wishers, the opposite quay was crammed with some two or three thousand people shaking their fists, brandishing sticks, and calling down curses as the boat with the Prince and Princess on board drew away to the calm of the sea. Such an expression of mass hatred had seldom occurred before, even in Ireland. It says volumes for the determinedly ostrich-like attitude adopted by the loyalist element, both English and Irish, that next day the headline in the *Daily Telegraph* ran 'Royal Visit to Cork, Enthusiastic Reception in the City'.

The blackest cloud on the political horizon, however, was not Ireland but Egypt and the Sudan. The crisis there had dragged on ever since 1881, too long a time for anyone of the Princess's impatient temperament. To Ponsonby she made the surprising confession that she enjoyed talking high treason sometimes and meddling in politics, which she well knew she had no business to do. She was, she explained, 'tired of Egyptian bother' and bored by the dilatory policy adopted by her friend Gladstone – 'Why don't you take the place at once and have done with it? Anybody but dear William would have done so long ago.'[6] Throughout 1884 her letters to Prince George are full of comments on the situation in Egypt and the Sudan and descriptions of the excited atmosphere at Marlborough House where 'they are rushing in and out from the War Office all day long'.[7] She fully shared in the general feeling of shock and horror when in February 1885 came the news of the fall of Khartoum and of General Gordon's death – 'Indeed it is an *awful* misfortune that Khartoum has fallen into the hands of the Mahdi, and our poor General Gordon, the greatest hero of our time, most probably killed and when his relief seemed so near. If only we had gone out there long ago all this might have been spared.'[8]

The Princess was much concerned for the comfort and well-being of the British troops in Egypt and the Sudan. 'The National Society for Aid to the Sick and Wounded in Time of War' had been founded in 1872 with Princess Christian as its Chairman. In the same month that Khartoum fell the Princess of Wales started her own branch of this Society, whose main object was to be the supply of comforts to the sick and wounded. She herself, however, was determined to send comforts to all the troops, whether sick or well. Nobody dared to point out to her that the National Society, being affiliated to the Red Cross, was strictly forbidden by the terms of its constitution to do anything to help the fighting men. Although its activities were to this extent irregular the Princess's branch was a triumphant success. Florence Nightingale herself had understood the necessity for looking after the welfare of the troops not only when they were ill but also when they were well; nothing organised, however, had been done in this way until the Princess founded her branch of the National Society, which sent out books, games, amusements and small comforts to the men behind the actual battle front, to help make more tolerable the empty hours of the hot Egyptian summer. The Princess herself gave a 'Doecker' hut (made, of course, in Denmark), prototype of the many recreation huts run by such bodies as the Y.M.C.A. during the two World Wars of the present century. 'In no previous campaign have I seen anything like it,' one enthusiastic brigadier wrote home, 'and there can be no doubt about the high appreciation the Army entertains for what the Society has done.'[9] Two river launches were also bought to help in the transportation of the wounded, one of them, suitably named the *Alexandra*, doing valuable work in the remote regions south of Aswan where the Princess herself had spent such happy days during her Egyptian holiday.

This troubled period was further saddened for the Royal Family by the death of Prince Leopold on 28 March, 1884. During his many periods of illness – he had suffered from haemophilia – his sister-in-law, the Princess, to whom he was particularly devoted, had done all she could to cheer and amuse him and to bring some pleasure into his life. Now she grieved for his young wife and family and for Queen Victoria, faced with the loss of a second child only five years after Princess Alice's death. It was on the Princess's arm that the Queen leant during Prince Leopold's funeral in St George's Chapel, and afterwards it was the Princess who led her, weeping bitterly, back to her carriage – 'Dear Alix, so kind and helpful'.

Throughout this year Queen Victoria was much concerned about the love affair of her grand-daughter, Princess Victoria of Prussia, and the Prince of Bulgaria, Alexander of Battenberg, known in the family as 'Sandro'. Although Prince Alexander had originally owed his position in Bulgaria to Russian influence he had afterwards quarrelled with Russia; for this reason Bismarck opposed his marriage with a Prussian princess, as indeed, did everyone who looked at the question from a political point of view. The only people on the side of the lovers were Queen Victoria and her daughter the Crown Princess, who both found Prince Alexander charming. Matters stood thus when one of the Princess of Wales's rare indiscretions added fuel to the flames. In conversation with his sister-in-law the Czar made some very derogatory comments on the Prince of Bulgaria, remarking that it merely amused him to watch the poor man writhe in his struggle against an inevitable fate. The Princess repeated these remarks in a letter to one of her Hessian relations, through whom they ultimately came to the ears of Prince Alexander himself, with the result that the tension between Bulgaria and the Czar became even more acute. In the end Prince Alexander lost both his bride and the Bulgarian throne; after a fantastic episode when he was abducted, presumably by Russian agents, he abdicated in August 1886. Shortly afterwards he and Princess Victoria, who had been deeply attached to one another, agreed that their engagement must be abandoned.

In a letter to Prince George the Princess gave her own version of Prince Alexander's abduction: 'They say it is a Russian plot, but who knows it is not the work of Mr Bismarck himself? He put him there, and finding he did not do exactly as he wished, he may have whisked him off now and cleverly put the blame apparently on Russian shoulders!!!'[10]

The Princess's hatred of Germany was as strong as ever. About this time Ponsonby overheard a small but significant passage of arms at Balmoral between her and Prince Louis of Hesse:

> 'When something arose he kept on insisting violently, "Ja, ja es war Dannische nicht Deutsch". The Princess of Wales quietly replied, "Nein, es war Deutsch". The Grand Duke hallooed his reply that it was Danish, Danish, Danish (I don't know what). The Princess grew hard and cold as I had never seen her, simply saying "nein". This he met with a long explanation to which she became utterly deaf, and further discussion was hopeless, at which she turned with a smile to her daughter as if to say "I've settled him!" '[11]

Meanwhile, Prince Alexander's brother, Prince Henry of Battenberg, had also fallen in love, his choice being Queen Victoria's daughter, Princess Beatrice. On first hearing this news the Queen was horrified, for she had planned to keep this youngest child permanently at home by her side. She discussed the matter with the Princess of Wales, now her frequent *confidante*, who gave her own views in a letter dated 24 August 1884. In spite of her sympathy with the Queen's feelings it is clear that she was really on the side of Princess Beatrice. After saying that she and the Prince had talked the matter over and were in complete agreement she wrote:

> 'I must not close my letter without telling you, dearest Mama how much I felt your again having placed so much confidence in me on a subject which I know has given you *such pain* even to mention to anyone, as you have always nursed the hope of keeping your one little ewe lamb* entirely to yourself. I can therefore well understand what a terrible shock it must have been to you when you heard she had formed a new interest. We must hope, however, that it will all be for the best, and that she will continue for many a long year to be the same help and comfort to you that she

* Queen Victoria had three other daughters alive.

has hitherto always been. Please remember that whenever it is a comfort to you to open your poor *lonely overburdened* heart each word that you say will always be sacred to your most devoted and loyal child – Alix.'[12]

In the event the Princess's hopes were realised. The Queen took a great liking to Prince Henry or 'Liko', to give him his family nickname, who was quite prepared to agree that he and his wife should make their home with her. For once the *cliché* came true; instead of losing a daughter Queen Victoria gained a loved and loving son.

The Princess of Wales's own children were now reaching an age when their love affairs could cause anxiety to their parents. Mrs Stonor, one of her ladies-in-waiting, had died in 1883, leaving four orphan children. The warm-hearted Princess, who had been much attached to their mother, made Harry and Julie, the two nearest in age to her own sons, as her special charge. Most of their holidays were spent with the royal children, who treated them almost as brother and sister. Now Prince George had fallen in love with the attractive Julie, a commoner and a Roman Catholic.

Nothing is more difficult to handle than the lovely, brittle fabric of first love. Some parents might have treated this boyish romance with a heavy hand, others would have committed the opposite blunder of laughing it out of court. The Princess dealt with the situation deftly and with exquisite delicacy. She took great pains to do or say nothing that could tarnish the lustre of her son's idyll whilst making perfectly clear that in the nature of things it must remain an idyll and nothing more. Wisely, she stressed her own great liking for Julie, 'such a pretty simple unaffected dear', and with that strange disregard for her own position that was so typical of her, she appeared genuinely surprised to discover that Julie was 'always the same and comes to me, old Motherdear, for everything'. In the same letter she writes explicitly of the insuperable nature of the barriers between boy and girl: 'There it is and, alas, rather a sad case I think for you both, my two poor children! I only wish you could marry and be happy, but, alas, I fear that cannot be.'[13] In lighter mood she can laugh with, but never at, her son, as on the occasion when he is photographed 'looking just like a loving couple' with his cousin 'the brat', Princess Charlotte of Saxe-Meinengen, and Julie, apparently, does not '*quite* approve of the combination'.[14]

If Lady Geraldine Somerset is to be believed, Prince George's father was almost as much taken with Julie Stonor as was Prince George himself. Several times she speaks of his liking for this pretty young girl and once she goes so far as to remark 'dear Papa and both sons are by way of being more or less in love with her'.[15] The truth was that the whole family were devoted to Julie, who was to remain a life-long friend to them all and especially to the Princess.

As Sir Harold Nicolson puts it, 'his affection for Miss Stonor rendered Prince George immune from any other compromising associations during the years when he was absent from home'.[16] In this respect he was influenced not only by his affection for Julie but also by his affection for his mother. 'I must say it is good of you to have resisted all temptation so far,' the Princess wrote on 10 May, 1886, 'and it is the greatest proof you could possibly give of how much you wish to please me that you should have done it for my sake and the promise you gave me of your own accord a few nights before you left. No words can express how grateful I feel to God for having given me such a good son in every way. God will reward you for it here and hereafter.'[17] A few months later she wrote, 'I am so pleased and touched at all you tell me about yourself and how faithfully you have stuck to your word and promise you gave your old Motherdear.'[18]

The behaviour of Prince George's father was very different. Lady Geraldine mentions his 'three reigning young ladies at present, Miss Chamberlain, Miss Tennent, and Miss Duff' and quotes the Duke of Cambridge as saying 'how strange this new line of the Prince of Wales is, taking to young girls and discarding the married women'. At Sandringham in January 1886 the Princess fell ill of diphtheria, a disease which left her with a permanent tendency to throat trouble. The Prince, however, came up to London, where, as in 1867, 'his mania for amusing himself' whilst his wife was lying ill caused some unfavourable comment.[19] The Princess herself was giving cause for some slight scandal by her intimacy with Lady Lonsdale, who had been involved in a notorious divorce case, a friendship which the Queen rather naturally viewed with considerable disapproval. The Princess told Ponsonby that she did not particularly care for Lady Lonsdale but that she was determined to see fair play. In her championship of someone whom she believed to be an injured party she would listen to no one, not even to Mrs Gladstone, who rather unwisely tried to intervene.

The year 1887 was bright with the splendour of Queen Victoria's Golden Jubilee. Of actual material splendour there was perhaps less than might have been expected since the Queen decided not to wear her crown and robes of state at the Thanksgiving Service. Distressed by this decision the Royal Family sent the Princess of Wales, whom they knew to be a special favourite, to persuade the Queen out of a bonnet and into a crown. In less than no time the Princess emerged from this interview, totally discomfited – 'I was never so snubbed in all my life.' So, bonnetted, Queen Victoria drove to the Abbey, and with her in her open carriage drove the Prince of Wales and the Princess, 'dear Alix, who is quite a daughter to me'.[20]

In 1888, the year after the Jubilee, came the celebrations in honour of the silver wedding of the Prince and Princess. At a family dinner-party the Princess appeared radiant in white and silver. She had insisted on fastening a real orange beside the spray of orange-blossom in her hair, protesting that she was now no bud but the ripened fruit. Few are the women of forty-three who could wear an orange on their head and yet look more lovely than ludicrous.

The more formal official celebrations for the silver wedding were cut short by the news of the death of the German Emperor, William I. The new Emperor, Frederick III, Queen Victoria's son-in-law, reigned only ninety-nine days, dying on 15 June from cancer of the throat. At the Queen's personal request the Princess of Wales swallowed her hatred of Prussia and attended the funeral in the company of her husband, Prince George, and Oliver Montagu. She deeply pitied her sister-in-law, now the Dowager Empress Frederick; 'hers is a lonely life and a terribly sad one, all her plans and ambitions crushed and nothing left but remembrance of the past.'[21] The new Emperor, 'that young fool William', was no comfort at all to his mother but rather the reverse, setting himself against the Liberal ideas which had been so dear to his father. 'He gets more foolish and conceited every day,' the Princess wrote; 'evidently he wants to show and teach the world how an Emperor should behave!!!'[22]

The Princess might well be grateful that her own sons in no way resembled the obnoxious William. 'Yes, indeed,' she wrote to Prince George on 22 April 1888, 'we are a most happy family and I thank God for having given me such good and affectionate children who are my real comfort in this world.'[23] Whatever his faults may have been, Prince Eddy was never an undutiful son. 'Eddy is a dear good simple boy,' Queen Victoria had written, 'and there is no fear of his ever becoming undutiful to me or his parents. He is very steadily inclined.'[24] Dear, good, and simple Prince Eddy may have been but steady he certainly was not. As Mr Pope-Hennessy puts it, 'among the few things Prince Eddy really cared for was every form of dissipation and amusement';[25] he had no serious tastes whatsoever to weigh on the other side of the scale. He was curiously immature for his age, his time at Cambridge having failed to awake in him the slightest interest in anything intellectual or bookish. The Army did rather more to develop his character. After Cambridge he joined the Tenth Hussars, where his fellow officers did their best to shake him out of his apathy, urging him to play polo, to act as galloper, and to join in the various regimental activities. He was modest, cheerful, and very attractive to women; he could talk well enough when he chose, but he totally lacked any power of concentration. Ponsonby noticed that even his conversation would 'tail off', and that he had a trick of perpetual fidgets amounting almost to a nervous tic.

The Princess's daughters formed rather a shadowy trio, often referred to by the unpleasing collective nickname of 'the Hags'. Their mother had been at some pains to have them taught music; otherwise their education seems to have been almost entirely neglected. In public they appeared diffident and shy; in private they were less inhibited, romping about the corridors at Sandringham and indulging in the family passion for practical jokes. On 27 July 1889 the eldest of them, Princess Louise, married the Earl of Fife, whom Queen Victoria rather reluctantly created a Duke. Nevertheless, this marriage pleased the Queen who was always glad when her descendants married outside the narrow family circle, and especially glad when they married Scotsmen. The bridegroom was eighteen years older than the bride, a fact which was made the more conspicuous by the extraordinarily youthful appearance of the bride's mother, whom one of the journalists reporting the wedding described as 'instinct with the spirit of youth'.

In the spring of 1890 the Princess's second son, Prince George, accompanied his father on a visit to Germany. Various episodes on this tour aroused the Princess's wrath. Strangely enough she, who had herself been brought up a Lutheran, blamed her son for taking Holy Communion at a Lutheran service. 'I am really sorry you should have done so,' she wrote in reproof, 'as with you it must have been a perfect *farce* as you have often told me you could not understand a word of German. How could you suddenly have got so *learned* [as] to be able to take part in such a sacred ceremony – and although you imagine it is exactly the same as our English service, certainly the forms are different, the doctrines also.'[26] Later she was to make a similar protest when the Queen sent Prince George as British representative to a *Luther Fest* – '*Why* you were sent by Grandmama I cannot make out as England is not Lutheran but *Anglican*.'[27] Not for nothing had the Princess attended All Saints, Margaret Street. More predictably, she was horrified to hear that her son had been made Honorary Colonel of a Prussian regiment – 'my Georgie boy has become a real, live, filthy, blue-coated, *Picklehaube* German soldier!!!' Magnanimously, she added a word of forgiveness, 'It was your misfortune, not your fault.'[28]

Hatred of Germany combined with her Danish sympathies to make the Princess take a deep concern in an agreement which was in process of negotiation between England and Germany. England was to have a protectorate over the East African Sultanate of Zanzibar in exchange for the North Sea island of Heligoland, an island which had belonged to Denmark until the Napoleonic wars and whose inhabitants were still Danish-speaking. On 13 June 1890 Ponsonby sought an interview to discuss this subject with the Prince of Wales, who sent for his wife as soon as the word Heligoland was mentioned. From this point the interview was conducted entirely by the Princess, her husband's part being limited to expressing agreement with her opinion. She expressed great pity for the population of Heligoland thus handed over to German rule, pooh-poohed Ponsonby's assurance that their rights would be properly safeguarded, and stigmatised the agreement as 'a knuckle-down to Germany' and a betrayal of British interests.

Among the Rosebery papers in the National Library of Scotland is a memorandum on the subject of Heligoland written on Marlborough House paper in a hand difficult to identify but closely resembling that of Charlotte Knollys. The memorandum itself is endorsed 'By the Princess of Wales'. With it is a pencilled note in the Princess's own hand, ending with the postscript, 'I am much flattered by Lord Rosebery's remarks'. Presumably he had complimented her upon the memorandum, which she would have sent to him as a personal friend, rather than to Lord Salisbury, then Prime Minister and Foreign Secretary. Two little notes show the easy terms of that friendship. The first, written in 1888, runs, 'Received from Lord Rosebery, the sum of ten shillings, in tardy payment of a debt of honour'. The second is dated 27 March 1890: 'Here is your picture of Her Most Gracious Majesty the Queen, "beautiful for ever" and varnished by my own skilful hands – and I hope to the complete satisfaction of its owner. Picture-cleaner and varnisher – Alexandra.'[29]

Rosebery was sufficiently impressed with the memorandum, which he described as 'a very respectable document',[30] to send it on to Gladstone, who also treated 'this remarkable and very confidential document'[31] as if it were the Princess's own production. It was also suggested that it should be sent to Lord Wolseley and to Sir Geoffrey Hornby as representing the military and naval interests involved. If the memorandum is really the Princess's work – and there seems no reason to doubt her authorship – it goes to prove that she had a better brain and a more able pen than she is generally credited with. For that reason it is worth giving in full:

> 'Heligoland is an Island in the South-east of the North Sea, and belonged from time immemorial to Denmark, until the British Government demanded the cession of the island at the Peace of Kiel in 1814, at the same time that Norway was severed from Denmark.

The island is more or less a barren rock, and one may well ask why the Government of Great Britain should have insisted on taking possession of it when Denmark still held the whole East Coast of the North Sea as far as the Elbe with no Naval Ports. Nor had Germany any Navy at all, and Holland was reduced to insignificance. That the British Government insisted on having Heligoland clearly shows the great foresight of the Minister then at the head of Foreign Affairs, and time now shows how right he was. Germany is at present in possession of the Coasts of Sleswig and Holstein, as well as of the ancient territory bordering the North Sea, and has acquired both sides of the mouth of the Elbe. She has built an important Naval Port in the Bay of Jahde, and has begun the construction of the great canal from Kiel to the Elbe which will enable her to bring her Fleet, stationed at Kiel, into the Elbe and the North Sea in a few hours' time. But Heligoland dominates the whole of the German Coast and the mouths of the great rivers flowing into the North Sea, with the Bay of Jahde, and a British Fleet stationed at Heligoland, can, in time of war, blockade all the outlets from Germany to the North Sea, and reduce her Fleet and Commerce to inactivity. This eventuality may be remote, but if this possibility was foreseen in 1814, surely it ought not to be lost sight of by a British Minister in 1890. Moreover there can be no doubt that Germany has in view the annexation of Holland. In the treaty of alliance between Prince Bismarck and Count Andrassy in 1879 the former indeed demanded and obtained from Austria a free hand which allowed him to do what he liked with Holland. There may be statesmen in this country who would look upon such an event with a certain amount of indifference, but when they consider that the mouths of the Schelde, with Flushing, belong to Holland (not Belgium) it is difficult to believe that such indifference, with what might be the consequence in regard to Antwerp and Belgium, should really exist. Germany, in possession of Holland, can construct a Naval Arsenal (and will certainly do it) at Flushing within a few hours' sail from the Thames. But England, in holding Heligoland, prevents a German fleet from operating against Holland and from reducing the country in a short time both by land and by sea.

In a defensive point of view it may be said that Heligoland in the hands of England covers the East Coast of these islands against any attack, while in the hands of Germany it would be made the basis of operations against England, and our Government in a short time, or at all events in a few years hence, would have to apply to Parliament and to the pockets of the taxpayer for the millions of money which would have to be expended in Fortifications that it would be necessary to erect along the coast in order to defend it against Foreign invasion.

If England cedes Heligoland to Germany, a precedent would at once be created for Spain to claim Gibraltar (another *barren* rock and a very expensive one) and Italy Malta, and there would indeed be but little reason for our retention of Cyprus which Germany might ask for as a convenient Station for her communications with her East African Colonies. At all events the opinions of the naval and military authorities as to the strategical value of Heligoland to England (and to Germany) should be submitted to the Crown before Diplomatic negotiations are completed.

June 1890.'

The slightly shaky grammar of the memorandum and the Danish spelling of place-names all seem to point to the Princess as its sole and unaided author. As to its substance, she was mistaken in her estimate of the importance of the Zanzibar Sultanate, but it was a mistake shared by the vast majority of her contemporaries. Where Heligoland itself was concerned historians are to this day undecided as to whether its retention would or would not have been of advantage to England during the First World War. In face of Ensor's statement that 'the island, when fortified, became the keystone of Germany's maritime position for offence as well as for defence',[32] it is interesting to read a little pencilled note in the Princess's writing preserved with the memorandum: 'Yes, certainly show it to the Naval and Military people although I fear as Lord Rosebery says it is all too late but still they might prevent the Germans from *fortifying the Island* which would at any rate be some point gained.'

Chapter thirteen

THE DUKE OF CLARENCE

1890 and 1891 were to be unhappy years for the Princess, troubled by the love affairs both of her husband and of her elder son. On his arrival home from India in May 1890 Prince Eddy was created Duke of Clarence and Avondale. He had returned looking wretchedly ill; it was clear that his dissipations were beginning to undermine his health. The obvious solution would seem to be marriage, but where was a bride to be found? His own choice would have been his pretty cousin 'Alicky', Princess of Hesse, daughter of Princess Alice, but she would have none of him. Queen Victoria then suggested another cousin, 'Mossy', Princess Margaret of Prussia, candidly admitting that Princess Margaret was 'not regularly pretty'. Perhaps for this reason Prince Eddy refused to consider her; instead, in flat defiance of clear and positive warnings from his wise grandmother, he proceeded to fall in love with the most impossible of all princesses, Hélène d'Orléans.

Nothing could be said against Princess Hélène personally; she was both good and attractive and she would have made Prince Eddy an admirable wife had she not been a Roman Catholic and the daughter of the Comte de Paris, a pretender to the French throne. Although the political obstacles in the way of such a marriage were difficult enough the religious ones were insuperable. There was no getting round the fact that the British Constitution forbade the heir to the throne to marry a Roman Catholic. The Princess of Wales, however, with incredible folly smiled upon the romance. Believing Prince Eddy to have been heart-broken by Princess Alicky's refusal she could not bear to see him thwarted yet again, and she much preferred the daughter of a French pretender to any German princess. So she looked on benevolently whilst his sisters pointed out to him how very much in love with him Princess Hélène really was, and Princess Louise, now Duchess of Fife, arranged that the two should meet each other frequently at her house at Sheen, pressing home her point by inviting Princess Hélène to Mar Lodge, her Scottish home. There, in August 1890, the pair became engaged.

The Princess of Wales may have been foolish in encouraging this impossible match but, given her determination to see the pair married, her handling of the situation was very adroit. The first obstacle in the lovers' way was Queen Victoria's formidable disapproval. No sooner had they told the Princess of their engagement than, with feminine guile, she insisted that they should there and then go to Balmoral and, trusting to the Queen's warm heart, appeal to her to give her consent. The Princess would listen to no protests from her reluctant son but, ordering a carriage, she pushed the pair into it, at the last moment thrusting a picnic lunch in after them to sustain their fainting spirits. All went as she had hoped and predicted; the Queen, taken by storm in this fashion, capitulated at once to the appeal of young love and gave the couple her blessing.

Princess Hélène was prepared to change her religion if necessary and to become a Protestant. The Princess of Wales could see no reason against such a step; had not her own sister changed her religion and joined the Orthodox Church on her marriage? The Comte de Paris, however, would not hear of such a suggestion. Princess Hélène herself only made matters worse by a personal appeal to the Pope who could only say that, come what might, she must remain a Roman Catholic. 'All we can do now is to wait and see what time can do for us and trust in God to help us,' the Princess of Wales wrote to

Prince George; 'in the meantime they go on corresponding and loving one another from a distance.'[1]

Prince Eddy may have gone on loving Princess Hélène from a distance but meanwhile he was loving someone else at closer quarters. In love, as in everything else, he was incapable of concentrating on one subject for any length of time. When he was supposedly yearning for Princess Hélène he was in fact writing a series of naively affectionate letters to the pretty Lady Sybil St Clair Erskine. His mother, however, knew nothing of this development; to her he was simply her lovesick boy over whom her heart constantly grieved.

Whilst Prince Eddy was in trouble over his love affairs, his father was in even worse difficulty. In September 1890, at a house-party given for the Prince at Tranby Croft, in Yorkshire, one of the guests, Sir William Gordon-Cumming, was accused of cheating at baccarat. This episode led to a law suit in which Gordon-Cumming claimed damages for slander and called the Prince as a witness. No other scandal did so much damage to the Prince's reputation or made him more unpopular with the nation at large. So much has been written about the affair that it is surely not necessary to rake over this old muck-heap yet again but merely to point out that the Princess was wholeheartedly on her husband's side and supported him loyally both in private and in public. In a letter to Prince George about 'that *horrid* Cumming business' she refers to Gordon-Cumming as 'that brute' and 'vile snob', and writes, 'You were quite right to think that as usual Papa through his good nature was dragged into it and made to suffer, for trying to save with the others together this worthless creature, who since then has behaved *too abominably* to them all.'[2]

This unhappy period was made more cheerful by the arrival of a first grandchild; on 17 May 1891 the Duchess of Fife gave birth to a daughter. In a letter to Prince George the Princess describes her rush to her daughter's bedside in the early hours of the morning and her delight when 'at five o'clock, thank God, I was a happy grandmother and held my little naked grandchild in my arms!! It squeaked like a little sucking-pig.' In this same letter she writes that Prince Eddy's engagement is at an end, commenting, 'to me too it is a horrible grief, I own, as she would have made the most perfect wife for Eddy in every way.'[3]

The hearing of the 'Baccarat Case' lasted from 1 June to 9 June. Judgment was given against Gordon-Cumming, a result which did nothing to make the Prince more popular; as the Queen wrote, 'the light which has been shed on his habits alarms and shocks people so much'.[4] On the other hand, his wife's loyalty to him provoked much favourable comment, one article in the *Review of Reviews* being specially worth quotation:

> 'The Prince of Wales' tenderness to his wife during her illness, his constant attention to her wants, the pains which he takes to keep her informed of all that is likely to amuse her, these are all strangely at variance with the popular conception which has gone abroad. The Prince and Princess have more tastes in common than most people imagine, and no wife could be more indignant at the injustice with which her husband has been assailed in the last few months than the Princess. . . . There is not in her the stuff of a Victoria or an Elizabeth. But perhaps on that very account they live on much more affectionate and harmonious terms than they might have done had she been otherwise.'

The writer of this perspicacious article did not know that the 'affectionate and harmonious terms' existing between husband and wife had been disturbed by another and, for the Princess, a far more wounding scandal than the Baccarat Case. A wife finds it much more easy to forgive her husband's gambling habits than his involvement in the affairs of another woman. The tangled business of Lord Charles Beresford and Lady Brooke was well under way before ever the Prince went to Tranby Croft. Frances Brooke was an attractive and unscrupulous woman. Describing in her memoirs the conventions and habits current in her youth, she wrote, 'We obeyed our parents, respected our elders, and kept our promises, even our marriage vows.'[5] Nothing could be farther from the truth where her own marriage vows were concerned. Frances Brooke had had an affair with the Prince's old friend, Lord Charles Beresford, and when the liaison ended she had been foolish enough to write him a most indiscreet letter. By accident this letter fell into the hands of Beresford's wife, who saw it as a useful weapon to use if ever her rival should be minded to make further trouble. She therefore deposited it with the famous solicitor, George Lewis, who knew more than any man about the scandalous secrets of Victorian Society. With remarkable effrontery Lady Brooke appealed to the Prince of Wales to help her recover this compromising document. After his experiences with Lady Mordaunt and Lady Aylesford the Prince should have learnt the wisdom of keeping clear of compromising letters, but he found Frances Brooke very touching in her role of beauty in distress. Foolishly, he rushed into the fray and demanded that George Lewis should destroy the letter.

Quite properly, George Lewis refused to part with his client's property, even at the request of the Prince of Wales, but he nevertheless allowed the Prince to read the letter. The hot-tempered Irishman, 'Charlie' Beresford, was not unnaturally furious at this piece of royal interference; he called his one-time friend a coward and a blackguard to his face and was only just restrained from striking him. The Prince retaliated by imposing a social boycott on the Beresfords, which fell especially heavily on Lady Charles, a beautiful woman who much enjoyed the pleasures of Society. In July 1891 Lord Charles took the only revenge which was open to him by threatening to publish an account of the whole sorry affair, 'publicity being evidently our only remedy'.

This threat was the more dangerous because by now Lady Brooke had taken Mrs Langtry's place as the Prince's recognised mistress, recognised, that is to say, by Society but not by the Princess, who never extended to Frances Brooke the toleration she had shown Lillie Langtry. The Princess herself had much to trouble her mind; whilst her husband's good name was thus threatened by a most unpleasant scandal her son's dissipated habits and general instability had reached a pitch when they could no longer be ignored. Prince Eddy resembled no one so much as his Hanoverian forebears, the 'wicked uncles' who had been the bogey-men of Queen Victoria's youth. Like them, he could never be trusted to behave quite like other people, especially where the emotion of love was concerned, falling passionately in love with one woman, and in less than no time, just as passionately in love with another, and almost invariably selecting someone who could not possibly be regarded as a suitable bride for a royal prince. Again like his great-uncles, he possessed a certain charm, especially for women, but he was dissolute and essentially trivial, in racing language 'not quite up to the weight'. What was to be done with this unsatisfactory young man?

By now the Prince had lost patience with his son. Impelled by the same motives which led so many Victorian fathers to ship their black sheep off to Canada or Australia he planned to send Prince Eddy on a tour of the more remote Colonies. The Queen, however, expressed her strong disapproval. After his father, Prince Eddy was heir to the English throne; in her view the English sovereign must be a good European, with a command of European languages and a knowledge of European countries and personalities. None of these things did Prince Eddy possess; 'He and Georgie are dear, good boys but *very* exclusively English, and that is a great misfortune.'[6] The difficulty was that although Queen Victoria knew something of her grandson's failings she did not realise how very far he was from being 'a dear good boy'. The Prince feared to expose Prince Eddy to the alluring temptations of European cities, but how was he to make this point clear to the Queen? 'It is difficult to explain to you the reasons why we do not consider it desirable for him to make lengthened stays in foreign capitals,'[7] he wrote in some embarrassment. The Princess meanwhile set her face against both a European tour and an extended visit to the Colonies. Her son was a naughty, bad boy, but, she argued, nothing was so likely to reform naughty, bad boys as a mother's influence. Let him therefore remain with his regiment, which was conveniently stationed as near home as Ireland, so that she could keep him under her maternal eye.

The Prince, however, vetoed this plan, holding that it would be waste of time for Prince Eddy to remain any longer in the army. He was in an unhappy situation; only two months had passed since the Baccarat Case and at any moment news of the much more compromising Beresford affair might burst upon the public. How could he admonish his son without laying himself open to the obvious retort about dwellers in glass-houses? At the beginning of August the Prince and Princess were together at Cowes, where they must have had ample time and opportunity to discuss the question of Prince Eddy's future. The Prince, however, would not face a final confrontation with his wife on this subject. On 14 August he left for Homburg; four days later his Secretary, Francis Knollys, sought an interview with the Princess.

Francis Knollys had been charged to put three plans before her, the final decision on Prince Eddy's future to be hers. The first scheme was a Colonial tour, the second a combination of Colonial tour with a Continental one, the third, and most a surprising, an immediate marriage with Princess May of Teck. This suggestion was not a completely novel one; as far back as 1886 Ponsonby had noted apropos of possible brides for Prince Eddy, 'Princess May seems out of the question as the Prince and Princess of Wales have no love for the parents and the boy does not care for the girl.'[8] Although Ponsonby was wrong in supposing that the Princess did not love the Duchess of Teck, everyone agreed that the Duke would not be an ideal father-in-law. Poverty, enforced idleness, and constant brooding over the morganatic 'taint' in his pedigree had combined to make him touchy and ill-tempered, whilst a severe stroke which he suffered in 1884 had slightly affected his mind. Moreover, whatever might be the Princess's views, there was no doubt about the Queen's disapproval of any Cambridge connection. To Princess May herself, however, no objection could be taken; she had looks, brains, character and common-sense, whilst the difficulties she had encountered in her home life had taught her tact and given her a surprising maturity of judgment. After a long discussion the Princess chose the third alternative; her son should marry Princess May. Having thus settled Prince Eddy's future she left next day for Denmark.

The happiness of her holiday was disturbed by rumours reaching her from England about the Beresford affair. Lady Charles's sister, Mrs Gerald Paget, had written what Sir Philip Magnus describes as 'a defamatory pamphlet', telling the whole sorry story from her sister's point of view. Although apparently only three copies were made, these three circulated freely, even in America. Far too many people 'in Society' now knew the story; it was even said that the Duchess of Manchester had read the pamphlet aloud to her guests at a dinner-party. Publicity had always been what the Princess most dreaded; she could manage her matrimonial affairs well enough so long as they did not become matter for public gossip and comment. These rumours, coming on top of the open scandal of the Baccarat Case, were for once more than she could endure; she cancelled her return to England, which had been fixed for 13 October, and left for Livadia in the Crimea, where the Czar and Czarina were about to celebrate their silver wedding.

No one supposed that had all been well between husband and wife the Princess would have chosen to attend her sister's silver wedding rather than be present at the festivities planned for her husband's fiftieth birthday, on 9 November. That occasion was spoilt for the Prince of Wales both by his wife's absence and by the damaged condition of his home; on 31 October a fire destroyed the top floor at Sandringham and badly damaged the dining room and the precious Goya tapestries. On 12 November another disaster occurred; Prince George fell ill of the dreaded typhoid fever.

'This dangerous illness,' writes Sir Philip Magnus, 'brought the Princess of Wales home with all speed from the Crimea.'[9] The inference is that had it not been for her son's illness she would have remained abroad much longer. When she arrived in England on 22 November she had, in point of fact, returned only a few days earlier than the date on which her husband was expecting her. 'I get good accounts of Alix from Livadia,' he had written on 11 November to his sister the Empress Frederick; 'and she will probably stay there till 19th and then come home.'[10] The rebuff which the Princess had administered to her erring husband had been intended as a very gentle one.

In their shared anxiety over their son's illness husband and wife forgot their differences. The Princess was now once again ready to stand beside her husband in all his troubles, even in those which he had brought upon himself. 'She warmly supports the Prince in everything connected with this unfortunate affair and is anxious to do all in her power to assist him,'[11] Francis Knollys wrote on 19 December 1891. A settlement of 'this unfortunate affair' seemed as far off as ever; in fact it was not until March 1892 that the letter which had been the cause of so much trouble was handed back to Lady Brooke.

Somewhat surprisingly, Prince Eddy's affairs provided the one bright spot in a dark outlook. The Queen had enthusiastically welcomed the idea of a marriage with Princess May; this being so, the reaction of the young people themselves was the only remaining difficulty. A month or so earlier Ponsonby had written of Prince Eddy, 'I am told he don't care for Princess May of Teck and she appears to be too proud to take the trouble of running after him for which I rather admire her.'[12] Ponsonby, however, was proved wrong in his judgment; Prince Eddy was willing and anxious to marry Princess May, so anxious in fact, that, meeting her at a house-party at Luton Hoo, he proposed and was accepted a full month earlier than the date on which his parents had planned that the engagement should take place.

'Beloved Mama,' the Princess wrote to Queen Victoria, 'this time I do hope that dear Eddy has found the *right bride.*' Her letter is full of praise of Princess May – 'she will be one of us at once and the fact of her being English will make all the difference and carry the whole nation with them' – but in her happiness over her son's choice she still cannot forget 'the sad tragedy and blighted life of that sweet dear Hélène'.[13]

The wedding-day was fixed for 27 February 1892. On 4 January Princess May and her parents travelled to Sandringham for the celebrations which were to mark Prince Eddy's twenty-eighth birthday. Three days later, although feeling very unwell, Prince Eddy insisted on taking part in a shoot. As he walked away from the house he chanced to glance back and, seeing his mother at a window, waved his hat in greeting. For many years the Princess kept that hat hanging up in her bedroom. He came back early looking very pale and complaining of a bad headache, and next day collapsed with influenza. On his birthday he came downstairs to receive his presents, but felt so ill that he was obliged to go back to bed. 'I still see him all the time before my eyes,' the Princess wrote to her parents, 'as he went up the stairs for the last time in his life and turned his head to give me his friendly nod, which I must do without forever now.' The next day the doctor, pronouncing him to be seriously ill with inflammation of the lungs, summoned a specialist and two nurses.

For the next two days, Sunday and Monday, Princess May was allowed to pay him frequent visits, but on Tuesday he was so much worse that the doctors, urging the need for perfect quiet, forbade any visitors except his parents. Ever since the beginning of his illness he had shown himself particularly gentle and obedient towards his mother who had been almost constantly at his side – 'everything I asked him to do he did and took everything from my hands'. Now he became delirious, raving incessantly. To her this was unspeakably painful; '*Nothing* is so terrible as to hear a person that one loves raving in that way',[14] she had written long ago at the time of Major Grey's death. Now her mind went back to the black hours of her husband's delirium during his attack of typhoid fever, but she comforted herself with the hope that as the father had recovered from a desperate illness so his son might do likewise.

It was not to be. At eight o'clock on the morning of 13 January, after an all-night vigil in the sick-room, the Princess woke her husband to tell him that she despaired of their son's life. Another specialist arrived; buoyed up by his opinion, the Prince of Wales continued to hope, although everyone else knew that all hope had vanished. He wandered restlessly in and out of his son's room where the Princess sat by the bedside, refusing to move until well after midnight, when the doctors persuaded her to take a little rest. Hardly had she lain down on her sofa than she was summoned back; Prince Eddy was dying. 'It was as if I myself must die at that moment, and yet I had to master my tears and my deep, deep despair, and be calm. Although the tears were running down I spoke to him, but, Oh, he no longer heard me, and yet he was still talking, but only with great difficulty and effort and with that terrible rattle in his throat.' The Prince of Wales joined her, followed by the dying man's brother and sisters, and by Princess May. The tiny bedroom, so ludicrously inadequate for the heir to the throne, was now crammed almost to suffocation point. For hours they waited, watching his painful death-agony, whilst the nurses put ice to his head and his mother wiped the sweat from his face – 'All we could hear were the sounds of terrible agony in his throat and chest and our own sobs.' Three times the watchers were sent out of the room as he suddenly rallied, but each time 'it was only for a few minutes, as a candle flares up once or twice and at length slowly dies out'. Even now the Princess could not believe that God would allow her son to be taken from her. Her simple faith was not shaken, 'but it is hard, so hard and Our Lord's ways are past understanding'.

Suddenly Prince Eddy exclaimed, 'Something too awful has happened – my darling brother George is dead.' His mother wondered whether the words meant that he knew himself to be dying. Afterwards the thought was to be a comfort to her when she grieved to remember that, because his illness had come on so suddenly, 'to my great sorrow, I never managed to speak to him of death'. She had, however, the comfort of hearing their own parson from Sandringham Church repeat the prayers for the dying. The watchers by his bedside had been there more than seven hours when Prince Eddy asked, 'Who is that?' and, murmuring the question over and over again, sank at last into the quiet of death.[15]

The Princess spoke truth when she wrote sadly to Queen Victoria that she would never recover from the shock of her son's death. He had been lethargic, dissipated, impervious to education and manifestly unfitted to the high position for which he was apparently destined, but he had also been amenable, home-loving and affectionate. More important by far, he was her first-born child; she had also felt for him the peculiar tenderness which a mother keeps for the weakest and most unsatisfactory member of her flock. The two days and nights spent in sleepless watching by his bedside, the ghastly realisation that what had seemed merely a trivial illness could and would end so catastrophically, the long and painful death-agony – all these memories made up a recurrent nightmare which was to haunt her for the rest of her life. The blow was doubly heavy because it came just at the time when her son's future appeared to be happy and assured. For years he had been a source of anxiety to his parents; now, at the very moment when they had succeeded in steering him into the safe harbour of marriage with a thoroughly desirable bride, death suddenly snatched him away.

On hearing of Prince Eddy's death the ever-faithful Oliver Montagu came at once to Sandringham. Meeting him, both the Prince and the Princess broke down in tears. They seemed to him to be completely shattered by their grief, finding comfort only in the sight of their son's body; before he left, Montagu was taken not once but three times to see the corpse. Sorrow had brought husband and wife very close to one another and emphasised the strength of the bond between them. A paper-covered booklet still exists, its price marked as 2/11, containing a sermon preached at Sandringham Church on 24 January, the Sunday after Prince Eddy's funeral. Inside is an inscription in the Prince of Wales's handwriting: 'To my dearest Wife, in remembrance of our beloved Eddy, who was taken from us! "He is not dead but sleepeth." From her devoted but broken-hearted husband, Bertie.'[16]

'Bertie and I followed him on foot Friday night at eleven o'clock to our own little church,' the Princess wrote to Queen Victoria; 'today we all took the Sacrament with him still near us.'[17] For her the worst moment came when she saw her son's coffin carried out of Sandringham Church and felt that now indeed he was leaving his home for ever. She had wished that he should be buried at Sandringham, beside the baby John who had lived only for one day. The Queen, quick to sympathise with anyone bereaved, agreed that she might have her wish, but the Prince of Wales insisted that his son must lie at Windsor among his peers. At Windsor therefore the funeral was to be; against Queen Victoria's wish, the Princess intended to be present, not indeed in public but in the gallery known as 'the Queen's Closet' from which the Queen herself had watched the wedding of Prince Eddy's parents. Even now the Princess did not quite lose her lightness of touch; 'I shall hide upon the staircase, in a corner, unknown to the world,'[18] she announced almost airily. So with her daughters, and with the Princess who was to have been her daughter-in-law, she watched her son's funeral, finding comfort in the beauty of the music, Purcell, Croft, Chopin and Sullivan, an eclectic selection of her own choosing.

On the grandiose tomb erected to the Duke of Clarence's memory there hung until quite recently a wreath of *immortelles* inscribed simply, 'Hélène'. And Princess Hélène it is who deserves to have the last word on the subject of the Duke. In November 1892 Queen Victoria had a conversation with this charming girl who had so faithfully loved her not very lovable grandson. '*Je l'aimais tant,*' said Princess Hélène, adding, somewhat surprisingly, '*il était si bon.*'

After the funeral the Prince of Wales took his wife and daughters to Osborne; 'poor dear Alix looks the picture of grief,' the Queen noted in her journal on 2 February, adding later, 'dear Alix looked lovelier than ever in her deep mourning'. From Osborne they went on to Eastbourne taking with them Princess May. Another guest was Lord Rosebery, who had never recovered from the shock of his wife's death two years previously. No two people could have been less alike than the extroverted, unintellectual Princess of Wales and the brilliant Rosebery, one of the most complex characters of his generation, but they had in common the experience of sudden, overwhelming bereavement. In June 1893 Rosebery wrote her a moving letter. After begging her to attend a party at the Foreign Office he continued:

> 'I can well believe that Your Royal Highness shrinks from everything of the kind, for I so truly enter into your feelings. Had I the choice, I should not be at the F.O., either giving parties or leading the life that I lead. But I have not the choice, and perhaps it is for the best.
>
> Your Royal Highness's position is of course totally different, and I only mention mine for the purpose of showing my humble and heartfelt sympathy. Great grief seeks its refuge in seclusion, and such as I might well seclude ourselves without notice. But Your Royal Highness cannot, and the reflection of the pleasure afforded by your appearance and the popularity it adds to the Monarchy, which shadows the living as well as the dead, may I hope induce you to come among us.
>
> Nothing after all can recall the past, but it should be the shrine to which we retire at times, not the cell in which we live; and so I earnestly hope that Your Royal Highness will sometimes put aside your sad memories to show yourself to those who love you so sincerely.
>
> I am half inclined to tear this letter up, but I leave that

to Your Royal Highness. But I would pray you to forgive my earnestness and my freedom. I am afraid I practise very badly in my humble sphere what I preach. Our cases are, however, very different; and I only write this as one who knows but too well the *fatal passion for retirement engendered by sorrow*, and as one warmly and sincerely devoted to Your Royal Highness, and sympathising with your grief as much as one in my position dare sympathise with one in yours.'[19]

'I quite agree with you *how* difficult and painful it is, after a *great* sorrow to begin life once more,' the Princess replied to this letter, 'but you may be sure that no selfish shrinking on my part will prevent me doing the duty which lies so clearly before me. Nothing after all can *change* or *lighten* our sorrows which are always and ever present wherever we are and whatever we do to our life's end!', and she signed herself, 'Yours very sincerely, a fellow sufferer.'[20]

In May 1892 Prince George was created Duke of York. Since he was now his father's heir his matrimonial plans had suddenly become matters of great importance. Rumour was already coupling his name with that of Princess May; the Duke, however, fancied himself in love with his attractive cousin 'Missy,' Princess Marie, daughter of Prince Alfred, now Duke of Edinburgh. She would have none of him, somewhat surprisingly preferring to marry the heir to the Rumanian throne rather than the heir to the British one. The Princess of Wales was delighted when 'Missy' announced her engagement to Prince Ferdinand; she regarded the Edinburgh family as intolerably Germanic, the Duke of Edinburgh being heir to his uncle, Duke Ernst of Saxe-Coburg-Gotha, and she had no wish to have any of the Edinburgh girls for a daughter-in-law. She was not the best of friends with 'Missy's' mother, one difficulty being the Duchess's claim, as daughter of a Czar, to take precedence over a mere Princess of Wales. A few years later, after the Duke of Edinburgh had succeeded to his uncle's title, Francis Knollys wrote to Ponsonby on this subject, 'I cannot imagine anything more unpopular than the Queen trying to arrange the Duchess of Coburg, the most unpopular Princess in England, taking precedence over the Princess of

Wales, the most popular Princess not only in England but in Europe.'[21]

'At times it is a fearful struggle for me to appear bright among them all [and] a fearful longing comes over me at times for both my boys,' the Princess wrote on 3 October to the Duke of York, who was now at Heidelberg, battling with the intricacies of what his mother called 'that old *sauerkraut*, the German language'.[22] She nevertheless spent a comparatively happy autumn holiday at Mar Lodge, with Oliver Montagu there to instruct her in the art of salmon fishing. For some time he had been failing in health; now he was persuaded to winter in Egypt to see whether the milder climate might not bring some improvement. Once there, however, he grew rapidly worse, and at the end of January 1893 he died in Cairo.

For the Princess the blow was a peculiarly heavy one, coming so soon after the death of her eldest son. 'So God has taken to himself our dearly beloved friend Oliver,' she wrote in eulogy and farewell, 'the best and truest of men, one to be relied on in every relation of life, faithful, discreet and trustworthy, gentle, kind, just and brave, and noble both in his life and death. God bless him for all his ever-thoughtfulness for others.'[23] Thus nobly she summed up the character of the man who had loved her for a quarter of a century, never asking for any return. But although they had not been lovers they had been very close to one another; the world looked on Oliver Montagu as a play-boy but she had seen the more serious side of his character. 'I was so touched by you saying you thought I had had some good influence on your dear nephew's spiritual life,' she wrote to his aunt, Lady Sydney; 'we have, it is true, often talked over sacred matters together, and I have always thought him such a good, *high principled, religious* man.'[24]

The Prince of Wales and the Duke of York attended Oliver Montagu's funeral at Hinchingbroke, the Princess going there privately the previous day. She had already sent Lord Sandwich a little cross, begging that it might remain overnight on the coffin so that 'I may take it away with me tomorrow as a sad remembrance of my faithful friend'.[25] Among the family memorials in the chancel of Sandringham Church is a tablet to Oliver Montagu. For at least twenty-two years – the last extant letter on the subject is dated 1915 – the Princess sent flowers on the anniversary of his death, asking Lord Sandwich to see them laid on 'your dear and never-to-be-forgotten brother Oliver's grave'.[26]

Prince Eddy was gone, and Oliver Montagu too, so that she clung the more closely to her one remaining son. The nation at large expected the Duke of York to marry Princess May; the Teck parents were loud and tactless in their advocacy of this idea, but the Prince and Princess of Wales, whilst fully approving of the proposed bride, could not as yet bring themselves to contemplate a marriage which might be construed as an affront to the memory of their dead son. Princess May, finding herself in a most awkward position, behaved with her customary good sense and restraint. The Duke himself had not as yet recovered from the shock of his brother's death, which had come upon him when he was barely convalescent from his attack of typhoid. His health and spirits had been so badly affected that his mother decided to take him with her on a Mediterranean cruise to visit her relations in Greece, arguing that he needed 'a complete change and rest before settling down in life'[27], whilst for her own part she longed to have her son all to herself yet once again before he took to himself a wife.

On arrival at Athens they found the King of Greece embroiled in constant quarrels with his sons, persistently refusing to recognise their right, as grown-up men, to have some control over their own lives. The situation was peculiarly painful to the Princess of Wales, who had always set such store by family unity. Meanwhile, the Duke of York was taking the opportunity to discuss his own problems with his favourite Aunt, Queen Olga of Greece, who was insistent that he ought to propose at once to Princess May. His mother felt that she could not bear to be in England at the actual moment of betrothal, certain though she was that Princess May would make her son an ideal wife, so she lingered at Venice whilst he travelled on to England. On 3 May 1893, in the garden of the Fifes' home at Sheen, where Prince Eddy had not so long ago courted Princess Hélène, the Duke of York proposed and was accepted. Though the arrangement could not properly be called a love-match it merited that title far more than a marriage between Princess May and Prince Eddy would have done. The two had had ample time to get to know one another so that their marriage could be securely based on a mutual liking and respect which was to develop with the years into a deep love between husband and wife.

On hearing the news the Princess wrote to Princess May a warmly affectionate letter:

> 'God bless you both and let me welcome you once more as my dear daughter. God bless you and grant you all the happiness which you so fully deserve with my Georgie and which was denied you with my darling Eddy. I am sure as you say his spirit is watching over you now and rejoicing with us and that the clouds have been lifted once more from your saddened young life and that you may yet look forward to a bright and happy future with the brother he loved so well. For my own self I need hardly speak as you know *how* much I have always loved you and how glad I am that you will still belong to us and I know we two will always understand each other and I hope my sweet May will always come straight to me for everything.'[28]

The last sentence unconsciously reveals the weakest points in the relationship between the Princess of Wales and her daughter-in-law. No young woman likes to be so dependent on her mother-in-law that she must 'always come straight to me for everything'; yet the Princess never saw how irritating this patronising attitude could be. As for understanding one another, she was hardly equipped to understand a girl as serious-minded and as self-contained as Princess May. Princess May, however, was well accustomed to dealing with just such a character as the Princess of Wales. The Duchess of Teck greatly resembled the Princess in her gaiety, her inconsequence, her lack of financial sense, her fantastic unpunctuality, her gift of getting in touch easily with all sorts and conditions of people, and also, it might be said, in the warmth of popular feeling she evoked, loyal affection springing up everywhere she went like a flower in her path. Princess May's experience with her mother must have been a real help to her in her relations with her very similar mother-in-law.

THE END OF THE OLD ORDER

The Duke of York and Princess May were married at the Chapel Royal on 6 July 1893. 'Poor Aunt Alix looked rather sad in church – one can quite understand why,'[1] wrote the Czarevitch Nicholas. The honeymoon was spent at Sandringham, at York Cottage, which was to be the young couple's future home. The choice was a strange one, for the shadow of Prince Eddy's death still hung over Sandringham. His room was kept exactly as if he were still alive, even the soap being changed whenever it showed signs of deterioration. The only additions were a Union Jack draping the bed on which he died and a glass-fronted wardrobe in which his various uniforms hung displayed. And if York Cottage was a strange choice for the honeymoon it was an even stranger one for a permanent home. Not merely was it ludicrously unfit to serve as a royal residence; it was so small and so badly planned as to make an unsuitable home for any growing family, royal or otherwise. The Princess of Wales appears to have had little to do with the choice of a house, delighted though she was to keep her son so near at hand; the Prince had given York Cottage as a wedding present to the Duke of York, who was charmed with it. He was blind to its inconveniences, blind too to the defect which most distressed his wife, its pedestrian and irredeemable ugliness. The heir to the British throne had no objection to living in a building painfully reminiscent of a seaside boarding-house. He loved Sandringham and wished to make his home there; York Cottage was at Sandringham and to York Cottage he could see no possible objection.

One objection in fact weighed more heavily than all the others put together, and that was the total lack of privacy. York Cottage is situated not in the park but in the actual garden of Sandringham House; mother-in-law and daughter-in-law were almost literally on each other's doorsteps. The temptation to be for ever dropping in was one which the Princess made no effort at all to resist; 'I sometimes think that just after we were married we were not left alone enough,' Princess May wrote in 1894 with masterly understatement, 'and this led to many little rubs which might have been avoided.'[2]

'Many little rubs' are a commonplace of the early days of married life. Too much has been made of differences which were in fact no more and no less than the differences which occur in ninety-nine families out of a hundred, even when the two women concerned are more temperamentally akin than were these two. The Princess genuinely loved her daughter-in-law and she made a real, if slightly ineffectual effort to remember that her son was no longer a small boy and her exclusive property but a grown-up married man. From the time of his engagement the tone of her letters to him changes; they become more restrained, less possessively affectionate, and seldom does the old note recur until she herself is an old and very unhappy woman. If indeed in these early days there had been serious friction between Princess May and her mother-in-law it would certainly not have escaped the notice of Princess May's 'Aunt Augusta', the Grand Duchess of Mecklenburg-Strelitz. Aunt and niece kept up a regular correspondence; even though Princess May was discretion itself in her letters the Grand Duchess was quick to mark and comment upon anything amiss. In these earlier letters she has nothing but good to say of 'dear Alix', whom she met briefly in February 1895 and described as being 'darling as ever, so affectionate and dear',[3] high praise indeed from the slightly astringent Grand Duchess.

The real difficulty lay not so much with the Duke of York's mother as with his sisters. Princess May had been brought up as the only girl among three brothers, all of them lively, intelligent and normally mature. Her sisters-in-law, on the contrary, were lethargic, uneducated and childlike, not to say childish, in their tastes and amusements. The Duchess of Fife, the only one of them yet married, was so tongue-tied with strangers as to make conversation with her a penance. Fishing was her only real interest although, as Lady Warwick rather cattily remarked, 'she would turn to music when open-air pursuits were not possible'. Princess Maud was generally regarded as the liveliest of the three but she was also the youngest and therefore a less important member of the family than Princess Victoria, the eldest daughter at home. Delicate, hypochondriacal, and already slightly embittered, Princess Victoria possessed a quick and none too kindly tongue. She did not spare her sister-in-law; 'Now do try to talk to May at dinner, though one knows she is deadly dull,' she admonished a guest at Windsor. This critical and unkind attitude so inhibited Princess May that even such an acute observer as Ponsonby could echo Princess Victoria's unjust judgment: 'I have sat next to the Duchess of York for the last three nights,' he wrote to his wife in September 1894, 'she is pretty and what you would call voluptuous, but decidedly dull.'[4] Surprising though it is to find the future Queen Mary described as 'voluptuous' it is yet more surprising to find her described as 'decidedly dull'.

Part of Princess Victoria's bitterness can be put down to the fact that 'Cousin May' was now a married woman whilst she herself remained a spinster. The Princess of Wales made no sort of effort to find husbands for her unmarried daughters. In 1894 Princess Victoria was twenty-six, Princess Maud a year younger, so that the Empress Frederick had good reason to write, 'it really is *not* wise to leave the fate of these dear girls *dans la vague* for years longer'. She suggested that various German princes, including 'young Lippe' and Prince Max of Baden, might be invited to England, adding, however, that Prince Max might be reluctant to come, 'having heard that *Germans* are at a discount in our dear Alix's favour'.[5] The Empress was right; the Princess of Wales was determined that no child of hers should marry a German and she showed very little desire that her daughters should marry anyone at all. Queen Victoria replied that the Prince of Wales had told her that he was powerless in the matter because 'Alix found them such good companions that she would not encourage them marrying, and that they themselves had no inclination for it', to which the Queen added the sage comment, 'I think he is mistaken as regards Maud.'[6]

Princess Maud it was who ultimately married. There had been some talk of her cousin, young Prince Christian, afterwards King Christian X, but in the end her husband was to be another Danish relative, Prince Charles, a naval officer and according to Lord Esher, 'a very nice young fellow, brave and modest'.[7] As a girl Princess Maud had been cheerful and gay but after marriage she became a grumbler, bewailing her grievances. Although the Prince of Wales gave her a house at Appleton near Sandringham to use as a holiday residence, she had naturally to make her permanent home in Denmark, a country she disliked, and she was the more miserable because her husband's service with the Danish navy took him away from her for long periods. The Princess rightly had no patience with her daughter's lamentations – 'she must on *no* account forget that she married a *Danish* Prince and a *naval* man and *he owes* his first duty both to *his country* and his profession.'[8]

For Princess Victoria matters did not go even so far propitiously as they had done for her sister. She wished at one time to marry a member of the Baring family but she was forbidden to think of marriage with a commoner. Rumour has it that in later life she fell in love with her father's equerry, Sir Arthur Davidson, but that for the same reason this match too was judged impossible.

One unlikely person was talked of as a husband first for Princess Maud, and later for Princess Victoria. During his short premiership that sick and unhappy man, Lord Rosebery, toyed briefly with the notion of marrying again. 'Marriage frightens him – he cannot believe in a fresh disinterested affection,' Esher wrote, adding, however, that Rosebery ought to marry because 'I suppose in these days a Prime Minister cannot have a mistress'.[9] Since this is hardly the frame of mind in which a man should set about courting a royal princess nineteen years his junior the Princess of Wales did well to be shocked when Rosebery appeared to consider himself a possible suitor for Princess Victoria's hand.[10]

Princess Victoria was to remain the unmarried daughter at home. It cannot truthfully be said that she was happy in that position, or that her mother, who nevertheless loved her dearly, treated her with sympathy or proper consideration. The Princess of Wales would keep a bell by her side and ring whenever she wished to summon her daughter to her side. 'Poor Toria was just a glorified maid to her mother,' wrote her Russian cousin, the Grand Duchess Olga. 'Many a time a talk or a game would be broken off by a message from my Aunt Alix, and Toria would run like lightning, often to discover that her mother could not remember why she had sent for her, and it puzzled me because Aunt Alix was so good.'[11] Good the Princess certainly was, but her goodness was not informed by imagination, a quality in which she was almost wholly lacking. As so often happens with unimaginative people she was apt to behave selfishly, in spite of her overflowing love and kindness, because she could not put herself into the position of the other person. Although her daughters counted for less with her than her sons she genuinely loved them all, and Princess Victoria in particular, but in her relationship with them she appears at her very worst, possessive, inconsiderate, and blandly uncomprehending of any point of view but her own.

With Princess Victoria and Charlotte Knollys as her constant companions the Princess of Wales spent much of her time at Sandringham during the 'locust years', as Sir Philip Magnus calls them, from 1893 to 1901 – 'years of inanition', says Mr Pope-Hennessy. There she occupied herself with visiting 'my poor people', keeping a benevolent eye on the carving school she had established for boys on the estate, arguing with gardeners who preferred grand bedding-out displays to 'my poor innocent inexpensive little flowers', and discussing church and parish affairs with the local parson. Every Saturday a list of the hymns to be sung at the Sunday services was submitted to her, and she would firmly strike out any which did not meet with her approval, substituting either

Peace, perfect peace or *Abide with me*. In fact, she behaved like a typical English country lady, and like many another country lady, she was growing just a little eccentric. But it was a gentle, gay eccentricity which made her yet the more lovable. She still mourned her eldest son – and who is to say how much she grieved for Oliver Montagu? – but she wore her rue with a difference. Never again was she to appear in bright colours, but unlike Queen Victoria, casting gloom all around her with the blackness of her dress, the Princess wore mourning so unobtrusive as to go almost unnoticed. In white, in silver, in blue-grey and the palest, most exquisite mauve, she glided through the panelled halls of Sandringham, more lovely and more *distraite* than ever, answering at random to half-heard queries, scattering smiles and impulsive kindnesses on anyone who crossed her path. One day it chanced to be a Scottish footman, homesick at Christmas-time among these alien splendours. 'Nobody must be lonely in *my* house,' she exhorted him, pressing into his hand a pair of gold cuff-links; 'you will get your proper Christmas present later, but these are something personal to you from me.'

No wonder that servants worshipped such a mistress although she was not always an easy person to serve. She could not be unkind but she could be inconsiderate and she was always unpredictable. Sometimes she would put her servants' interests so far above her own as to make both them and her appear ridiculous; at others, she would behave as if they could have no interests at all except the interest of serving her. About the turn of the century she had as her dressers two daughters of a woodman on the Sandringham estate called Temple. Because Temple was a widower needing a daughter at home to look after him she would go to great pains never to take both girls away with her from Sandringham at the same time. One of these girls, Bessie Temple, was a special favourite. Some of her experiences with the Princess would be incredible were they not true. On one occasion during a Scottish visit Bessie was given a room inconveniently far from that of her mistress. In the middle of the night the Princess summoned her, and for some reason or other desired her to stay in the room till morning. Bessie prepared to lie down on the sofa; the Princess, however, insisted that Bessie must sleep in her bed whilst she herself took the sofa, and it was only with the greatest difficulty that she could be persuaded of the incongruity of such an arrangement. Yet when Bessie became engaged to a member of the crew of the royal yacht time and again she had to put off the date of her wedding because the Princess insisted that she must travel with her on yet another and another journey – 'Just this once, Bessie; I cannot possibly do without you *this* time.'

On one occasion she presented Bessie with a beautiful grey silk frock, remarking that she herself no longer needed it as she had a new one almost exactly similar. For that very reason Bessie took great care never to wear the frock when she was anywhere near the Princess. One day, however, she was faced with the question, 'Why do I never see you in that pretty frock?' 'Because, Ma'am, I do not want to appear dressed the same as Your Royal Highness.' 'Nonsense! That is exactly why I gave it you; I *want* us to look just alike.'

The Princess was never extravagant or careless over clothes and some of the economies learnt during her penurious youth remained with her always, her maids being expected to darn her stockings, sometimes even her handkerchiefs. She once insisted that 'six good brocade dresses' should be unpicked and cleaned, and used to cover furniture at Sandringham. For patriotic reasons she dressed chiefly in London, where her favourite dressmaker was Redfern, but occasionally she allowed herself a shopping expedition to Paris. There she would patronise Doucet, then a great name in the world of fashion, and also the lesser-known Fromont of the Rue de la Paix.

For entertainment there was always music. In 1896 she went with her daughter and Charlotte Knollys to hear 'the beautiful Wagner music' at Bayreuth where she enjoyed behaving like any ordinary person, sitting in the stalls instead of in a box, and rushing out between the acts to snatch a meal in a nearby restaurant. A sentence in a letter to Prince George recalls forgotten social customs – 'We ladies had to tear our hats off the moment the curtain went up and put them on again when the curtain dropped, an awful nuisance but part of the play.'[12]

Like many women of her generation the Princess made a hobby of painting both in water-colours and oils. It must be admitted, however, that there is a considerable difference to be seen between her own unaided efforts and those pictures which she completed under the 'supervision' of a drawing-master. She was more successful with the camera, or 'photography machine', as she would sometimes call it, and to the end of her life she remained an enthusiastic and skilful amateur photographer.

About the year 1900 a golf-course was laid out in Sandringham Park. The Princess never grasped the rules of this game, regarding it as a kind of hockey allowing of much light-hearted scrummaging, the winner being the player who first succeeded in propelling his or her ball into the hole, regardless of the number of strokes played. In 1895 she sent Arthur Balfour, a great golfing enthusiast, one of the oddest Christmas cards that any Cabinet Minister can have received from a royal personage. The picture shows two hands clasped upon a golf-club and underneath is written:

The merry season LINKS our hands
With IRON bands today,
So PUT a smiling face on, friend,
And DRIVE dull care away.
May fickle fortune never TEES
Nor BUNKER you nor foil
Your plans, but stick to you until
You finally STRIKE oil.[13]

Indoors, bridge had now superseded whist as the favourite game. For several years after Prince Eddy's death dancing was frowned upon, but in 1897 the ebullient Daisy Cornwallis-West, afterwards Princess of Pless, succeeded in breaking down this ban, in spite of a slight show of disapproval on the part of the Princess.

This placid existence was interrupted in November 1894 by the news that the Czar had fallen seriously ill at Livadia. Although the Prince and Princess travelled out to the Crimea with the utmost speed a telegram announcing his death reached them at Vienna. Princess 'Alicky' of Hesse was also on her way to Russia; she had at last overcome her scruples against joining the Orthodox Church and had agreed to marry the Czarevitch Nicholas, who had been for a long time devotedly in love with her. Now the funeral of the old Czar and the wedding of the new Czar were to take place almost simultaneously.

To the Princess of Wales the first meeting with her widowed sister was 'unspeakable agony'. Through the nineteen days of funeral ceremonies she was always at the Empress's side, even sleeping by night in her bedroom. The occasion which the Princess herself found most moving was the moment when, late at night by the light of flickering torches, the Czar's coffin was carried over the threshold of his home by his own relatives and then borne on the shoulders of his faithful Cossacks to the little church on top of a neighbouring hill. Next day, as the booming of guns echoed round the mountains, the funeral procession made its slow way to the waiting ships. For two and a half hours the Princess and her sister walked behind the coffin down a rough path strewn with evergreens. 'The sun shone gloriously,' she wrote to Queen Victoria, 'and the sea was sparkling in its rays whilst the whole road was lined with thousands of weeping people who fell on their knees and crossed themselves reverently as their beloved Emperor was carried by them for the last time.'[14]

At Moscow the coffin was taken to the cathedral of Michael the Archangel within the Kremlin, the procession stopping at every church along its route – and there were many. Two days later the whole proceeding had to be gone through again in reverse on the way to the train for St Petersburg. Here the procession took more than four hours to make its way to the fortress church of St Peter and St Paul. For the second time the Princess witnessed the funeral ceremonies of a Czar in that strange baroque church, nearer in spirit to Vienna than to Russia, lit by thousands of candles guttering in great chandeliers of blue enamel, gilt and crystal. The corpse lay with its face exposed for seven days, 'a barbarous and unseemly custom', Arthur Ellis wrote to Queen Victoria, complaining also of 'the *thirty-ninth* repetition of the same mass'.[15] At the end of the final funeral service, which lasted for four hours, all the Royalties had to kiss the dead man in a last farewell. Not surprisingly, the Empress broke down completely on her return to the Anitchoff Palace. Once again it was for the Princess to comfort and soothe; 'I cannot think how the Empress would have got through these terrible days without her,' Charlotte Knollys wrote to Queen Victoria, adding, 'the Prince has also won golden opinions by all the kind feeling he has shown'.[16]

The Czar's funeral was followed almost immediately by the wedding of his successor; 'I am not sure that the wedding was not sadder than the funeral,' wrote Charlotte Knollys, remarking, however, that it was 'a magnificent sight'.[17] The two sisters, the Dowager Empress and the Princess, both appeared at the wedding dressed entirely in white; the Princess's face betrayed the effort she was making not to break down, whilst the Empress wept openly throughout the ceremony.

During her stay in Russia the Princess celebrated her fiftieth birthday. Although Mary Gladstone wrote of her at a Drawing-Room as 'carrying off the palm for youth and beauty, sweetness, sadness and grace',[18] whilst Lord Carrington described her appearance, 'in a black and white striped silk gown, looking too pretty – about thirty-five, apparently',[19] she had in fact reached an age when life is inevitably saddened by the deaths of friends and relations. The next death in her family circle was, however, an unexpected one. In 1896 Princess Beatrice's husband, Prince Henry of Battenberg, died of fever whilst on active service in the Ashanti campaign. The blow was a bitter one for Queen Victoria, who had come to rely greatly on this son-in-law; again it was the Princess of Wales who comforted and consoled her. The next year saw the breaking of a strong link with the past when the Duchess of Teck died on 27 October. On hearing the news the Princess rushed over to White Lodge, taking with her no attendant lady and bringing only what would now be called 'a grip', intent on arriving there as soon as possible to help and comfort the bereaved Duchess of York.

For the Princess of Wales herself the saddest blow of all came with the death of her mother, Queen Louise, on 9 September, 1898. When she was called to Denmark to her dying mother the Princess was forced to leave her husband barely convalescent from a painful accident. In July the Prince had slipped and fractured his kneecap. Writing to the Duke of York the Princess describes the concourse of doctors and surgeons – 'they say to themselves "this kneecap we truly lay" as they do with a foundation stone'. Seldom or never did she complain of her own lameness, but a sentence in this same letter shows what she had really suffered from her handicap: 'I only hope to God he may not get a stiff leg like mine, which is, I confess, an *awful* bore and nuisance, and one's wretched leg seems always in the way – and makes everything one would like to do *so* awkward – such as riding, running and bicycling, etc., and stairs are always detestable and before a lot of people it is odious.'[20]

The Princess was so exhausted by the strain and sadness of her mother's last illness that even the Prince of Wales, who was never an alarmist, expressed serious fears for her health. She dawdled interminably over the business of sorting Queen Louise's papers and possessions, exasperating the Duke of York, who had remained with her in Denmark and was now fretting over the loss of his shooting. The Prince of Wales too was growing impatient; 'I must honestly tell you that your Papa is *very* anxious that Motherdear should return home now,' the Duchess of York wrote; 'I do hope you may be able to persuade her to come soon.'[21]

Although the Prince never liked to be parted from his wife for very long his anxiety over her in no way prevented him from amusing himself with other women. In 1895, Frances Brooke, now Countess of Warwick, suddenly and unexpectedly became converted to socialism. Whether for this reason, or because the Prince was becoming a little bored with her charms, the affair between them began to show unmistakable signs of cooling off. Society with a capital 'S' was what mattered most to Lady Warwick, even in her socialist phase; now that doors were no longer open to her as the Prince's mistress her social position would be extremely precarious if the Princess were to continue to refuse to receive her. With this in mind, Lady Warwick wrote the Prince a letter in which she declared that although she knew that unkind gossip had reached his wife's ears yet she was convinced that the Princess was too noble a character to listen to slander or to bear malice. This letter touched the Prince so much that he showed it to his wife, which of course was exactly what Lady Warwick had intended that he should do. Displaying the wisdom of the serpent, the Princess burst into tears, expressed her sorrow for Lady Warwick's sad plight, and declared her own certainty that 'out of evil good would come'. She even agreed to receive her defeated rival – she could now afford to be magnanimous – and the Prince wrote off at once to give the good news: 'I know my darling that she will now meet you with pleasure, so that your position is, thank God! better now than it ever was since we have been such friends, and I do not despair in time that you and she may become quite good friends.'

The Prince had a plan by which he hoped to bring about this improbable friendship; 'We must endeavour to get up some object in common – some philanthropic one I mean – which may have a common interest to both.' The Princess, however, quietly put an end to this ingenuous scheme. 'In case you should hear from Lady Warwick asking you to become President of a Charity of hers, refuse it,' the Duke of York wrote to his wife; 'Motherdear has done so and wishes you to do the same.'[22] But although the Princess was not prepared to see herself or any member of her family sitting on a charitable committee with her husband's ex-mistress, she nevertheless appeared to him to be all sweetness and forgiveness. 'Certainly the Princess has been an angel of goodness through all this,' he wrote to Lady Warwick, 'but then she is a Lady and never could do anything that was mean or small.'[23]

Seven weeks after this idyllic ending to his connection with Lady Warwick the Prince of Wales dined for the first time with Mr and Mrs George Keppel, a handsome young society couple. George Keppel, brother to Lord Albemarle, came of a family closely connected with the Royal Family by ties of service and friendship. His wife Alice was an attractive woman of twenty-nine; between her and the Prince, to use Sir Philip Magnus's tactful phrase, 'an understanding arose almost overnight'.[24] Discreet and intelligent, loyal and in no way self-seeking, Alice Keppel was universally popular. Her family life was a happy one and its happiness was not destroyed by her love-affair with the Prince. In appearance she was handsome rather than beautiful, with fine dark eyes, a full but well-proportioned figure and surprisingly small hands and feet, of which she was very vain. Her voice was loud, suddenly descending to a whisper, then rising almost to a bellow when she wished to emphasise a point.

Mrs Keppel's many good qualities won her general acceptance; Sir Philip Magnus writes that she was invited to almost all the houses which the Prince visited except Hatfield and Welbeck – and, be it said, also Arundel, since the Duke of Norfolk set his face against her no less strongly than did the Duke of Portland and Lord Salisbury. Some of the feeling against Mrs Keppel among these members of the older aristocracy was due to their affection and sympathy for the Princess, whose attitude towards Mrs Keppel is popularly believed to have been one of almost superhuman charity and forebearance. This view is not absolutely correct. At times she could rise to heroic heights in her dealings with her husband's mistress but there were moments when she was less saintly. Every year the Prince and Princess attended Cowes Regatta Week on board the royal yacht, an occasion to which they both looked forward eagerly, the Prince because he enjoyed racing in his famous *Britannia*, the Princess because it was the one time when she had her beloved son, the Duke of York, all to herself. (The Duchess, being a shocking sailor, wisely stayed away.) 'How are things going on in general?' the Duchess wrote one Cowes week, 'I mean, does peace reign or have you had a difficult time?'[25] Peace had reigned all the fortnight and there had been no rows of any kind, her husband replied, adding, 'Alas, Mrs K. arrives tomorrow and stops here in a yacht, I am afraid that peace and quiet will not remain.'[26] 'What a pity Mrs G. K. is again to the fore!' the Duchess commented. 'How annoyed Mama will be!'[27]

The Princess most assuredly did not like Mrs Keppel, but she was grateful to her for keeping the Prince entertained and therefore good-tempered, and for banishing the spectre of boredom which haunted him perpetually. A tiny anecdote illustrates her tolerant, faintly teasing attitude. One day she chanced to look out of the window at Sandringham just as her husband and his mistress were returning from a drive in an open carriage. The Princess herself never lost her graceful slimness but Alice Keppel, her junior by twenty-five years, had already grown very stout, whilst the Prince of Wales had long merited his disrespectful nickname of 'Tum-Tum'. The sight of these two plump persons sitting solemnly side by side was too much for her equanimity; calling to her lady-in-waiting to come and view the joke with her, she dissolved into fits of laughter.

The Princess found increasing compensation for the trials of her married life in the family of grandchildren growing up at York Cottage. 'My blessed grandson David', afterwards King Edward VIII, was born in 1894, Prince Albert in 1895, Princess Mary in 1897 and Prince Henry in 1900. She had always been one to spoil rather than to discipline children, a tendency which can be a positive virtue in a grandmother. The Duchess of York did not altogether approve of such indulgence but she was a sympathetic and sensible young woman and she allowed the Princess to have the children with her as much as she wished. Not so the Duchess of Fife. The differing attitudes of daughter-in-law and daughter did not pass unnoticed; 'I was so glad to show Louise and Macduff how fully you trust your precious children to my care, and how fondly I look after them,'[28] the Princess wrote on 13 November 1897.

This year of 1897 was the year of Queen Victoria's Diamond Jubilee. The Princess had her own ideas as to how that anniversary should be celebrated; in a letter to the Lord Mayor of London she suggested that a fund should be opened to provide a dinner 'for the poorest of the poor in the slums of London', enclosing, of course, a substantial donation of her own. Such impetuous generosity was typical of her and so was the disregard of hard financial fact. So many appeals had recently come before the public that inevitably this particular one fared badly. The scheme might have broken down altogether had it not been for the generosity and also, said unkind critics, the flair for self-advertisement displayed by the millionaire tea-merchant, Thomas Lipton, who wrote a cheque to cover the considerable deficit between the amount subscribed and the amount actually required. The Princess was naturally grateful to him for coming to the rescue of her scheme; when he received a knighthood in the next Honours List it was rumoured that it had been given him at her request.

For the Princess herself the Jubilee rejoicings were overshadowed by anxiety for her brother the King of Greece. On 17 April hostilities had broken out between Turkey and Greece. Neither side really wanted war; the Turks were urged on by Kaiser William II whilst King George of Greece, as always, trusted to the Great Powers to intervene before it was too late. The Turks proved much too strong for the Greeks; disaster followed disaster and the King sent frenzied telegrams to his sister begging her to use her influence with the Queen and with the British Government on behalf of Greece. She, of course, was powerless. 'The Princess of Wales is in a terrible state of mind over the Greek business but keeps herself in wonderful control,'[29] Lord Carrington wrote on 8 May. On 17 May the Greeks were defeated at Domokos; the road to Athens lay open to the Turkish army. Panic seized the city where anti-monarchist feeling rose to dangerous heights. In the evening of that same day the Princess rushed to Windsor in a final attempt to enlist Queen Victoria's sympathy and help. 'The Princess of Wales came down last night in an awful stew about Greece,' the Queen's lady-in-waiting, Marie Mallet, wrote to her husband, 'imploring the Queen to do something to stop the war and stay the hand of the triumphant Turks.'[30] The Queen could do nothing, nor, indeed, did she show very much interest in the matter; 'We live for nothing but the Jubilee and seem to ignore the doings of the world in general,' Mrs Mallet wrote on 14 June, 'and we snort at the Greek question.'[31]

Later in the year the Prince and Princess paid a last visit to the Gladstones at Hawarden. Gladstone had always been grateful for what he described as 'the unbounded kindness which we have always received from your Royal Highness and not less from the beloved Princess of Wales',[32] a kindness which had done something to compensate for the Queen's unfriendly attitude. When Gladstone died on 19 May 1898 the Princess wrote a long letter to Mrs Gladstone in which she described him as 'that great and good Man whose name will go down in letters of gold to posterity as one of the most beautiful upright and disinterested characters that has ever adorned the pages of history.'[33] She herself attended his funeral service in Westminster Abbey, where the Prince acted as pall-bearer, regardless of the Queen's protests. A little crucifix, which had belonged first to Gladstone, then to his wife, hung always beside the Princess's bed, treasured for the sake of these two old friends.

Affairs in Greece continued to alarm the Princess, who was particularly anxious about the position of her nephew Prince George, whom the four Protecting Powers had appointed High Commissioner in Crete. Balkan troubles, however, were overshadowed by the growing threat of war in South Africa. Like her husband, the Princess had been open in her support of the Jameson Raid and when Jameson was standing trial she had written to the Duke of York: 'So papa saw poor Doctor Jameson. I wish I had. I am *so* sorry for him and think he must be so humiliated now. I do hope they will all be let off.'[34]

'This horrid African War' broke out in October 1899. The Princess's particular *bête noire*, Kaiser William, was openly pro-Boer; she was therefore extremely annoyed that he should be due to visit Sandringham in November, and she mocked aloud when she discovered that he was to bring with him a special barber to curl his famous moustache. Her own concern was with the care of the sick and wounded. 'On December 12th 1899,' Dame Beryl Oliver writes in *The British Red Cross in Action*, 'the Princess of Wales decided to select and send twelve nursing sisters to South Africa,' and from this small beginning sprang the body afterwards known as Queen Alexandra's Imperial Nursing Service. Later on, she sent out a further twenty of 'my military nurses' at her own expense, though complaining that she was not allowed to make her own selection – 'I still regret not having chosen my *own* nurses'.[35]

A hospital ship was also to be bought out of the balance of funds collected in the Princess's name during the Egyptian campaign. She took a deep interest in this scheme, concerning herself, contrary to her usual habit, with small practical details of equipment and administration. She enquired whether there was to be a chaplain on board, and demanded to know why there was to be no navigating officer – 'How can they do without a navigating lieutenant? To me who have been so much at sea, it seems quite an impossibility.'[36] She herself ordered special mattresses for the bunks, and she greeted with enthusiasm the arrival of several cases of champagne – 'As for the champagne, I am sure it will be the most welcome gift for the poor wounded officers, who generally live upon it at home.'[37] Many difficulties were encountered culminating ignominiously enough with the collapse of the ship's boiler; at last, however, the hospital ship *Princess of Wales* set sail for Cape Town, where she saw much useful service.

In the spring of 1900 anti-British feeling in France was so pronounced that the Prince decided to cancel his Easter holiday on the Riviera and to accompany his wife to Copenhagen. As their train was standing in Brussels railway station a youth called Sipido fired a shot through the carriage window, the bullet passing straight between the Prince and the Princess. 'There was no time for anyone to be frightened, except the Princess's little Chinese dog, who was terrified by the explosion,' wrote Charlotte Knollys, who had also been in the carriage; 'the Prince never even changed colour and the Princess behaved beautifully.'[38]

On 30 July the Prince's brother Alfred, now Duke of Saxe-Coburg-Gotha, died of cancer. At Frederichshof his sister, the Empress Frederick, was slowly and very painfully dying of the same disease. In August, when on her way once again to Denmark, the Princess visited her sister-in-law. 'God bless you, darling,' she wrote on leaving, 'and may you suffer less is the prayer of your loving sister Alix.'[39] In October yet another blow fell; Prince Christian Victor, elder son of Prince and Princess Christian, died of enteric fever in South Africa. Painfully tired, unable either to eat or sleep, Queen Victoria struggled on for a few months. The end, however, was near; on 15 January the Princess found herself hurrying to Osborne, where she joined her husband, summoned hastily from London. The Kaiser, subdued and very much on his best behaviour, arrived on 20 January. Two days later, in the dusk of the winter evening, Queen Victoria died surrounded by her family, the Princess kneeling beside her and holding her hand.

EDWARDIAN QUEEN

The Prince of Wales was King at last, and the Princess, Queen Consort, a title she disliked and refused to use – 'she means to be "the Queen",'[1] wrote Lord Esher. It was King Edward's great misfortune that he had had to wait so long for his inheritance. The real *raison d'être* of a Prince of Wales is his future kingship; he has no position of his own in the constitutional scheme and only such specific duties as the Sovereign chooses to allot to him. He is, as it were, an actor standing in the wings of the stage waiting for his cue, which may not come until the last act of the play. Not till the age of fifty-nine could King Edward begin the real business of his life and he was to die before his sixty-ninth birthday. Fate allotted him nearly sixty years of expectancy for less than ten of fulfilment.

Because of his mother's refusal to associate him in any way with her work as sovereign, those years had not been a time of active apprenticeship but of empty waiting; now, in late middle-age, he had to set about learning the difficult trade of kingship. For him Queen Victoria's death meant a radical alteration in the pattern of his life, but for his wife the change was not so clearly marked. The difference in the position of a Princess of Wales and a Queen Consort is not one of kind but of degree. Queen Alexandra's duties would still be social and charitable ones and her new dignity did not mean that she would have any closer connection with affairs of state. Nevertheless, she had her own personal contribution to make to the Edwardian conception of monarchy. Queen Victoria had done very much to raise the standing of the throne in popular estimation; perhaps never before in English history had the monarch been so respectable and respected. However, when she died she was an old lady of eighty-one who had lived for many years secluded from her people, a revered but distant figure. Inevitably the monarchy had come to be regarded as old-fashioned, shut in upon itself, a little stuffy. It was for the new King to let in some fresh air, to throw the shutters open on the light of common day. This was his great achievement; and some of the credit for it must in fairness be given to his wife.

His popularity had always fluctuated wildly; not so hers. Long ago the nation had taken her to its heart and through all the changes of fortune she had never lost her hold upon the affection of the people. Everybody loved her, not merely the masses but also the intellectuals with whom she had so little in common, and the older aristocracy who were the last people to be dazzled by the glamour of royalty. Had she ever shown any resentment against her husband his peccadilloes would have had a much more disastrous effect upon his popularity; because she accepted them without question the nation was prepared to accept them also for her sake. Nevertheless, they presented a stumbling-block. Although some people might like King Edward better for what Wilfrid Blunt called his 'pleasant little weaknesses' (which were, after all, the little weaknesses which many men would like to indulge in themselves), a large section of the population, and one that was growing every day more influential, remained completely out of sympathy with his attitude towards life. Sir Philip Magnus writes of him that, 'cherishing warmly until the last the traditional values of an older Merrie England which had its roots in the countryside, he was increasingly perplexed when confronted by the changing values of a population which contained in 1914 only eight per cent. who continued to work on the land.'[2] If King Edward was perplexed by an industrial generation, that generation, both masters and men, were perplexed and shocked by him in their turn. At the time of the Tranby Croft scandal an old coachman, who had been for many years in the service of a well-to-do Manchester family, shook his head and remarked, 'God will never allow such a wicked man to come to the throne.' His employers would certainly have echoed that sentiment, perhaps in the form of a prayer. Whatever their own private behaviour may have been, men of this stamp demanded that the morality of public characters should be above reproach. Although everybody loved King Edward for his *panache* and delighted to see the monarchy take on a new shape better suited to the twentieth century, the man in the street, and more especially the men in the streets of the northern cities, demanded that the sovereign should continue to uphold a nineteenth-century standard of morals.

This of course King Edward could not and would not do; he was no hypocrite and he would not pretend to being any more moral than he actually was. It was left to Queen Alexandra to preserve for the throne its aura of Victorian respectability without in any way detracting from its new, more decorative Edwardian air; she proved in her own person that royalty could be both glamorous and good. She eased the transition from the old world to the new because men of both worlds could find in her the qualities they sought for in a queen. She was the smartest of all Edwardian beauties and yet as virtuous as Queen Victoria; combining the more free and easy manners of a new generation with a beautiful and queenly stateliness, she was at once both dignified and approachable.

Her remarkable beauty was, of course, one of Queen Alexandra's greatest assets. Simply to look at her was a rare pleasure. Those who saw her at the state opening of King Edward's first Parliament never forgot her appearance, dressed in deepest mourning, her fair complexion set off by a heavy black veil surmounted by a miniature diamond crown. A spectator at the 1906 state opening when asked, sixty years later, to describe the Queen's appearance, simply replied, 'She was the most beautiful person I ever saw.' In 1906 Queen Alexandra was already sixty-one; as late as 1909 Margot Asquith could write, 'the Queen, dazzlingly beautiful, whether in gold and silver by night, or in violet velvet by day, succeeded in making every other woman look common beside her.'[3] 'Lovely and gracious', 'so beautiful with her sly, sideways look', 'ineffably beautiful', 'slender, graceful and beautiful' – these are only some of the innumerable expressions of admiration lavished upon Queen Alexandra in her sixties.

Only in beauty and in a certain touching innocence – 'Alix is so innocent, she can't believe in such wickedness,'[4] the Grand Duchess Augusta once wrote of her – did Queen Alexandra outshine her contemporaries. Her letters faithfully reflect the life and thought, if thought it can be called, of the typical Edwardian Society lady; she read the same books, enjoyed the same plays, held the same views on life in general, as did most of her fellows. Had she been more serious and intellectual, preferring George Moore to Marie Corelli, Bernard Shaw to Pinero, she would not have personified as well as she did the Edwardian ideal of womanhood. The very mediocrity of her mind, flitting, impermanent, butterfly-like, made her the more typical of her generation. The Edwardian age, for all its *bravura*, was essentially a mediocre one, a plain between two mountain ranges. Neither its personalities nor its events are of the first order of importance. Bonar Law and Asquith, Galsworthy and H. G. Wells, are not to be named in the same breath as Disraeli and Gladstone, Dickens and Thackeray, whilst episodes such as the Suffragette Movement, the Parliament Act, the Curragh Mutiny, pale into insignificance before the events of 1914–18. The great Victorians have gone; the giant catastrophe is yet to come. Our chief interest in the Edwardians is an ironic one – 'Alas, regardless of their doom the little victims play.'

To their credit be it said, the Edwardians played with immense style and gusto; they did not hesitate to make hay whilst their sun shone so brightly. Queen Alexandra thoroughly enjoyed her position, although to old friends such as Lady Macclesfield she made the usual conventional remarks (and doubtless she believed that she meant them) about preferring a peaceful life and a more private station – 'with a heavy heart I have to lead this new life with all its many responsibilities'.[5] Whilst Queen Victoria lay unburied she refused to allow herself to be called 'the Queen' and forbade anyone to kiss her hand. Her grief was a perfectly honest emotion; she had been genuinely fond of her mother-in-law and at the private service of committal at Frogmore Mausoleum she was the only person, except for the very young and impressionable Duke of Coburg, who could not refrain from tears.

Although a real affection had existed between the two women the situation had not always been an easy one. For thirty-eight years as Princess of Wales Alexandra had lived under the tremendous shadow of Queen Victoria; now at last she came out into the sun. Up to now she had been under the necessity of seeking the Queen's approval even in trivial matters; she had had to walk delicately, remembering always to subordinate herself, careful never to take too much of the limelight. Always she had been obliged to defer to the Queen's tastes, the Queen's wishes, the Queen's prejudices. True, if a difference had arisen between them she had nearly always won her point, but only by the exercise of much tact and persuasion. The discipline had been quite severe but it had been salutary. By nature Queen Alexandra was extremely obstinate; it had been good for her character to be forced to subordinate herself and to give way to another. This, however, she need do no longer; now it was for other people to give way to her. 'It is queer, her determination to have her own way,' was Lord Esher's puzzled comment. 'As Princess of Wales she was never, so she says, allowed to do as she chose. "Now I do as I like" is the sort of attitude.'[6] With her husband's accession a subtle change comes over Queen Alexandra. Sir Philip Magnus writes of 'her wilful and charming way'; from now onwards she does not cease to be charming but her wilfulness grows more and more apparent. She becomes – it must be said – a little spoilt.

In small matters Queen Alexandra would no longer brook any dictation. Nobody knew what was the correct dress for the Queen Consort to wear at the Coronation; the last Queen Consort had been Queen Adelaide and only the Grand Duchess Augusta had any clear recollection of King William IV's Coronation. Historians were consulted, records were turned up, but Queen Alexandra cared for none of these things. Where clothes were concerned she would bow neither to the dictates of history nor to the demands of fashion. 'I know better than all the milliners and antiquaries,' she wrote to Sir Arthur Ellis, 'I shall wear exactly what I like and so will all my ladies – *Basta!*'[7]

The Queen proved equally obstinate about the business of moving into Windsor Castle and Buckingham Palace. At Windsor she was determined to occupy the State Apartments, an idea vetoed by King Edward, who chose to live in the rooms which had been occupied by his parents. Esher noted that 'there was quite a sharp difference of opinion'. Being himself something of a connoisseur he also noted that in discussing the arrangement of the rooms the Queen showed 'excellent taste', a quality with which she is not generally credited.[8] She was delighted by the discovery of many treasures hidden away unused. 'Our rooms will be beautiful when furnished with all the splendid, fabulous furniture in the Castle,' she wrote to the Duke of York; 'I have been fishing out such beauties from every imaginable corner,' adding with naive and rather touching pride, 'I do not think even the Rothschilds could boast of anything better or more valuable.'[9] Among all the rooms at Windsor thus furnished with priceless furniture and pictures Queen Alexandra kept one small room to be hung entirely with her own amateurish water-colour sketches.

Perhaps because her wishes had been crossed at Windsor the Queen became the more stubborn when faced with the prospect of moving to Buckingham Palace, a building with which she was curiously unfamiliar. When Lord Esher was showing her round he noted with astonishment that she had never been into Queen Victoria's private rooms, which Queen Victoria herself had in fact used very seldom. For a long time Queen Alexandra obstinately refused to consider moving, a refusal which much troubled the King. He even went so far as to appeal to the Grand Duchess Augusta, begging her 'as an English Princess' – the old lady was very proud of her descent from King George III – 'to tell Alix it is a duty and a necessity to live at the Palace'.[10] In the end, of course, Queen Alexandra was obliged to agree to the move. She wrote to the Duke of York, describing her feelings at the prospect of leaving her beloved Marlborough House: 'That I feel will finish me. All my happiness and sorrow were here, very nearly all you children were born here, all the reminiscences of my whole life are here, and I feel as if by taking me away a cord will be torn in my heart which can never be mended again.'[11]

What most worried Queen Alexandra was the question of finding proper accommodation for Charlotte Knollys at the Palace and the difficulty of fitting all her own innumerable keep-sakes and treasures into the comparatively small space available for her private use. Once these problems were solved she very quickly reconciled herself to her new home. She made her rooms at Buckingham Palace very charming if over-crowded even by the standards of her own day. Mary Drew described the sunny sitting-room with its big bay window, the profusion of flowers everywhere, and, amongst the vast collection of framed photographs, one of her own father, Gladstone.[12]

Buckingham Palace and Windsor Castle were completely renovated; at Balmoral, however, Queen Alexandra declared her intention of keeping Queen Victoria's arrangements more or less unaltered. 'I dreaded very much at first coming up here without our beloved Queen, whose favourite home it was,' she wrote to Lady Macclesfield; 'one misses her at every step and corner and it seems almost like sacrilege sitting here writing at *her* table and living in *her* rooms with all her things about me. I will not have any of her things and treasures touched here, all shall remain as she placed them herself.'[13] Filial piety, however, was not strong enough to put up with the Balmoral drawing-room where Queen Alexandra decided to replace the tartan carpets and curtains with others of more restrained pattern and colour. Otherwise, she bore as best she could with her predecessor's taste. A letter written in 1910 to Queen Mary, who had just become, in her turn, mistress at Balmoral, shows how much this restraint cost her: 'I wonder whether you have made any alterations in your rooms upstairs – as I confess dear Grand-Mama's taste in wallpapers was rather sad and very doubtful!! that washed out pink moiré paper in the sitting-room is *sickly* and the one in the bedroom *appalling* but I never liked to touch anything of hers so left it all exactly as she had it.'[14]

Queen Alexandra had never been fond of 'dear old melancholy Abergeldie', and of recent years she had gone there as seldom as possible. Balmoral, however, was a different matter;

she found the Scottish holidays, previously something of a penance, becoming more and more of a pleasure to her. 'Motherdear is so happy at Balmoral, and is in tearing spirits and enjoys everything like a child,' wrote the Duchess of York; 'it is quite a pleasure to see her and she looks younger and lovelier than ever, a perfect marvel.'[15]

Whether at Buckingham Palace, Sandringham, Windsor or Balmoral, Queen Alexandra was very much mistress, even matriarch, in her own home. Perhaps because she allowed him so generous a measure of freedom outside the family circle, within that circle King Edward usually bowed to his wife's will. He might be King of England but she was the domestic autocrat. The King approved of regularity and liked to fix plans well in advance; his wife, however, was a born improviser and she would not always accommodate herself to such arrangements. 'I cannot get Alix to agree to plans made so long beforehand, but what would suit *my* plans best would be to arrive at Copenhagen on April 21st,' King Edward wrote on 8 February 1908 to his brother-in-law, King Frederick of Denmark. Two busy monarchs might be expected to fix the date of a state visit at least two months in advance; the King, however, continues almost in the manner of a henpecked husband, imploring his brother-in-law's help, 'though Alix has not at present agreed to the date she might be influenced by your agreeing with me.'[16] Lord Esher recorded an earlier occasion when, in the middle of an important business discussion, a message came from Alexandra, then Princess of Wales, demanding her husband's presence, to be followed by a second message so peremptory that the Prince fled hastily, the business left undone.

Usually, of course, it was Queen Alexandra who kept King Edward waiting. Her fantastic unpunctuality both irritated and inconvenienced her husband, yet she made not the slightest effort to mend her ways. 'Keep him waiting; it will do him good!' she remarked airily to Sir Sidney Greville when the King had already waited for half-an-hour, fretting lest he should be late for an important engagement.[17] Shortly after King Edward's accession the Queen was to help him to receive addresses and deputations. The deputations were due at noon but at one o'clock there was still no sign of Queen Alexandra.

'The King sat in the Equerries' room drumming on the table and looking out of the window with the face of a Christian martyr. Finally at 1.50 p.m. the Queen came down looking lovely and quite unconcerned. All she said was, "Am I late?" The King swallowed and walked gravely out of the room.'[18]

The King's liking for ceremonial and correctitude, his restless search after constant entertainment and occupation, combined with the Queen's spontaneous gaiety to make their life at Buckingham Palace or Windsor, Balmoral or Sandringham a unique blend of magnificence and informality. Gone was the boredom which had so afflicted Queen Victoria's Court, but the grandeur remained. Dinner, for instance, was a splendid function. The King took in the Queen, who almost invariably arrived late. The ladies glittered with tiaras and jewels of all sorts, the gentlemen with orders and medals. Talk was free and animated although those who sat beside host and hostess did not always find it so easy to make conversation. King Edward was difficult to amuse, more particularly as he disliked to talk of abstract subjects, and all too often he would start drumming on the table with his plump fingers, a trick of his which indicated acute boredom. Queen Alexandra's dinner partners also had their difficulties, chiefly due to her deafness. As deaf people are apt to do, she tried to cover up her handicap by talking ceaselessly herself. She had a charming habit of watching what went on at the dinner-table and if she saw anyone laugh she would laugh with them, giving a little wave of her hand as if to show that she too had heard and enjoyed the joke. After dinner there was none of that endless standing about which had been the peculiar trial of Queen Victoria's evening parties; instead there would be bridge for those who wished to play, whilst, as Esher noted with relief, 'the non-players *sit* and talk'. Usually there would be two bridge tables; at the King's table the stakes would be reasonably high, at the Queen's the play would not be for money. On one informal occasion in May 1901, when the King and Queen played at the same table, a wrangle ensued over what points they should play for, the Queen maintaining that she would not play for money as her income had not yet been voted her by Parliament. In the end they agreed to compromise on playing penny points, King Edward winning eleven pence, Queen Alexandra losing seven pence.

When the mood took her, however, Queen Alexandra could play surprisingly high; some years previously Lady Geraldine had recorded that the Duke of Cambridge had been at a house-party at Goodwood where 'the Princess played very high loo, the Duke was fortunate and won £100.'[19] On another occasion the Duke commented on '*the boldness* with which the Princess plunges'.[20] At Chatsworth in January 1907 she astonished the company by insisting on playing baccarat, though perhaps not realising what game was intended, since Lord Rosebery persisted in referring to it as 'Lotto'. This particular visit to Chatsworth included Twelfth Night celebrations, when dinner was turned into a Christmas-like festivity complete with crackers. Arthur Balfour did his best to oblige by perching a paper cap on his head but he was clearly out of his element. Not so Queen Alexandra; 'she was wonderful at this sort of thing and made everybody play up so that the fun became fast and furious'.[21] At another Chatsworth party she first danced a waltz with the Portuguese diplomat, the Marquis de Soveral, and then insisted that everyone should kick off their shoes to see what difference this made to their height. She went round trying on everybody's shoes, even the men's pumps, yet still remaining 'always graceful in all she does'.[22]

Her waltz partner Soveral was perhaps Queen Alexandra's favourite among her husband's men friends. 'The Blue Monkey', to use his nickname, was immensely popular with women. An extremely able and astute man, he was nevertheless always prepared to play the fool to order. On one occasion the Duchess of York came upon Queen Alexandra and Soveral at 'the merchant's', or village shop, at Crathie, the Queen intent on buying caps for all the men then staying at Balmoral, and trying the caps one by one on Soveral to see which were the most becoming.

This simplicity and total lack of affectation misled, and still misleads, many people into supposing Queen Alexandra to be less astute than she really was. A case in point is an account of a visit she paid to Luke Fildes's studio in 1901 to see his state portrait of King Edward: 'She stood looking at it for a long time, a smile playing over her lips. "I like it *very* much. I think it is *very* good. I know that expression *so* well. It is *just* like him when he begins to feel drowsy." '

Realising that he had somewhat tactlessly stressed the Hanoverian droop of the King's eyelids Fildes immediately altered the portrait. 'A helpful suggestion though an unintentional one' – so his grandson and biographer describes Queen Alexander's remark. But was it in fact completely unintentional?[23]

For the younger members of the household life at Court was now far more amusing than it had been in Queen Victoria's day. At this period the Queen's Household included six Maids of Honour. Queen Alexandra, who always liked the company of young people, much enjoyed having these girls about her. She took a special interest in the two Vivian sisters, Dorothy and Violet – 'my heavenly twins' as she would call them. These twins, dressed exactly alike, were one of the prettiest and best-known sights at Court. The Queen treated them almost as if they were her daughters – 'she was more than a mother to me', one of them wrote long afterwards – taking a lively but serious interest in their health, their clothes, and their love-affairs. When Dorothy Vivian became engaged to a promising Cavalry officer called Douglas Haig, Queen Alexandra arranged that the wedding should be celebrated at Buckingham Palace. As the bride and bridegroom were about to drive away someone tied the traditional old shoe on to their carriage. 'No, no! They must have this one,' the Queen cried out, hopping forward with her own elegant slipper in her hand.

The Maids of Honour never accompanied the Queen to Sandringham because on less formal occasions King Edward preferred to be without them. Though she herself was short the Queen liked to have the tall Maids of Honour with her on great occasions such as Ascot Week or state visits from foreign royalty, so that the unfortunate shorter girls would find themselves saddled with the dreary 'Mausoleum Waiting', which entailed attendance at the annual memorial services for Queen Victoria and the Prince Consort.

Apart from this particular grievance the only complaint which the Maids of Honour had to make was concerned with the arrangement, or lack of arrangement, of their duties.

Every afternoon the Maid of Honour must be waiting in readiness for the Queen to send for her and not till after four o'clock did etiquette allow her to enquire as to whether she would in fact be needed. As often as not she would then discover that the Queen had already gone out, forgetting all about her existence. She was never informed as to the dates and times when she would be in attendance on the Queen of an evening, so that she might be in her bath or dressing for some particularly delectable party when a Royal Messenger would arrive – in London the Maids of Honour were never resident at Buckingham Palace – to say that she was urgently needed by the Queen and that the Palace carriage would be round in twenty minutes. Such a lack of system would seem typical of anyone as unmethodical as Queen Alexandra; in point of fact, however, an exactly similar complaint was made by Queen Victoria's Maids of Honour.

The frequent periods of Court mourning presented special pitfalls. On one occasion a particularly grand function was to take place the very day before full mourning ended. The ladies of the Household asked Queen Alexandra whether they were to be allowed to emerge from unrelieved black on this occasion; she, however, merely replied that such questions bored her intensely and that they must do exactly as they pleased. After much debate it was decided to play for safety and to remain in full mourning. That night, the Queen appeared, a little late as usual, dressed in white from head to foot, glittering with diamonds, a glorious vision, as of course she had always intended to be, against the inky blackness of her Court. During periods of mourning theatre-going was of course forbidden; for some reason this ban did not extend to opera, which Queen Alexandra much preferred, and after the death of her father, King Christian IX, for months on end she attended the opera nearly every night.

Although Queen Victoria's relatives and descendants, 'the old Royal Family' as they were sometimes called, made no complaints about the changes at Windsor and Balmoral, they did not feel themselves to be quite so welcome at those places as they had been under the previous régime. Deeply attached though they were to Queen Alexandra, who had never shown them anything but kindness and affection, they could not but notice her open preference for the company of her own Danish relations, just as another and earlier 'old Royal Family', the descendants of George III, had much more openly and bitterly resented Queen Victoria's preoccupation with the Saxe-Coburg-Gotha family.

The break-up of the old, closely-knit family circle was in fact inevitable. King Edward had no such strong family ties as those which had bound Queen Victoria to half the royalties of Europe. The brother and sisters nearest to him in age and affection were dead, the relationship with Prince and Princess Christian had always been a difficult one, whilst Princess Louise was an embittered, difficult character, soured by an unhappy marriage. Although Princess Louise had once been her favourite sister-in-law, Queen Alexandra was now inclined to take the side of the husband against the wife. She had actually invited Lord Lorne to Sandringham on the occasion of his silver wedding, an anniversary which Princess Louise preferred to spend alone abroad. The brother-in-law who had meant most to Queen Alexandra was Prince Leopold. He too was dead; there remained only the Duke of Connaught and Princess Beatrice, both of them so much younger than King Edward that no very close intimacy had ever been possible. But although the English throne could no longer provide a focus and a rallying-ground for Queen Victoria's vast army of relatives, there was never any suspicion of a rift within the family. For political reasons only Queen Alexandra had always cold-shouldered Prince and Princess Christian; for both political and personal reasons she cordially disliked her nephew Kaiser William II. With these exceptions she was on the best of terms with her husband's family, and especially with her young nieces. In the words of one of the Maids of Honour, 'King Edward was bored by bread-and-butter Misses'. His teasing manner and pointed personal remarks could sadly embarrass a shy young girl, unable to answer back. Queen Alexandra, on the contrary, could never say a hurtful word. Warm, gay, sympathetic, she delighted in showing kindnesses to young people and in sending them presents, usually extremely inappropriate ones. They in their turn laughed a little at such oddities and loved her very dearly.

NAVAL AND MILITARY

Her brilliant social life was what the world chiefly saw of Queen Alexandra; there was, however, a reverse side to the medal. Part of Soveral's attraction for her lay in the simple fact that he spoke distinctly and in a tone of voice which she could almost invariably hear. Her deafness had grown into a barrier cutting her off from the world at large and more especially from the gay society in which both she and King Edward delighted. How could she, for instance, appreciate the private theatricals then so much in vogue when not a word was audible to her? How could she take her part in the interplay of wit and gossip where everything depended on the aside, the casual hint, the quick repartee? For years Queen Alexandra had put up a gallant fight against her increasing deafness and now she made an effort to learn lip-reading, taking lessons in company with the young Duchess of Marlborough, who was also deaf. Unfortunately she made but little progress in this very difficult accomplishment. On the whole, she tended more and more to relax, to abandon the effort to keep up. It was so much easier to stay quietly at Sandringham in the company of dear Charlotte Knollys, with whom no effort whatsoever need be made.

This summer and autumn of 1901 her mood of withdrawal

was strengthened by King Edward's curious reluctance to let her take her proper share in the social and ceremonial work of the monarchy. His refusal to allow her to play any conspicuous part or to attend official functions without him was remarked on every hand. Queen Alexandra herself complained to the Grand Duchess Augusta that he insisted on taking everything upon himself, and she was specially distressed when he would not allow her to present awards to Red Cross workers, which she had always done herself when Princess of Wales.

Faced with this unhelpful attitude on his part Queen Alexandra made less and less effort to share in her husband's life and interests, withdrawing more and more frequently to Sandringham, or further afield to her beloved Denmark, or to the Mediterranean for yachting cruises. Members of the Royal Family began to worry because she left King Edward to himself so often and for so long at a time. 'When she gets *stuck* at Sandringham it is difficult to move her,' the Duchess of York wrote to the Grand Duchess Augusta; 'I had so hoped that in her new position as Queen all this would have improved. It does not look well for her so constantly to leave *him* alone as she does.'[1] Meanwhile King Edward's attachment to Mrs Keppel was obvious and accepted; 'the King has been making a good many small "Mrs George" dinners lately,'[2] Lord Lincolnshire wrote in February 1902. On one point, however, Queen Alexandra was quite determined; her husband was not to have any more dealings with Lady Warwick. Although she was no longer King Edward's mistress, Lady Warwick still saw herself in the role of the power behind the throne, and she was constantly interfering in matters which were in no way her concern. Because the situation was giving rise to gossip Queen Alexandra decided to intervene. She herself wrote Lady Warwick 'a very kind letter', to be followed up by a call from Lord Esher. 'He told me,' wrote Lady Warwick, 'with charming courtesy and frankness, that he thought it would be well for all concerned if my close connection with great affairs were to cease as it was giving rise to hostile comment which distressed Queen Alexandra.'[3] So, tactfully, did the Queen contrive that the King's ex-mistress should fade out of the picture.

Except where Greece was concerned, Queen Alexandra herself did not meddle in politics. King Edward was well aware that such matters were not his wife's strong point, and wisely he did not encourage her to take an interest in them. Unlike Queen Victoria, King Edward was particularly careful to let his heir see the contents of the official boxes. 'You can show them to May, too,' he told the Duke of York. 'But Mama does not see them,' the Duke objected. 'No,' the King replied, 'but that is a very different matter.'[4]

Little though she usually concerned herself with matters of state, private friendship did, however, induce Queen Alexandra to take sides in one of the most acrimonious political controversies of the day. The nation at large may have scouted the possibility of war, but from 1904 onwards politicians agreed with military and naval experts in believing that before very long Germany would challenge Britain's Colonial supremacy and command of the seas, just as she had already challenged Britain's industrial pre-eminence. In face of this German threat the modernisation and expansion of the British Navy became an issue of the first importance and one on which the Navy itself was sharply divided. The leader of the reforming party – indeed, he might almost have been said to be that party in his own person – was Admiral Sir John Fisher; his chief opponent was Admiral Lord Charles Beresford, once King Edward's personal friend, but now very much out of favour with him because of their quarrel over Lady Warwick's letter.

Dislike of Lord Charles may have helped to make the King into a strong supporter of Fisher's reforming party although, as Sir Philip Magnus writes, 'he was scrupulous in exhibiting an attitude of regal impartiality and he never forgot that he had a duty as sovereign to exclude any element of personal prejudice.'[5] In an attempt to renew their old friendship Lord Charles made frequent personal approaches to the King, only to be politely rebuffed. Queen Alexandra was more forgiving – after all, she had less to forgive – and in August 1908 at the end of a visit to the Channel Fleet, then under Lord Charles's command, she went so far as to write him a friendly letter, clearly intended as an olive branch. The meeting at Corfu to which the Queen referred had been in fact anything but a 'charming time' for Lord Charles, who had incurred a severe reprimand for failing to put on full-dress uniform to receive the King of Greece on board his flag-ship:

> 'I came across these photos done of you and your ship off Corfu two years ago and thought you might like to have them in remembrance of that charming time. We all of us did enjoy our visit to Portland and seeing your *beautiful* ships in such *splendid* order and spick and span every one of them. Without flattery both the King and myself thought we had never seen such perfect order and discipline in any of our fleets.
>
> Let me wish you every success in your naval career, and let me repeat once more what I said before, one should *always* try to sacrifice one's personal grievances and remember Nelson's words, England expects every man to do his duty.'[6]

In reply Lord Charles thanked 'his most revered Queen' for a letter which had given him 'the most unbounded pleasure', and added, 'personally, Your Majesties' visit put new life into me as I had just been attacked in a most cowardly manner in my absence by statements that were absolutely untrue', his attacker presumably being Fisher.[7] Clearly he had no intention of sacrificing what the Queen had described as his 'personal grievances', or of interpreting Nelson's signal in terms of Fisher in command at the Admiralty, so that nothing came of her tentative efforts at peace-making.

Although for old time's sake she tried hard to remain on friendly terms with Lord Charles, Queen Alexandra was in fact one of Sir John Fisher's most ardent partisans. Her attitude was based on a personal friendship which seems to date back only to 1904, when Fisher became First Sea Lord. They must, however, have met earlier, because King Edward had for long had a great admiration and affection for Fisher, whom he appointed on his own initiative a member of a three-man committee set up in 1903 to enquire into the re-organisation of the War Office. Fisher was an able man but he was also a simple one, and it was his simplicity which appealed so much to Queen Alexandra, herself a very simple person. Admiral

Sir Reginald Bacon wrote of him that 'he spoke, wrote, and thought in large type italics', and no one who has read Queen Alexandra's letters will deny that she did the same. The two of them had much in common; they were both enthusiastic, impetuous, single-minded, and they were both upheld by a firm, uncomplicated religious faith. Equally significantly, they both loved laughter, and they both laughed at the same jokes.

One thing in particular bound them together, and that was their mutual hatred of Germany. Queen Alexandra's heart warmed to a man who never forgot what he described as 'our betrayal of Denmark when the Germans took Kiel and Schleswig-Holstein', and who had concocted a fantastic plan to anticipate any declaration of war by a landing of British troops in those lands which had once been Danish. The Kaiser actually believed that this plan might be carried out; 'Fisher can no doubt, land 100,000 men in Schleswig-Holstein', he wrote in 1906, 'and the British Navy has reconnoitred the coast of Denmark with this object in view.'[8] As late as 1917 Fisher was writing to Queen Alexandra, 'There is yet time to re-conquer Schleswig-Holstein and the Kiel Canal. It should be done now! I guarantee I could do it!'[9]

Fisher habitually referred to the Queen as 'Blessed Queen Alexandra' whilst she in her turn would address him as 'Dear Admiral Jack' and later, 'My Beloved Lord Fisher'. She enjoyed his flamboyant epistolary style and exchanged with him many letters and joking telegrams. Fisher was, of course, the originator of the Dreadnought, a ship which marked a revolution in naval design. His original plan had been to lay down four new Dreadnoughts every year; in 1906, however, the Liberal Government queried the necessity for even as many as three. In July of that year when Fisher requested a seat in the Royal train the Queen telegraphed: 'Yes with pleasure I will give you a seat in my train if you will give us a fourth Dreadnought.'[10] Fisher replied: 'Humbly beg to inform Your Majesty that four Dreadnoughts will be built and building on Your Majesty's next birthday, December 2nd,* so therefore humbly hope to be allowed the seat so graciously offered in Your Majesty's train.'[11]

*Mistaken date, actually 1 December.

When the Queen's birthday came round Fisher's telegram contained no reference to Dreadnoughts. It read: 'Your Majesty is sixty-two today may you live until you look it is the fervent wish of your humble admirer.'[12] Queen Alexandra replied: 'In your kind telegram you wish me too long a life it would take me three hundred before I could look sixty-two after your reckoning.'[13]

In 1909, when Fisher was under heavy attack, both at home and abroad, Queen Alexandra sent him a telegram not nearly so innocuous as her earlier, joking messages: 'It is all right as I knew pure invention and G – lies Alexandra.'[14]

This telegram was sent not in cypher but *en clair*, which was unwise, to say the least, since everyone knew what the Queen of England meant when she referred to 'G-lies'. Queen Alexandra was sometimes indiscreet in her open championship of Fisher, especially in 1908, at the time of the correspondence between the Kaiser and Lord Tweedmouth, then First Lord of the Admiralty. Lord Esher, a staunch supporter of Fisher, had written a letter to a body known as the Imperial Maritime League in which he declared that Fisher was the most dreaded man in Germany, feared by everyone from the Kaiser downwards. A copy of this letter unfortunately reached the Kaiser, who took great exception to this statement and wrote personally to protest to Lord Tweedmouth. Fisher's enemies made the most of the resulting political crisis, *The Times* coming out strongly against him in a powerful leading article. Queen Alexandra was hot in his defence. 'I have just been with the Queen and her sister,' Fisher wrote on 7 March: 'they sent for me and they are full of fury over the whole business and the utter meanness of *The Times*.'[15] Later he wrote: 'I had a private seance with Princess Victoria by her wish at Buckingham Palace, and she told me about all Society being worked up against me but the King and Queen and herself solid as a rock, but George rather wobbly.'[16]

Queen Alexandra was concerned with military as well as with naval reforms, but in a more practical and less controversial manner. In any account of her life her connection with the Army Nursing Services and with the Red Cross must be an episode deserving a special place to itself. Because nursing had always been one of her great interests it was natural that when she became Queen she should make it her particular concern. As early as February 1901 she sent for Sydney Holland, the Chairman of the London Hospital, to discuss with him the re-organisation of the Army Nursing Services. She told him that she wished to see a really efficient Army Nursing Service, with herself at its head, and she asked him to draw up a scheme for such a service in consultation with the Boer War hero, Lord Roberts.

The position was a delicate one because a small Army Nursing Service was already in existence with Princess Christian at its head. The Princess was persuaded to resign in favour of Queen Alexandra, retaining, however, her headship of the Army Nursing Reserve, which she administered in an efficient if autocratic manner – 'If anyone ventures to disagree with Her Royal Highness she has simply said, "It is my wish, that is sufficient," which always ended the discussion.'[17] Queen Alexandra's Imperial Military Nursing Service was established in 1902 under the control of a Nursing Board with the Queen as President.

The Queen's personal interest in this matter was so great that no trouble was too much for her to take; she even copied out in her own hand fifteen pages of comment by Lord Roberts on the proposed scheme, forwarding them to Holland with the all-too-pertinent remark, 'I only hope you will be able to read them'.[18] She personally devised the badge to be worn by the Q.A.I.M.N.S. nurses, a cross as borne on the Royal Arms of Denmark, surmounted by an Imperial Crown, and the cipher 'A' within the cross.

Difficulties, however, arose when the newly-formed Territorial Army wished to have its own Nursing Service and Nursing Reserve. The Territorial Army was the brain-child of the Secretary of State for War, Richard Haldane, afterwards Lord Haldane of Cloan; it was therefore natural that his very able sister, Elizabeth Haldane, should concern herself with the establishment of a Territorial Army Nursing Reserve. For nearly four years her scheme hung fire because difficulties cropped up at every turn. Queen Alexandra was growing impatient; in June 1906 she sent for Lady Roberts, who was to be her chief adviser on Army Nursing affairs, and in a private talk stressed how anxious she was to know whether anything was in fact being done about a scheme for the expansion of the Nursing Service in time of war. Lady Roberts told her that the matter was under consideration both by the Secretary of State and by the Nursing Board. 'I don't want to influence the Board,' the Queen answered, 'but I should like the members to know that I am in favour of a Reserve being formed *while yet there is time*.'[19] Lady Roberts replied that the chief opponent of such a scheme was the Queen's old friend, Sydney Holland, and she urged the Queen to use her influence with him.

Holland was duly persuaded to change his mind; other difficulties, however, still remained, chief among them being the position of Princess Christian. Understandably enough, Queen Alexandra's assumption of the Princess's place at the head of the Army Nursing Service had provoked considerable ill-feeling. This had much distressed King Edward, whose one desire now was to prevent any recurrence of the friction between his wife and his sister. Lady Roberts and Elizabeth Haldane had their hands full smoothing down differences and trying to keep some control over the vagaries of Queen Alexandra herself. 'I have very often smoothed things down when she has run counter to authority,' Lady Roberts wrote to Miss Haldane, 'before your brother came with his soothing influence matters were sometimes *very* difficult and not always pleasant.'[20]

At one moment the Queen veered right round to Holland's point of view and opposed the formation of any organised Nursing Reserve for the Territorial Army. Once, however, she had been brought to agree with this scheme she became enthusiastic for its success, and only perturbed about what seemed to her to be unnecessary delays in putting it into practice. As she remarked to Lady Roberts, she could not understand 'why such a fuss should have been made to get my consent and then nothing has been done'. Lady Roberts noted that the Queen 'always likes to be told the *reason why* about everything'[21] and that there was nothing she more disliked than being kept in the dark on any subject.

All at last seemed set fair for the formation of the Territorial Army Nursing Reserve when Queen Alexandra herself raised one serious difficulty. It had been proposed that the

Princess of Wales should become President of the new Reserve. To this the Queen would in no wise agree and on 8 April 1908 she wrote Lady Roberts an extremely stiff letter:

> 'I received your letter two days ago telling me of Mr Haldane's proposal to start a separate and special nursing service for the Territorial Army with an independent President. This I regret to say I cannot agree to. I am President of all Military and Naval Hospitals and Nurses, and at my death the whole concern will pass into the hands of my dear daughter-in-law, so as always to be kept together and under one head. This new Territorial scheme must therefore be kept on the same lines as our present one, and one of the ladies acting as Chairman, either Lady Derby or the Duchess of Montrose, will kindly have to report to me, the same as you do, everything that takes place.'[22]

Lady Roberts saw in this letter the baleful influence of the Empress Marie, whom she suspected of urging her sister to insist on keeping the headship of all the Nursing Services for herself. Nothing, however, could be done except to accept the situation with the best grace possible. Six months later two small matters connected with the proposed uniform threatened to cause still further trouble. Queen Alexandra had chosen khaki, but the nurses themselves objected to wearing anything so unbecoming. No sooner was this difficulty settled than trouble arose over the wearing of the red cape which had hitherto been regarded as sacred to the first line nurses of the Regular Army. In the end, however, everybody was more or less satisfied; the nurses found themselves wearing a becoming grey outfit 'with touches of red', and Queen Alexandra kept to herself the Presidency both of the Nursing Board of the Regular Army and the Advisory Council of the Territorial Army Nursing Service.

One major difficulty which the Queen was determined to see solved was the lack of suitable accommodation for military nurses. So passionately did she feel about this subject that her letters to Holland became even more picturesquely incoherent than usual; 'I have made a *coup d'état* and taken the bull by the horns at once by seeing Mr Haldane today, told him as well as I could about our Military Nurses' Homes,'[23] she wrote on 18 December 1905. The Queen's literary style may have been peculiar, but her determination was not to be resisted; although Brodrick and Arnold-Forster, two previous Secretaries of State for War, had refused the nurses better accommodation, as a result of her intervention they were soon provided with proper quarters everywhere. She concerned herself too with smaller problems of personnel and administration, in especial with the personal difficulties of individual nurses. One nurse, for instance, who had been causing trouble she describes as 'a perfect viper' and orders an immediate enquiry into her behaviour; another more desirable character, who had been dismissed the Service on account of ill-health, she insists must be admitted as soon as possible into Midhurst Sanatorium.

The Queen also took a serious interest in the Red Cross as the voluntary body concerned with military nursing. At the beginning of the new reign Red Cross affairs were in a state of ambiguity and confusion. The National Aid Society, in which Queen Alexandra as Princess of Wales had taken such an effectual interest at the time of the Sudan campaign, was in fact, if not in name, the Red Cross Society in England, treated as such by the International Red Cross in Geneva. In 1899 a Central British Red Cross Committee had been established, its object being 'to maintain among voluntary aid societies in time of peace an organisation which will enable them to render prompt and efficient aid in time of war to the sick and wounded, in the manner best suited to supplement the Army Medical Service.' As might have been expected, relations between this committee and the National Aid Society were not amicable. The obvious answer to the problem would have seemed to be for both societies to die a voluntary death and to resuscitate themselves as a single body; pride and prejudice, however, barred the way. The intervention of a higher authority was needed to compel them to settle their difference, and in this matter there could be no higher authority than a royal one.

As Prince of Wales, King Edward had taken a real interest in Red Cross matters; now, however, his time was so fully engaged that of necessity the Red Cross became primarily Queen Alexandra's concern. In March 1905, Lord Esher, the *éminence grise* of King Edward's reign, summoned Lord Rothschild, Sir Sydney Holland, and other notables of the Red Cross and the medical world, to a consultation at Buckingham Palace to discuss means of breaking the deadlock between the two Red Cross societies. Four months later it was announced that Their Majesties had decided that the various bodies concerned with Red Cross work throughout Britain and the British Empire should be amalgamated into one body, to be called The British Red Cross Society, the King to be its Patron and the Queen its President. The Queen herself would preside at the first Council Meeting, which was to be held at Buckingham Palace.

Queen Alexandra was filled with apprehension at the prospect of addressing 'this tremendous meeting', telling the Duke of York that when she rose to her feet to read her speech she felt ready to sink under the table with fright. Wisely, she began by stressing her personal interest in the problem – 'It has been on my mind ever since the South African War, and I became the President, to try and re-organise the Red Cross Society on a more practical and sound basis.' After detailing the new arrangements and expressing her warm approval of them she returned once more to the personal note, 'I therefore now appeal to all the women of the Empire to assist me in carrying out this great scheme, which is essentially women's work, and which is the one and only way in which we can assist our brave and gallant Army and Navy.'[24]

'Thank God it all ended well,' Queen Alexandra wrote next day to her son; 'they were all very kind about it.'[25] Well they might have been, since the Queen's personal participation had helped to resolve an almost insoluble problem by throwing over the new arrangements all the glamour of royal approval and patronage.

One of the first schemes set on foot by the newly-organised British Red Cross Society was the raising of Voluntary Aid Detachments, the V.A.D.s who were such familiar figures in the first World War. Here again, Royal influence played its part; women of rank and position – and these two things were all-important in Edwardian England – were anxious and willing to do all they could to further the scheme once they knew that the Queen was taking a personal interest in it.

Perhaps the climax of Queen Alexandra's efforts for the Red Cross came in June 1907, when the eighth International Conference of Red Cross Societies was held in London. Socially it was a brilliant occasion. The delegates were entertained at Windsor Castle, at the Mansion House and at many of the great London mansions such as Lansdowne House and Chesterfield House; they attended a Court Ball and a gala performance at Covent Garden, and on the last day of the Conference a reception was given for them at Buckingham Palace. At this reception a Japanese delegate, Baron Ozawa, delivered a message from the Emperor of Japan praising 'the great humanitarian work' of Queen Alexandra, and declaring that his Empress hoped to follow her example. The trained and dedicated social workers of today may smile to find Queen Alexandra's kindly patronage described in such terms; in her own age and generation, however, nothing more arduous would have been expected or desired of her. Unlike her sister-in-law, Princess Christian, or her daughter-in-law Queen Mary, she took little interest in practical details nor had she any talent for organisation. Her gifts were of a more personal nature. She had a quick, genuine sympathy with those who, in the Prayer Book phrase, were in 'need, sickness, or any other adversity', and she had the rare power of making her sympathy immediately apparent to the sufferer. The wounded soldier or the sick child knew instinctively that she felt with and not merely for them, that she really cared. In the same way she could put herself immediately in touch with nurses or workers in the cause of charity. She made them feel that she was personally interested in their problems and delighted by their achievements; a word or a smile from her was enough to soothe hurt feelings, to spur on the indolent, or to reward the devoted. Although it would be ridiculous to set Queen Alexandra up as an important figure among the workers for humanitarian causes, none the less she played the comparatively small part which fate allotted her with sincere feeling and with a charming personal touch; she was, in fact, the perfect patroness.

CORONATION POSTPONED

For Queen Alexandra the first year of her husband's reign was not, on the whole, a happy period. In April, on her way home from Copenhagen, she paid another brief visit to the Empress Frederick, writing to the Duke of York, 'She was a sad sight indeed, in such constant terrible agonies that it made me simply miserable to see her.'[1] When the Empress died on 5 August Queen Alexandra accompanied King Edward to Germany for the funeral, taking with her a wreath of flowers from Windsor, the home which the dead woman had loved so dearly.

Another cause of sadness was the impending departure of the Duke and Duchess of York on an eight months' tour of Australia, South Africa and Canada. The prospect of this long separation distressed the Queen so much that King Edward chivalrously took it upon himself to persuade his ministers to allow the tour to be abandoned; very properly, however, they insisted that the plan should be carried through. When all allowance has been made for the difference between a journey to the Antipodes in 1901 and a similar journey today it is impossible not to admit that Queen Alexandra's attitude was a selfish and a short-sighted one. Selfishness is not a quality with which she is usually associated; in her it was obscured by warm-hearted overflowing kindness. It is, however, all too easy to be both kind and selfish, especially in a position like Queen Alexandra's, where kindness can be indulged in without overmuch cost. 'Mama, as I have always said, is one of the most selfish people I know,'[2] her devoted son once wrote to his wife, not in a fit of exasperation but as his considered opinion. Now once again, as in the case of her treatment of Princess Victoria, Queen Alexandra's selfishness was due not to lack of feeling but to lack of imagination. She could not envisage the multitude of people to whom her son's presence would bring pleasure, inspiration, and a sense of fellowship within the bonds of Empire, nor could she realise how valuable the experience would be to her son himself.

The leave-taking on 16 March 1901 was a lachrymose occasion when even the Duke broke down in tears. Queen Alexandra, however, soon found consolation in the company of her grandchildren, who had been left in her charge. Both she and her husband were in their element as grandparents. The King, who could be terrifying to adults, was at his kindest and most gentle with children whilst Queen Alexandra herself retained so much of the child in her nature that she instinctively understood the working of the child-mind. Not that she was under any delusions about her grandchildren; she was devoted to her eldest grandson, 'David', but she was determined not to allow him to 'get grand' and she mocked at the notion that his questions were more clever and searching than those asked by other children.

For eight long months these four little children were, as Sir John Wheeler-Bennett puts it, 'grossly and enthusiastically spoilt by their grandparents'.[3] Their grandmother enjoyed nothing so much as arranging special treats, perhaps a visit to the Military Tournament, where four-year-old Princess Mary was once fascinated and horrified by a clown, or an excursion to Virginia Water: 'Little David caught his first fish and danced about with joy shouting all the time "This is the first fish I ever caught in my life" – then, turning round to the sailor, he said, "You must *not* kill him, throw him back into the water again!" which I thought so nice of him and shows a good heart.'[4]

At Sandringham that hot summer the grown-ups would sit out nearly all day under the trees, watching the children at their play. It was an idyllic existence but not one conducive to doing many lessons. The teaching of French had been entrusted to Mademoiselle Bricka, an intellectual lady who had been the Duchess of York's own governess, and a great influence on her during adolescence. Perhaps the Duchess had underestimated the difference between teaching one clever and conscientious girl and controlling three small unruly children; although she was beloved by her charges, Bricka never succeeded in instilling much French into their heads. She was not a person likely to agree well with a grandmother such as Queen Alexandra who could never be persuaded to take education seriously and who had no qualms whatsoever about interrupting schoolroom routine. Bricka poured out her woes to the Grand Duchess Augusta, who was soon sending her niece letters calculated to upset any parent's peace of mind. Both the Duke and Duchess of York wrote anxiously asking why Bricka had been left behind when the family moved to Sandringham. Queen Alexandra remained unperturbed by their protests: 'The reason we did not take her there was that Laking particularly asked that he [David] might be left more with his brothers and sisters *for a little while* as *we all* noticed how precocious and *old-fashioned* he was getting – and quite the way of *a single child!* – which would make him ultimately "a tiresome child".'[5]

Under Queen Alexandra's system, or rather, her lack of system, education certainly suffered, and so did nursery discipline, but for children accustomed to the quarter-deck manner of the Duke of York and to the somewhat withdrawn attitude of their loving but reserved mother, those eight months were a wonderful period of fun, freedom and development.

During this summer of 1901 one of the Queen's greatest pleasures was motoring. She was an enthusiast for this new form of locomotion although as a passenger she must have been a little disconcerting: 'I did enjoy being driven about in the cool of the evening at fifty miles!! an hour! I have the greatest confidence in our driver. I poke him violently in the back at every corner to go gently and whenever a dog, child or anything else crosses our way.'

In this same letter to the Duke of York she strongly discouraged him from attempting to lease the Houghton property; he therefore abandoned the idea of exchanging York Cottage for this beautiful house, a lost opportunity which his wife never ceased to regret.[6]

'Looking forward *madly* to seeing you again,'[7] the Queen wrote to her daughter in-law on 29 October. She was the more pleased to welcome back the travellers because, in common with others near to the King, she was troubled by a vague but anxious feeling that all was not well with him. Earlier on, the Duke of York himself had been worried lest the Queen should not be paying sufficient attention to symptoms of overstrain displayed by her husband; 'you must do all you can to help him and insist on him having a rest this autumn,'[8] he had written almost in reproof. The King, however, was not making it easy for anyone to help him. Of recent months he had become unaccountably short-tempered and irritable; he would listen to no advice nor would he spare himself any item of work, however trivial or unnecessary. Always a big eater, his appetite now assumed gargantuan proportions. He would never allow himself time to taste and appreciate the rich food which he so much enjoyed; although he had the reputation of a *gourmet* he was in fact much more of a *gourmand*. His figure had always been a sore point with him but now he suddenly grew so stout that none of his clothes would meet about him. Every day he reckoned to smoke ten, twelve or thirteen cigars so large and pungent that strong men blenched when he kindly pressed them to take one. Smoking on this scale was clearly bad for anyone who suffered as he did from chronic bronchitis. He had always been very abstemious about drink, but now he began to take a little too much, protesting with truth that although he did not enjoy what he drank he found it absolutely necessary as a stimulant. In vain did the Queen urge him to cut down his smoking, to eat less and to take more time over his meals; he paid not the slightest heed. So tired was he that he would drop off to sleep in his box at the theatre or opera, and once, to Queen Alexandra's great consternation, he fell asleep in the middle of luncheon. Overstrained and in a state of near-collapse, he was anything but an easy companion.

The Crown Princess of Prussia at the time of her marriage, 1858
a portrait after Winterhalter

Princess Alexandra and Princess Dagmar, 1856
from a painting by E. Jerichau-Baumann

The marriage of the Prince of Wales and Princess Alexandra of Denmark in St George's Chapel, Windsor, 10 March 1863
a detail from the painting by W. P. Frith, R.A.

Princess Alexandra, before her marriage

The Prince of Wales, 1861

The Princess of Wales and the Duke of Edinburgh (Prince Alfred), September 1868

The Prince of Wales, 1868

The Princess of Wales
by Richard Lauchert, 1863

A portrait of the Prince and Princess of Wales with Prince Albert Victor (Eddy) and Princess Louise
by Heinrich von Angeli, 1876

The Princess of Wales at Abergeldie with Prince Albert Victor (Eddy) and Prince George, 1866

A drawing by Arthur Ellis of the Princess of Wales, Miss Charlotte Knollys, and himself, out riding

Everybody's mind was now full of the Coronation, which had been fixed for 26 June 1902. As the day approached the King grew no better either in health or temper. On 5 June, when Queen Alexandra visited Westminster Abbey to see the preparations for the ceremony, Esher noted that the workmen were far more interested in her than in any other of the distinguished visitors whom he had escorted round. As she left the Abbey a small crowd cheered her long and loudly, to her undisguised delight. She had the more need of such encouragement because although her husband was now an obviously sick man, he was determined none the less, against the advice of his doctors, to go through with the long programme of functions which had already been arranged. Accordingly, on 14 June she went down with him to Aldershot to stay at the damp and uncomfortable Pavilion there in readiness for a big military review to be held on the sixteenth.

In the middle of the night of the fourteenth King Edward was seized with such pain that two doctors were sent for post-haste. Although it was clear that he was seriously ill, in a laudable but misguided effort not to alarm the public a bulletin was issued stating that he was suffering from nothing worse than lumbago. Queen Alexandra continued to fulfil her various public engagements. On the morning of the fifteenth she attended the Garrison Church, in the afternoon she visited three hospitals and a library, and only when these duties were done could she give her full attention to her sick husband. It was becoming more and more clear that the Coronation might have to be postponed, but King Edward would not hear of any such idea; 'I will go to the Abbey though it kills me' was his reiterated cry.

Obviously, however, he could not attend the review, where the Queen must deputise for him. Though not as shy as other members of the Royal Family she was always nervous on great public occasions such as the state opening of Parliament; now she was to take the salute at a review of 31,000 troops, the march-past to last as long as two and a half hours. Though in deepest anxiety for her husband she must present an absolutely unperturbed and unworried face to the public. She carried the situation off triumphantly, driving on to the parade-ground in an open carriage in spite of the rain which had threatened to spoil the occasion. It had been expected that the Prince of Wales* would take the salute with her, but instead he stationed himself behind her carriage, leaving the full honours to her alone.

When she returned to the Pavilion after that long day of strain and tension the worst was yet to come. Somehow or other the King must be got home to Windsor, although he was in no state to be exposed to the publicity of a railway journey nor to endure the bumps and shaking which were in those days an inevitable part of travel by motor-car. The twenty miles between Windsor and Aldershot had to be done at the slow pace of a horse-drawn carriage, the King and Queen alone in one carriage and the doctors following discreetly behind.

The next day was the first day of Ascot races, which Queen Alexandra was obliged to attend in order not to give grounds for public alarm. Disturbing rumours were, however, already current, and when she drove up the course she was received with complete silence, a mark of sympathy more moving than any cheers. Meanwhile, King Edward was growing yet more unmanageable as his physical condition worsened. On the Sunday he entertained a party of friends, including Mrs Keppel, insisting on showing them round the Castle himself. The more fervently they begged him to stop and rest, the farther and faster he walked with the result that by the end of the afternoon the guests were almost more exhausted than their host. Not unnaturally, after their departure the King suffered from complete prostration; his temperature rose, and by the following morning it was clear to everyone that he was gravely ill.

This was the day when the King was to return to London for his Coronation, driving in semi-state with a Captain's escort of the Household Cavalry from Paddington Station to Buckingham Palace. Ill though he was, this drive was something which King Edward refused to abandon. All along the route the people of London had gathered to give their sovereign a rousing welcome. Hats were raised, handkerchiefs fluttered, cheers rang out to greet a man in a state of high fever, hardly able to hold himself erect in his seat, suffering

* The Duke of York was created Prince of Wales on 9 November 1901.

agonies at every movement of the carriage. During that nightmare drive the Queen was at his side, bowing and waving incessantly. She gave no hint or sign of the anxiety which was consuming her, nor, lest the crowd should guess that something was amiss, did she even dare to turn a sympathetic or questioning glance on her husband as he sat beside her, smiling and suffering tortures. At last they were past the Guard of Honour drawn up in the forecourt of Buckingham Palace, but even here, in their own home, they could find no peace or rest. The Palace was already full of guests come for the Coronation, and that evening there was to be a dinner-party for two hundred people, followed by a reception.

King Edward was both obdurate and alarmed; he was determined to attend these functions yet at the same time he was 'worrying himself to fiddlestrings' at the thought of such an ordeal. Wisely, Queen Alexandra took the decision upon herself; the King was not to appear that evening and she alone would entertain their guests.

Three doctors had meanwhile arrived at the Palace. After examining their patient they decided that next morning, at the latest, they must operate for appendicitis. The Coronation could not take place. For a long time King Edward refused to bow to the inevitable, protesting that he would go to his crowning though it killed him, but at last he admitted defeat. Passively he allowed himself to be put to bed and given a sleeping draught.

For Queen Alexandra, however, the evening had only just begun. The doctors judged it kindest not to let her know of the impending operation until the morning, but what they thought fit to tell her of her husband's condition was enough to cause her almost unbearable concern. To the dinner and reception, however, she must go. In her autobiography, Queen Marie of Rumania, the 'Missy' with whom the Duke of York had once been in love, described Queen Alexandra as she received her guests, beautiful and gracious as ever but, wrote Queen Marie, 'I can still see the anxiety beneath her smile.'[9] Since nothing official had been said about the King's absence, heads were constantly turning towards the door in hopes that he might yet appear. Meanwhile, Princess Victoria threaded her way through the crowd, whispering to a few relations and intimate friends, 'Dear Papa is very ill.' The news came as a sudden dramatic shock, but still the party must go on, and not till well after midnight could Queen Alexandra at last take her leave.

Next morning when the King walked into the room which had been prepared for an operating-theatre, his wife was at his side and the surgeon, Frederick Treves, noticed with approval her calmness and self-control. There followed an odd and rather macabre little scene, which would be unthinkable today. Contrary to general belief, our grandmothers were not squeamish, counting it their right and their duty to be beside their relatives at moments when we should certainly absent ourselves. So now Queen Alexandra remained in the room whilst the anaesthetic was administered and as King Edward began to throw his arms about and to grow black in the face she struggled to hold him down, crying out in great alarm 'Why don't you begin?' To his horror Treves realised that she intended to be present throughout the operation. His reaction was eloquent of the changes that the last sixty years have seen both in surgical procedure and in etiquette. 'I was anxious to prepare for the operation,' he wrote afterwards, 'but did not like to take off my coat, tuck up my sleeves, and put on an apron whilst the Queen was present.'[10] However, when told she must leave, Queen Alexandra went without further ado, joining her son and her two daughters next door in her bedroom. There, forty minutes later, Treves came in to tell her that the operation had proved a complete success. For the second time in his life King Edward had been at death's door and had survived.

During his illness and convalescence Queen Alexandra spent every available moment with her husband. She had even to be gently dissuaded from attending the daily dressing of the wound, Treves remarking on the great interest she took in all surgical matters. In his opinion she had all the natural instincts of a nurse, but wisely she refrained from taking any part at all in the actual nursing. Her deafness, however, was a sad handicap; often when she came into the room King Edward would pretend to be asleep rather than exhaust himself by trying to make her hear. Gay and unselfconscious, making doctors and nurses laugh with her rather childish little jokes, she endeared herself enormously to them all. Trouble only arose once, when Treves chanced to mention the date of the postponed Coronation as having been fixed for 9 August. By some oversight, this was the first that Queen Alexandra had heard of the matter. Her indignation astonished Treves, who had come to regard her as a paragon of gentleness. The ceremony, she protested, concerned her almost as much as it concerned the King; she was to be crowned too, and she had every right to be consulted. To fix a date whilst King Edward still lay very sick was, she considered, to fly in the face of providence, and she would have them all remember that such matters did not rest in the hands of men but of God. She expressed herself so strongly on the subject that instead of an official announcement of the date, a very cautious bulletin was issued stating that if the King were sufficiently recovered it was hoped that the Coronation would take place some time between 8 August and 12 August.

Although most of the functions planned for this Coronation season were cancelled Queen Alexandra attended two reviews at which the Prince of Wales deputised for his father. Not surprisingly, she was looking a little tired and strained, but she was visibly delighted by the great welcome given her by the crowds. She also received many of the foreign visitors come for the Coronation who must now go away disappointed. Among them was the Rani of Partabgarh, who had broken every rule of caste and purdah in order to accompany her husband to England, the great wish of her heart being to set eyes on Queen Alexandra. 'All this I have done to see my Queen,' she protested to an English friend; 'don't let me return without seeing her, she is good and gracious, beg her to see me, let me see my Queen.'[11] Queen Alexandra's interest in India made her the more willing to grant this request; not merely did she receive the Rani but she secured her a place for the postponed Coronation. The Queen also made a point of inviting the Danish and Russian military delegations to visit her but when asked whether she also wished to receive the German delegation she replied with a most decided negative.

Although still confined to his bed King Edward would not

be denied the pleasure of receiving one distinguished arrival himself. On 12 July Lord Kitchener landed at Southampton on his return from the South African War, to be given a hero's welcome. That same afternoon he was taken to Buckingham Palace and into the King's bedroom, where the Queen was also waiting to receive him. Kneeling down beside the bed, Kitchener took the King's hand and kissed it; then, with some difficulty, the King invested him with the Order of Merit, hanging the insignia round his neck. Moved by the strange contrast between the soldier and the sick monarch, Queen Alexandra burst into tears.

King Edward's convalescence was to be spent on board the royal yacht at Cowes. Since he much disliked the idea of the public seeing him in his invalid state, great efforts were made to secure privacy for him on the journey, only to be nearly frustrated by the Queen's incorrigible curiosity. As she drove with him in a closed ambulance from Buckingham Palace to Victoria Station she persisted in peeping round the drawn blinds, bowing and waving to everyone who recognised her.

The three weeks spent on board the yacht were a happy and peaceful time. Queen Alexandra had Soveral to amuse her, and, better still, she had the Prince of Wales to make her laugh with the schoolboy jokes in which both she and he delighted. Although she much enjoyed smoking she usually took the very greatest care that no one outside her immediate circle should see her do so, but when Randall Davidson, then Bishop of Winchester, joined the party on board she amused and astonished everyone by persuading him to smoke a cigarette with her. In more serious mood, when they visited Osborne she took the Bishop into the room where Queen Victoria had died, and there the two of them held a little service. As Esher wrote, 'It is this mixture of ragging and real feeling that is so attractive about the Queen.'[12]

Just before the party returned to London Sir Frederick Treves persuaded Queen Alexandra to make a surprise visit to Netley Military Hospital, his idea being to catch the hospital authorities unawares so that the Queen could see for herself just how badly the wounded men from South Africa were being neglected. Nobody was there to greet the royal party when they scrambled ashore from their launch and made their way across a lawn where some of the patients were lying on the grass, listening to the strains of a bagpipe. When the Queen asked one man how he was getting on, to her immense delight he replied, 'Very well, Miss.' The sight of so many mutilated and limbless men moved her intensely. When Treves led up a burly Highlander, blinded in both eyes, she seized the man's hand and exclaimed, 'Dear man, I am so sorry, so sorry. How terrible it is! What can I do to help you?' Touched by her obvious and artless concern the man burst into tears. Regardless of the onlookers, the enormous Highlander and the small, elegant Queen stood holding hands and sobbing aloud like children. She could not be persuaded to leave him until she had led him back to his seat and done all she could to make him comfortable. Inside the hospital, as they toured the wards, Treves noticed the Queen's 'extraordinary powers of observation'. If the hospital authorities were equally impressed perhaps they may have been shamed into making some much-needed improvements.[13]

The postponed Coronation took place on 9 August. Because of her wistful interest in the India she was never to see Queen Alexandra chose to wear a dress of golden Indian gauze, embroidered in India, and out of compliment to her native Denmark among all her magnificent jewels she also wore the replica of the Dagmar Cross which had been given her on her marriage. Never had she seemed more beautiful than when she moved slowly forward after her crowning, the diamonds in her crown glittering and flashing, a sceptre in either hand, and spread out behind her the fantastic length of her violet velvet train.

To Queen Alexandra the chief meaning of the Coronation was a religious one. Her literal but quite genuine belief in the significance of the various rites is shown very clearly in the generally misquoted story about her anointing. The true version of this incident is still current in the family of Archbishop Maclagan of York, who, contrary to custom, crowned the Queen, the Archbishop of Canterbury being so frail that it was thought unwise to impose on him the double strain of crowning both the King and Queen. Before the Coronation Queen Alexandra sent for Archbishop Maclagan to explain to him her predicament. Like most women of her age and generation, she augmented her own hair with a *toupet*. If she were to be properly anointed she felt that the holy oil must actually touch her own body, not merely this erection of false hair; she therefore begged the Archbishop to be sure that some of the oil ran down on to her forehead. This he did; and on returning to Buckingham Palace she refused to wipe the oil off, wishing to bear the mark of her anointing as long as possible. From now onwards Archbishop Maclagan was '*my* Archbishop', and his photograph always stood on her writing-table.

Discussing the Coronation with Gladstone's daughter, Mary Drew, Queen Alexandra agreed heartily when that rather intense lady remarked that the ceremony must have seemed like the start of 'a new, a dedicated life'. She told Mrs Drew that at the Thanksgiving Service held after the Coronation at St Paul's 'she couldn't bear leaving before Holy Communion, and thought that in the circumstances it would have been better to omit it altogether.'[14] But since she could never fail to see the ridiculous side of even the most solemn occasion, she also told Mary Drew that she had been nearly soaked through by the rain on her way into St Paul's as she had not thought it right to put up an umbrella, and she made a good story out of the moment when the King tripped and all but broke his leg, an episode which might have made a ludicrous anticlimax to a service of thanksgiving.

THE REIGN OF KING EDWARD VII

The Coronation over, the King and Queen returned to Cowes for a short stay before setting out in the Royal Yacht on a cruise up the west coast of England and Scotland. The double drama of the King's illness and his Coronation had provoked a tremendous outburst of loyalty and affection towards him. At Douglas in the Isle of Man the crowds were so eager to see him that the pressure of people around the royal carriage became really alarming. King Edward, who hated any delay or failure in organisation, lost his temper and bellowed at the coachman; Queen Alexandra, however, remained imperturbable, speaking to the people nearest her as if they were personal friends, begging them to take the greatest care lest the children with them should be hurt or frightened in the crush. On this visit Queen Alexandra met the Manx author, Hall Caine; 'a curious-looking man, the same as his books', is her typically elliptical description of him. In this same letter to the Prince of Wales she mentions that among their guests on board the yacht was the 'very nice' young Austen Chamberlain.[1]

Mourning for Queen Victoria had overshadowed the London Season of 1901, that of 1902 had been wrecked by the King's sudden illness, and not until the summer of 1903 did the Edwardian social sun shine out in its full splendour. Buckingham Palace, shuttered and empty for so many years, now became a centre for splendid official ceremonies and gay social entertainments. Evening Courts took the place of less glamorous afternoon Drawing-Rooms, and for the first time in sixty years a magnificent state ball was held at Windsor Castle. At the end of the Season came a short but unexpectedly successful state visit to Ireland, and only when that was over was Queen Alexandra free to seek the peace and quiet of her old home in Denmark.

As a matter of course Princess Victoria accompanied her mother on this Danish visit. 'Toria has had to go to that vile D . . . k,'[2] the Princess of Wales wrote in an unusually outspoken moment. The dawdling habits of the Danish Royal Family and the total lack of intellectual stimulus at the Danish Court made a visit to Bernstorff or Fredensborg a form of slow torture for anyone as methodical, as energetic and as serious-minded as the Princess of Wales. Apart from the peculiar trials of life in 'vile D . . . k' the general difficulty of Princess Victoria's position was causing her family some concern. 'I had a talk with Victoria, so sensible, glad to have a rest by herself alone,' the Grand Duchess Augusta had written two years previously; 'how odd her mother don't feel that at thirty-three one requires a little freedom!'[3] The death of the old Duke of Cambridge in 1904 left untenanted the house at Kew which had been for so long associated with the Royal Family. The Grand Duchess was seized with the idea of handing it over to Princess Victoria as a retreat to which she could sometimes retire without her mother. Greatly daring, she broached the subject with Queen Alexandra but, as might have been expected, her idea met with little favour. Never at any time robust, Princess Victoria suffered more and more frequently from a variety of ailments, some of them possibly psychosomatic in origin. She was the most intelligent of Queen Alexandra's children and for this reason she suffered the more acutely from the frustrations imposed on her by the narrow limits of a life lived almost completely under the shadow of her mother.

That winter of 1903 the normal routine of Sandringham

was broken by what might have been a serious catastrophe. During the night of 10 December Charlotte Knollys awoke to find her bedroom full of smoke. She rushed downstairs to the Queen's room immediately below her own and finding that also smoke-filled, she shook Queen Alexandra awake, and, wrapping a dressing-gown around her, shepherded her to safety just before the fire took real hold. Two rooms were completely wrecked, but the estate fire-brigade succeeded in getting the blaze under control before any more damage was done. The Grand Duchess Augusta's comment on this episode is spiced with a typically pungent criticism of King Edward: 'I was horrified hearing of dear Alix's danger, too awful to think of! We must give credit to old Charlotte for *really* saving her life. What order will the King decorate Charlotte with to reward such readiness of thought and action? Though *he* was in no hurry to hasten to see Alix after her merciful escape.'[4]

Early in 1904 the Russo-Japanese War broke out. Although for the sake of her Russian relatives Queen Alexandra might have been expected to take the Russian side, her Danish blood made her quick to sympathise with a small nation in arms against a much bigger one. 'For a wonder in this war Motherdear is for the Japs!' the Princess of Wales wrote to the Grand Duchess. 'She is not nearly so Russian as she was and I don't think Aunt Minny can do much harm now in that way.'[5] At the close of the war Queen Alexandra even complained that the peace terms were unfair to the victors – 'I fear the poor brave Japanese made a bad bargain; certainly they ought at least to have kept the island they took and which formerly was their own.'[6]

The war had exposed the weakness of the whole Russian system of government and society, a weakness made yet more apparent by the unrest and uprisings which marked the year 1905. These troubles naturally filled Queen Alexandra with intense anxiety both for her sister and for her nephew, since she realised only too well how insecure was the Czar's position. 'Just now everything in Russia seems critical,' she wrote in November 1905; 'I fear the Constitution which at last poor Nicky has been forced to grant has come too late and then God only knows what will happen.'[7] The Queen was certainly not unaware of the earthquake that was brewing.

She also realised the harm that was being done by her husband's niece 'Alicky', now the Czarina Alexandra Fedorovna. The Czarina's blind devotion to the 'holy man' Rasputin is common knowledge; what is less well known is the fact that long before she ever met Rasputin she had already had recourse to 'faith-healers' in the hopes of producing a male heir, foremost among these healers being a Frenchman named Philippe Vachot. Queen Alexandra deeply disapproved of this man, who in fact turned out to be a fraud. In 1902 the Princess of Wales wrote to her husband telling him of 'a nice long chat' she had had with 'Motherdear' – 'We talked about the spiritualist's influence in Russia and she told me it is more Alicky who is under this horrid man's influence than Nicky, Aunt Minny is in despair.'[8]

Greece also was in turmoil, the position in the island of Crete being especially difficult. In 1898 the four Protecting Powers, England, France, Italy and Russia, had appointed Queen Alexandra's nephew, Prince George of Greece, to be High Commissioner in Crete. Although matters went well during his first term of office, after 1901 the situation progressively worsened. Prince George was accused of despotic and high-handed behaviour, an accusation which was repeated by the British press in an article appearing in the *Daily Chronicle*, written by a certain Professor Jannaris and headed 'Prince George of Greece Out-Sultans the Sultan'. On 30 September 1904 Queen Alexandra wrote from Bernstorff to the Prince of Wales, pointing out that Jannaris had a personal grudge against Prince George, who had refused to use his own influence to obtain for the Professor a post at the University of Athens, and protesting against 'all his *lies* and pure *inventions* about poor George which were re-copied and taken up by *The Times* and all our English papers.' She begged her son to go at once both to Francis Knollys and to the Foreign Secretary, Lord Lansdowne, and to explain to them the real truth about the campaign against Prince George – 'he, poor boy, has been calumnied' – a typical mis-spelling, this – 'in a most unjust and cruel way and is as innocent about it all as a baby.'[9]

Although the Queen was right in supposing that the attack on her nephew was an unfair one her championship could do him no real good. Of the four Protecting Powers, England was the one most definitely opposed to Prince George and his régime. Esme Howard, afterwards Lord Howard of Penrith, thus described his instructions on being appointed Consul-General in Crete in July 1903: 'I was given to understand at the Foreign Office before taking up my new post that the Prince was the favourite nephew of King Edward and Queen Alexandra and that it must be my particular job to let him down lightly.' Finally, in 1906, following Venizelos's uprising, Prince George was obliged to resign his office. Meeting her nephew after this forced departure from Crete the Queen described him as 'dreadfully pulled down' and 'very bitter'.[10]

Against these various political troubles disturbing the peace of the Queen's family there was to be set one important gain. On 7 June 1905 the union between Norway and Sweden was dissolved, leaving Norway free to choose between a monarchical or a republican form of government. If a monarchy were chosen the obvious choice for King would seem to be a Danish prince because of the ancient connection between Norway and Denmark, the most eligible candidate being Princess Maud's husband, Prince Charles. King Edward was most anxious to see his son-in-law on the Norwegian throne, and rather unwisely, he urged the Prince to take strong action. Queen Alexandra was, for once, the more cautious of the two. She chanced to be paying her usual summer visit to Denmark just at the time when this subject was being most hotly canvassed, and being so near the centre of events, she was in a better position than her husband to judge of the complexities of the situation. She therefore wrote both to the King's Secretary, Francis Knollys, and to the Prince of Wales to explain how matters really stood. Her letter to the Prince is dated 27 September 1905:

'I am glad you saw my letter to Francis as in it I explained how things were here and all facts about Norway and how impossible it would have been for Charles to have acted differently in his position here, and that it would have led to war between the three countries at once. It was very strained between the Swedes and Norwegians last week and they very nearly came to blows. Even we in Denmark knew very little about it.'[11]

All, however, was satisfactorily arranged; on 18 November Prince Charles was duly elected King of Norway, taking the title of King Haakon VII. Either as ruling sovereigns or as consorts descendants of old King Christian IX now occupied the thrones of England, Russia, Greece and Norway. 'Maud and Charles were received with open arms,' Queen Alexandra wrote of the welcome given to the new King and Queen, adding with proper grandmotherly pride, 'the success of Christiana is little Olaf (my little Hamlet) who took them all by storm.'[12]

Twice every year Queen Alexandra regularly visited Denmark. King Edward often accompanied her on her spring visit and took part in the family reunion on the old King's birthday, but he never came with her in the summer. Husband and wife were in fact spending more and more time apart. In 1905 Queen Alexandra for the first time paid an official visit by herself to a foreign country. Nothing could have been more successful than this visit to Portugal. At Lisbon she was rowed ashore from the royal yacht in a state barge manned by eighty oarsmen dressed in traditional red uniforms. She was entertained to official luncheons and dinners and to a gala performance at the Opera where, wrote Maurice de Bunsen, 'the audience simply went mad with delight at seeing her'. The Portuguese crowds, usually so quiet and undemonstrative, gave her a rapturous welcome wherever she went. They did not greet her thus enthusiastically because she was Queen of the country that was their oldest ally but because she was a beautiful and warm-hearted woman; to quote de Bunsen again, 'her personal charm carried everything before her'.[13] As a souvenir of her visit Queen Alexandra was given a picture in Portuguese tiles showing her arrival at Lisbon. She was in great difficulties as to where to display this handsome but unhandy gift, ultimately finding a place for it in her bathroom at Windsor Castle.

From Lisbon the royal yacht sailed to Gibraltar, where the Queen toured the Rock and also visited the Dowager Queen Isabel of Spain, 'dear Granny Isabel' who was living in retirement near Seville, 'where she leads the life of Buffalo Bill'.[14] Meanwhile at home in England King Edward had been so ill with bronchitis that the Queen thought it her duty to forgo her usual visit to Denmark for her father's birthday, and instead to pick up King Edward at Marseilles to go with her on a Mediterranean cruise. His bronchitis was now a chronic condition and a constant source of anxiety, especially in bad wintry weather – 'these fogs are very bad for Papa who nearly chokes, it frightens me *dreadfully*.'[15] Queen Alexandra had been really anxious about her husband's health, describing him as looking 'very unwell and dreadfully pulled down',[16] but nevertheless she allowed him to go alone to Paris at the end of their three weeks' cruise whilst she sailed on to Athens to visit her Greek relatives.

At home in England much of the Queen's time was of course given to charitable causes. One of her favourite charities was the London Hospital, which she visited frequently, always referring to it as 'my hospital'. In 1899 she had arranged that 'her' hospital should pioneer the use of the Finsen Lamp, a Danish invention for the treatment of lupus. As Lady Macclesfield had long ago discovered, she could be remarkably obstinate and, although the Hospital Committee and the medical staff were less than enthusiastic, this was an issue on which she was not prepared to take 'no' for an answer. She insisted that doctors and nurses should be sent to 'my dear little Copenhagen, which is a pretty, cheery town',[17] to study the new methods, and she herself gave the hospital its first Finsen lamp, which proved to be of real help in the treatment of this disfiguring disease. The Hospital authorities, gracefully admitting defeat, decided to engrave on this lamp the words 'Nothing like Perseverance', an inscription which would have been more true, though less polite, had it read, 'Nothing like Obstinacy'.

Another episode connected with the London Hospital is the well-known incident of 'the Elephant Man', John Merrick. Elephantiasis had turned this unfortunate into a hideous monster who had been exhibited as such at fairs and show-grounds, until at last he became a patient at the London Hospital. Queen Alexandra, then Princess of Wales, heard his pitiful story, and although warned that his appearance was literally terrifying, she made a special visit to the hospital in order to see him and talk to him. She never forgot him or lost interest and until his death, many years later, she would always send him a Christmas card with a message written in her own hand.

Such spontaneous, personal acts of kindness came naturally to the Queen. Charity in the more conventional sense of the word might almost be said to have been her hobby, so eagerly and with such zest did she give away her money. Her generosity was unending; not so her income. As Sidney Holland wrote, 'she gives to everyone who asks; she cannot refuse; she has intense sympathy for anyone who has done wrong.' People were all too quick to take advantage of this sympathy; a Windsor school mistress, for instance, who had embezzled money, wrote personally to the Queen to ask for help, and was promptly given it. Dighton Probyn did his very best to keep some sort of control over her charitable giving but she had ways and means of evading his vigilance. On one occasion she sent for Holland and, with a great display of secrecy, fished out from beneath her sofa cushions a crumpled envelope containing a cheque for £1,000 and a further £1,000 in notes, which she pressed into his hand as a gift for the London Hospital.

The summer of 1905 brought a special pleasure to Queen Alexandra with the birth of a fifth son to the Prince and Princess of Wales. Although this child, who was named John, was in the end to bring grief rather than happiness to his family, his grandmother was always to feel a special affection for him. In the coming autumn the Prince and Princess were to make an official tour of India. Since a visit to India was still Queen Alexandra's unrealised ambition a slight feeling of jealousy perhaps explains her unusually caustic comments on the Princess's careful and well-timed preparations for this journey. The date for departure had been fixed for 19 October. Three weeks could scarcely be considered too long a time to give to the preparation of a trousseau for a royal tour scheduled to last six months; yet on 27 September the Queen was writing thus to her son to condole with him on his wife's absence: 'So my poor Georgie has lost his May, who had fled to London to look in her glass!! What a bore and a nuisance, but I cannot understand why she should have gone so soon, as the dresses for India cannot take quite such a long time to do or try on either.'[18]

The Princess herself had written to her husband complaining of 'a hard day's work at tiresome clothes';[19] the Queen was therefore less than just in hinting that her daughter-in-law enjoyed 'looking in her glass'.

Such outbursts on Queen Alexandra's part were rare; on the whole, the relationship between mother-in-law and daughter-in-law was an amicable and affectionate one. Being a compassionate and an observant woman the Princess fully recognised Queen Alexandra's various trials and difficulties. In particular, she realised how frustrating and nerve-racking a handicap deafness must be, and, quietly and unobtrusively, she set herself to give what help she could to her mother-in-law. The Queen was warmly grateful for this perceptive kindness. 'You, my sweet May,' she wrote appreciatively, 'are always so dear and nice to me, and whenever I am not quite *au fait* because of my *beastly ears* you always by a word or even a turn towards me make me understand. I am *most grateful* as nobody knows what I have to go through sometimes.'[20] Inevitably some friction occurred between York Cottage and 'the Big House' at Sandringham but it was kept within reasonable limits, thanks to the Princess's discretion and to Queen Alexandra's real love for her daughter-in-law. 'You know well, my sweet Miss May, what pleasure it is to me to have you near me,'[21] she wrote, and again in another letter, 'you know well *how* fond I am of you, my dear child.'[22]

One fruitful source of trouble was the question of the children's education since mother's and grandmother's views on this subject were almost diametrically opposed. However, whilst the Prince and Princess were away in India matters went much more smoothly than they had done on the previous occasion when Queen Alexandra had been left in charge. She agreed very well with the nurses and tutors as she had not agreed with the unfortunate Mademoiselle Bricka. Although the boys' tutor, Mr Hansell, might complain that his charges often returned from the Big House hours late for lessons or bed, the little boys themselves knew well enough that when they pleaded, 'Grandpa and Grandmamma wanted us to stay,' they had an excuse which could not be called in question. The Queen wrote constantly to both parents, telling them about the doings of 'dear David, grown and such a sturdy, manly-looking little fellow, and little Mary also grown a good deal and sweet Bertie my particular friend.'[23] Remembering how the Duke of Connaught had been called Arthur after his godfather the Duke of Wellington, she suffered under the strange delusion that five-year-old Prince Henry should also be called after his godfather, Lord Roberts, always referring to him as 'little Bobs'.

Queen Alexandra could have had no greater treat than thus to be left in charge of these six children. It was unalloyed pleasure to watch young Princess Mary's prowess on horseback, or to drive to the meet to watch the elder boys start off on their first day's hunting, or of an evening to gather them all around her and to read aloud stories of Froggy and Bunny from the old books which had once been the delight of her own small sons. When bedtime came she would go upstairs and bath the little ones herself, 'to our mutual delight'. On wet days she would set them to painting pictures and on one occasion the elder children were allowed to attend a lecture by a Colonel Patterson, who had helped to build the Uganda Railway, and to shiver with delicious terror at his stories of man-eating lions. A visit to Windsor meant tremendous romps down the long corridors and in the convenient emptiness of St George's Hall, varied by games of charades – 'and occasionally they invite *Granny* to act too.'[24] No wonder that the Prince of Wales wrote home complaining half in jest that his children were being shockingly spoilt. 'You say I am no exception in spoiling my grandchildren,' the Queen wrote in mocking reply, 'and I say you are no exception in being impertinent to your mother which I consider much worse.'[25]

But however great was her delight in her grandchildren's company Queen Alexandra could not prevent her thoughts from turning towards India, 'the *one wish* of my heart to see'. Her letters to her son are shot through with longing for the country she so much desired to visit – 'I do envy you dreadfully and *never* shall cease regretting having been left behind when Papa went alone! I shall *never* forget or forgive it.'[26]

To the Princess she wrote in similar strain – 'I am glad you sometimes think of old me and *how* I would have enjoyed it all! Oh, if only I could go once before I die or before I am too old to enjoy it all thoroughly!'[27]

At home in England things were not going too smoothly. The winter of 1905–6 was a difficult period for industry when many people found themselves thrown out of work. As usual, Queen Alexandra concerned herself with the personal side of the problem without making any effort to understand the economic issues involved. She headed an appeal for gifts to a charitable fund to help the unemployed, an action which did not commend itself to the President of the Board of Trade, Gerald Balfour. 'I hope you will be able to say something to dissuade the Queen from trying to interfere with the delicate machinery of administration,' he wrote to his brother Arthur, then Prime Minister; 'so far as I can judge her only idea of assistance to the unemployed is by way of doles.'[28] Two months later the Conservative party suffered a heavy defeat in the General Election, Balfour himself losing his seat – 'anything so ungrateful as that I have never seen',[29] the Queen wrote to her son. What interested and infuriated her most in this election was the behaviour of her old rival, Lady Warwick, who campaigned actively on behalf of the Labour Party – 'and what do you think of that charming Lady Warwick mounting a waggon at the corner of the street and addressing her "comrades", the scum of the labourers, and then taking off her glove to shake and feel their horny hands!'[30] Politics, however, were always a secondary consideration with Queen Alexandra; it is typical of her that, just when excitement about the election was at its height, she should write pages to the Prince of Wales about the death of old Temple, the father of her two dressers.

At first the Queen was much perturbed by the size of the Liberal majority but, curiously enough, she, who was a thorough Tory in her opinions, always seemed to get on best with Liberal politicians, preferring Gladstone to Disraeli and Lord Rosebery to Lord Salisbury. Although she had liked Balfour well enough she was soon on far more intimate terms with Asquith, who succeeded Campbell-Bannerman as Liberal Prime Minister in April 1908. Asquith's second wife, the ebullient Margot Tennant, had cherished a great admiration for Queen Alexandra ever since the day when, as quite a young girl, she had met the then Princess of Wales at tea with the Duchess of Manchester. 'My heart beat when I looked at her,' Margot Asquith wrote years later. 'She had more real beauty, both of line and expression, than anyone I had ever seen, and I can never forget that first meeting.'[31] Queen Alexandra, however, did not find the wife quite so congenial as the husband. One sentence from the letter she wrote to Margot congratulating her on her engagement is too apposite not to be also a little malicious – 'Though he is Home Secretary I feel sure that you will soon be Home Ruler!'

On 29 January 1906 the King of Denmark died after only an hour's illness, so that, although he was eighty-eight years old, perhaps Queen Alexandra was justified in writing to the Princess of Wales that 'it all came so suddenly and unexpectedly'. Rather naughtily, she pleaded her grief as an excuse for retiring alone to Sandringham whilst King Edward went off to Biarritz – 'After all that sadness and terrible grief and sorrow for my beloved Papa, I must bury myself for a little while quite away from the world and its noise and bustle.'[32]

The old King's death meant that Queen Alexandra no longer had a home in Denmark. The new King was her brother Frederick, usually referred to, because of some childhood joke, as 'Freddie with the pretty little face'. Although she was fond enough of this brother she had never been really intimate either with him or with his wife, Princess Louise of Sweden, a slightly eccentric lady who devoted herself almost exclusively to the painting of illuminations on vellum. With these two installed at the Amalienborg and at Bernstorff and Fredensborg, Queen Alexandra could never feel herself at home there as she had in her parents' day; yet some sort of home in Denmark had come to be a necessity to her. She therefore decided to look for a house which she could share with the Empress Marie so that she and this favourite sister could spend their holidays there together. A pillared and rather elaborately elegant little villa was found close to the sea at Hvidore near Copenhagen and soon the two sisters were busy with decorations and furnishings. Opinions differed as to the result of their labours. 'I have never seen a more ghastly property,' wrote Lord Hardinge, 'there being no privacy, owing to the road passing close to the house, so that those on the road could look straight into the windows, whilst access to the sea could be obtained only by crossing the road.'[33] Hans Madol, however, refers to it as 'the lovely property' and, differing from Lord Hardinge even on the question of privacy, declares that the sisters could watch the passing ships, themselves unobserved, whilst Baroness de Stoeckel writes, 'If some kind fairy had asked me my wish I should have replied "Never to leave this enchanted spot".'[34] Whatever may have been other people's opinion, the two sisters delighted in their holiday home, where they could be entirely at their ease, picking fruit from their own trees or wandering along the shore in search of amber washed up by the tide.

For nearly thirty years political reasons had prevented the Empress Marie from visiting England; now in the spring of 1907 Queen Alexandra had the special pleasure of welcoming her to London for a stay of several weeks. Together they went sightseeing to the National Gallery and the Wallace Collection, they visited orphanages and hospitals, they saw several plays, and, most enjoyable of all, they motored down to Windsor to enjoy the sunshine and the spring flowers. 'Everything is so tastefully and artistically arranged,' the Empress wrote to her son; 'it makes one's mouth water to see all this magnificence'[35] – a strange comment to come from a woman whose life had been spent among the fantastic splendours of Tsarkoe Seloe and the Winter Palace.

The next year, 1908, after the Empress had again visited England, the King and Queen themselves visited Russia, although in fact they did not set foot on Russian soil. The King was to meet the Czar Nicholas on board the imperial yacht at Reval, the visit being planned with a view to counteracting the effects of the Czar's previous meeting with the Kaiser, and to draw closer the bonds of friendship between England and Russia. Sir John Fisher, who was to be one of the party, wrote off in high glee, 'the King has sweetly asked me to go to Russia with him which is lovely as the Queen has telegraphed for the Grand Duchess I am in love with to come and meet me.'[36] The lady in question was the Grand Duchess Olga, sister to the Czar, whom Fisher had met the previous year at Carlsbad, where he had taught her to waltz, greatly to King Edward's amusement. Fisher had a real mania for dancing and a habit of dancing the whole evening with the same partner, a practice strictly forbidden by the rules of Edwardian etiquette.

On 5 June the party set sail for Reval on board the royal yacht. Although the voyage was an exceptionally rough one the stormy weather did not affect the Queen who had long ago overcome her youthful tendency to seasickness. She always appeared looking immaculate, and she merely laughed when one afternoon a particularly violent roll of the yacht flung her right across the saloon to land up in the opposite corner amid the wreckage of the tea and the tea-service. When the royal yacht anchored in Reval harbour near the imperial yachts *Standart* and *Polar Star* for security reasons no one was allowed ashore, a prohibition which mattered not at all to the Queen, whose only wish was to spend as much time as possible with the Empress Marie.

Perhaps Queen Alexandra clung so closely to her sister because at home in England she was beginning to feel a little lonely and neglected. This state of depression may have been partly due to her health. The year 1909 opened badly for her with an attack of influenza so severe that the doctors forbade her to see anyone, even the Prince of Wales. The Princess of Wales described her mother-in-law as suffering very much from neuralgia and depression and feeling 'up to nothing', adding, however, 'I only hope she will be all right for Berlin for she ought to go there if she possibly can.'[37] Although a state visit to Berlin, of all places, was hardly calculated to relieve Queen Alexandra's depression or to hasten her convalescence, she could not refuse to go for fear of affronting the Kaiser. She made the very best of an unwelcome business and during the journey to Berlin she appeared to be in particularly high spirits. At dinner-time a sudden lurch of the train sent a dish of quails flying in all directions, one bird actually lodging in her hair. The company held their breath, fearing that quail and *toupet* were inextricably entangled. The Queen, however, was neat-fingered; she deftly removed the bird without any untoward accident and for the rest of the meal she kept the table in fits of laughter by describing how she was planning to arrive at Berlin *coiffée de cailles*.

During the three-day visit Queen Alexandra was very much on her best behaviour, hiding her hatred of all things Prussian behind a particularly charming smile. She gave no hint of her secret amusement when, on leaving the station, the horses behaved so badly that she and the German Empress were obliged to leave their carriage and take refuge in another, an episode particularly galling to the Kaiser, who feared that the Germans had 'lost face' in front of the horse-loving English.

Queen Alexandra was still far from well, but she forgot her own ill-health in anxiety for her husband. The arranged programme was far too heavy a one for King Edward, who was suffering from a bronchial chill. He refused to give way, battling gallantly against fever and exhaustion, but at a gala ballet performance at the Opera House he agreed that the Queen should deputise for him during the interval, when German custom obliged a visiting sovereign to go round saying a few words to all the notabilities present. She performed this function with supreme grace, enchanting everybody, although she could not hear a single word that was said to her; 'I have never seen anything better done,' reported Fritz Ponsonby.[38]

On their Mediterranean cruise this spring the King and Queen took the Empress Marie with them as their guest. She was particularly delighted by the chance to see something of Italy, a country she had never before visited. Landing at Baiae, the Queen and the Empress paid a call on the Duchess of Aosta. The occasion had a certain piquancy, since the Duchess was that same Hélène d'Orléans who had been sought in marriage both by Queen Alexandra's son the Duke of Clarence and the Empress's son the Czarevitch Nicholas. When King Edward returned to England the two sisters sailed on to Athens to visit their brother and his family. On this Mediterranean cruise the Empress was delighted to find the King, her brother-in-law, 'so courteous and pleasant, and in such good spirits.' His courtesy, however, was sometimes put to severe strain by the sisters' notorious disregard of time. Ponsonby gives a vivid account of their attempted ascent of Vesuvius on donkey-back. The King elected to stay behind in the little train, wisely refusing to entrust his bulky person to a donkey. The Empress, the Queen and Ponsonby mounted their beasts and set off up the mountain. Naturally, the best donkeys had been allotted to the two royal ladies so that Ponsonby was soon left trailing far behind. Suddenly he heard, far below him, the whistle of the train's engine; King Edward was growing impatient. With great difficulty Ponsonby urged his donkey on until he was within hailing distance of Queen Alexandra and could make her understand that the King wished them to return. She merely remarked that it was foolish to turn back when half-way there, and continued the ascent. The whistle sounded again and again, yet more shrilly. The frantic Ponsonby set off in an endeavour to overtake the Empress, who was by this time a mere speck in the distance. Somehow or other he managed to come up with her and to persuade both sisters to turn back. They set off at a smart pace down to the train, Ponsonby coming in a poor third on his tired and decrepit donkey: 'The vials of the monarch's wrath were therefore emptied on my innocent head; as I knew that his remarks were intended for others I didn't remonstrate.'[39]

It would seem churlish to cast any doubt upon the truth of this delightful tale. The fact remains that, in a letter to her son, the Czar, describing this same expedition up Vesuvius, the Empress definitely says that Queen Alexandra was carried in a chair by three men whilst she herself walked.[40]

This pleasant holiday in company with her beloved sister had not entirely cured Queen Alexandra's depression. A letter she wrote to the Prince of Wales from Balmoral the following August shows her mood very clearly:

> 'I do miss you my darling boy so dreadfully at times. Really on board the yacht at Cowes seems the only time we ever sleep under the same roof which makes me quite low and unhappy when thinking of how formerly we were so much together and to each other. Of course I know it can't be helped but that does not make it better. If I had not my darling Toria with me I should indeed be quite miserable and lonely as Papa is always so much away now from home.'[41]

Devoted as the Prince was to his Mother, even for her sake he was not prepared to leave the Duke of Devonshire's famous moors at Bolton Abbey and waste that precious fortnight which began on 12 August. 'I have actually had a long letter from Motherdear at Balmoral,' he told the Princess. 'She writes in rather a sad frame of mind and says she feels so lonely that none of us are there, but she doesn't understand of course about the shooting, grouse are always shot in August.'[42]

Queen Alexandra actually had a child living near to Balmoral since the Duchess of Fife's home was at Mar Lodge. This daughter was delicate, retiring, and almost pathologically shy; she would not join weekend parties at Balmoral, and she kept her children secluded even from their nearest relations.

As usual, the Queen cheered up on arrival in Denmark. From Hvidore she wrote happily enough both to her son and her daughter-in-law, describing the beauty of 'our lovely place here', and expressing her relief on hearing that King Edward, who had only arrived at Balmoral after her departure for Denmark, was looking particularly well during his Scottish visit and very much enjoying the shooting. Her one serious anxiety seemed to be for her brother, the King of Greece. She believed him to be seriously considering abdication, and, as so often before, she blamed Britain for the state of affairs in Greece – '*we* have utterly left him and his country in the lurch'.[43]

When Queen Alexandra returned to England she found the country overshadowed by the threat of political crisis. On the last day of November the struggle between the Liberal Government and the House of Lords reached a climax when the Lords threw out the Budget. The General Election which followed left the Liberal Government still in office, maintained there by Irish Nationalist support. The Liberals now determined to end the deadlock by introducing a bill which would drastically curtail the powers of the House of Lords, a measure which ultimately resulted in the Parliament Act of 1911. The House of Lords would have to pass any such bill and obviously that House would not vote for its own near-destruction unless overwhelming pressure was brought to bear. The King was sounded as to his willingness to create the necessary number of new peers to force the bill through, the theory being that, faced with this threat, the Lords must capitulate. Being extremely reluctant even to consider such a use of the Royal Prerogative the King worked his hardest to find a compromise solution, but all to no result. The matter distressed him as no political question had ever done before; his health worsened, and both his family and his doctors grew anxious. He refused, however, to take their advice and to leave England for his usual holiday in Biarritz until Asquith was able to assure him that no immediate crisis was impending. On 6 March he left England, planning to spend a few days in Paris *en route*. During his stay there he developed a bronchial chill and on arrival at Biarritz he collapsed.

Queen Alexandra was always justifiably frightened by these bronchial attacks; her anxiety, therefore, was intense. Although instinct prompted her to rush to her husband's side she feared that her sudden arrival might alarm him. She may also have been influenced by the knowledge that her husband had Mrs Keppel with him, a fact which might have made her own appearance on the scene both embarrassing and inopportune. She therefore contented herself with asking the Royal Family's doctor, Sir Francis Laking, to hold himself in readiness to travel out with her at a moment's notice. The King, however, slowly improved, until by the end of March he was well enough to enjoy a walk and a game of what Queen Alexandra spelt as 'crocket'. She wrote begging him to leave 'that horrid Biarritz' and to join her on a Mediterranean cruise, forgetful of the fact that for him this would be impossible since he could not put himself so far out of reach at a time of political crisis. With that touch of irresponsibility which was part of her nature, Queen Alexandra then decided not to wait to see him on his return from France but to leave immediately for a short holiday in Corfu with Princess Victoria. 'Dear Mama, fancy going all the way to Corfu for a fortnight, and what a fatigue just before the Season!'[44] wrote the Princess of Wales who would never have considered doing any such thing herself. A year or two earlier, when Queen Alexandra was off on a similarly brief and unpremeditated excursion, the Prince had written to his wife:

'Fancy going all the way to Scotland for only nine days and to Norway for three, what an expense and how impractical! Thank God you are not like that; it would drive me mad!'[45]

Before leaving England Queen Alexandra did something no Queen Consort had ever done before; she visited the House of Commons and listened to a debate, sitting in that part of the Ladies' Gallery which was known as the Speaker's Gallery. The Prime Minister, Asquith, opened the debate by moving 'that it is expedient that the powers of the House of Lords be restricted by law as respects bills other than money bills'. The Queen stayed for more than two hours, not leaving until she had heard Neil Primrose, son of her old friend, Lord Rosebery, speak in favour of the motion. She can in fact have heard little or nothing of any of the speeches, which makes it the more remarkable that she should have made such a departure from precedent.

When King Edward returned to England on 27 April Queen Alexandra had already arrived in Corfu. The following weekend he went down to Sandringham. That Sunday was a day of biting wind; he insisted, nevertheless, on taking his usual Sunday walk to inspect the farm and the pedigree stock. The result was a recurrence of his bronchial trouble; when he returned to London he was clearly a sick man. Word was sent to Queen Alexandra, who immediately left for home, but so little idea had she of the seriousness of her husband's condition that on arrival at Venice she and Princess Victoria toyed with the idea of staying for twenty-four hours. They decided, however, to travel straight on to England although neither of them imagined for a moment that the King was seriously ill.

During the few hours which she spent at Venice the Queen paid an informal visit to the English Hospital on the Giudecca, where a strange encounter took place. Among the patients there was that most fantastic of Edwardian literary characters, Frederick Rolfe, author of *Hadrian the Seventh*. His state of health was considered to be so hopeless that he had already been given the Last Sacraments. Warm-hearted and pitiful as always, the Queen paused to speak a few soothing and sympathetic words to the apparently dying man. The little incident must have caused some stir because a year later when Rolfe was evicted from his rooms for failure to pay the rent, a kindly hotel clerk wrote direct to Queen Alexandra 'to beg Your Majesty to grant Her interest to the English author, Mr Rolfe, who, being unable to satisfy his living expenses since last spring, is now wandering homeless on the Lido island in this piercing cold.' With her usual generosity the Queen immediately sent Rolfe a gift of money through the British Consul, who being a prudent man and knowing Rolfe, thought it as well not to divulge the name of the donor.

On arrival at Calais the Queen was handed a letter from the Prince of Wales which ended on a note of some alarm about the King's condition: 'His cough troubles him very much and he has slept very badly the last nights. I cannot disguise the fact that I am anxious about him, as one always must be when he gets one of these attacks and this one following so soon after the one he had at Biarritz. I know Laking is writing to you and I will say no more but thank God you are coming home tomorrow to look after him. God bless you, darling Motherdear.'[46]

Although Princess Victoria at once took in the gravity of the situation even now Queen Alexandra could not or would not realise that her husband's life was in danger. Whenever she had previously returned home from abroad, King Edward had always made a point of meeting her personally at the station, but now it was the Prince and Princess of Wales with their two eldest children who greeted her at Victoria. On arrival at the Palace the sight of her husband hunched in his chair, grey in the face and fighting for breath, shocked her into a realisation of the truth. Ill though he was, King Edward had personally given all directions for her reception at the Palace, and now he told her that he had a box reserved for her for the evening performance at Covent Garden, to which, of course she would not go, refusing to leave him.

Next morning, 6 May, the King insisted that his valet should dress him in frock coat and formal clothes before he received Francis Knollys and, later, Sir Ernest Cassel. Queen Alexandra chanced not to be in his room when, early that afternoon, he collapsed; she was immediately summoned as it was plain that death was very near. Now, in this extremity, the Queen rose to the full height of her generous nature; she sent for Mrs Keppel and herself arranged that, in one of his moments of full consciousness, she should be allowed the opportunity to bid him goodbye. She also gave orders that other close friends should be admitted to see him until, in the early evening, he lapsed into a coma. Just before midnight he died very peaceably, thirty hours after Queen Alexandra's return home.

WIDOWHOOD

Whilst King Edward lived his wife had been forced to share him with the nation at large, with Europe, and in another sense, with his various mistresses; now that he was dead for a day or two he was hers and hers alone. Esher described her moving about 'quietly but perfectly naturally' in the room where his body lay and talking 'with only a slight diminuition of her natural gaiety but with a tenderness which betrayed all the love in her soul, and oh! so natural feeling that she had got him there altogether to herself . . . In a way she seemed and is, I am convinced, happy.'[1]

Not Esher only but Fisher, Hardinge, Fritz Ponsonby, Asquith and other personal friends came at Queen Alexandra's request to have a last sight of their king, and to all of them she spoke calmly and with extreme simplicity. Esher and Francis Knollys had already spent several hours vainly trying to compose a suitable message to be issued in the Queen's name to the people of the Empire when a note came asking them to read a draft which she herself had composed. Written 'on four sides of large white note-paper without an erasure of any sort' it struck both Esher and Knollys as being 'perfect'; they therefore decided to publish it unaltered.[2] Although today this message might be considered too emotional and over-emphatic it exactly suited contemporary taste. For the most part its phraseology is conventional, but occasionally the Queen speaks with her own voice as when she begs her people to 'give me a thought in your prayers which will comfort and sustain me through all I still have to go through'.

The funeral was not held until a fortnight after the King's death, partly because of Queen Alexandra's extreme reluctance to part from her husband's body. As might have been expected, she behaved throughout the long funeral ceremonies with flawless dignity and composure, even managing to preserve her equanimity when, on her arrival at Westminster Hall, Kaiser William sprang forward with officious politeness to fling open her carriage door. Her natural spontaneous courtesy never failed; as she came out of St George's Chapel after the actual burial she noticed various old friends standing on the long flight of steps and held out her hand to them in silent greeting.

It was natural, but it was also unfortunate, that the Empress Marie should have been one of the first of the royal guests to arrive for the funeral and that she should have remained in England afterwards on a three months' visit to her widowed sister. In Russia the widow of the Czar took precedence over the wife of the new Czar; the Empress could not or would not see that the rules prevailing at the Russian court did not hold good elsewhere, and she urged her sister to claim a position and privileges to which she was no longer entitled. Faced with this predicament the new Queen behaved with her usual tact and courtesy, although the Grand Duchess Augusta was not so complacent. 'I understand every word, expressed or not,' she wrote to Queen Mary on 24 May, 'and have feared what you so justly allude to. May the pernicious influence soon depart, *then* I hope all will come right.'[3]

Almost inevitably difficulties arose over the question as to which pieces of jewellery belonged to the Queen of England and which to Queen Alexandra personally. King Edward's will did not help to clarify matters. According to his lawyers it had not been his intention to leave to his wife all 'his jewels, ornaments, articles of Art or *vertu*, curiosities and other chattels', but because he had not known which she would prefer to keep, he had left it to her to make her own choice, an arrangement which left the door open to all sorts of misunderstandings. The two pieces which gave rise to most difficulty were King Edward's Garter star and the famous diamond circlet usually worn by the Queen at the opening of Parliament, 'the lovely little crown', as the Grand Duchess described it. In accordance with precedent Queen Alexandra retained the Garter insignia for her lifetime, whilst the diamond crown was returned to Queen Mary in time for the 1911 opening of Parliament.

On one point King Edward's will was quite explicit; Sandringham House was left to Queen Alexandra for her lifetime. She has frequently been blamed for remaining on alone in 'the Big House' whilst her son, King of England and father of a large family, had to make do with the totally inadequate accommodation at York Cottage. It is difficult to see what else she should have done; if King Edward had left the house to her he had presumably intended that she should live in it. By so doing she was merely carrying out her dead husband's wish. If anyone were to blame it was King George himself; he could and should have found himself a more suitable country home in the Sandringham neighbourhood, but he was so sentimentally attached to York Cottage that he was oblivious of its ludicrous inadequacy and inconvenience.

But if Queen Alexandra was justified in remaining at Sandringham she was certainly to blame for her unwillingness to hand Buckingham Palace over to the new King and Queen. Ten years earlier King Edward had been at pains to ask the Grand Duchess Augusta to persuade his wife to move into the Palace; now Kaiser William took upon himself the ungrateful task of persuading her to move out of it. Usually the most tactless of men, on this occasion he made a commendable effort to put his point with care and discretion, stressing the comfort that his aunt might be expected to find in the return to Marlborough House, her home for so many happy years. Queen Alexandra heard him out with smiling patience, at the end of his speech remarking very sweetly, 'Willy dear, you know that you always speak rather indistinctly; I am afraid I have not heard a single word you were saying.'

Here, however, the trouble has been much magnified;

King George and Queen Mary in actual fact moved into Buckingham Palace in December 1910, only seven months after King Edward's death. The real difficulty was Queen Alexandra's inability to make plans and her refusal to keep to them once they were made. The person who suffered most from this lack of method was of course Queen Mary, herself the most methodical of women. The new Queen was not slow to recognise her mother-in-law's good points. Years later when her own son, the Duke of Kent, became engaged to Queen Alexandra's great-niece, Princess Marina, Queen Mary told Lady Airlie that the connection greatly pleased her because 'the women of the Danish Family have the art of marriage'. 'Look at Queen Alexandra,' she continued; 'could any other wife have managed King Edward as well as she did?' Queen Alexandra too appreciated Queen Mary's worth to the full: 'What a comfort it is to me that it is *May* and not someone who is not one of us!'[4] she exclaimed to Lady Geraldine and to Lady Katherine Coke she described her daughter-in-law as being '*more* than kind and dear'.[5] Different as they were by temperament a real *rapprochement* between the two women might well have come about in the highly emotional atmosphere of the period immediately following King Edward's death. Had it not been for the presence of the Empress Marie Queen Alexandra might have found her chief comfort and support in her daughter-in-law; as things were she naturally turned to her sister, who was herself a widow. In a letter to Queen Mary's brother, Adolphus, now Duke of Teck, the Grand Duchess Augusta pointed out that no very deep intimacy had ever existed between the old Queen and the new. Both were essentially shy characters, clinging closely to their own family but finding it difficult to make other friends. This being so, it was, in the Grand Duchess's opinion, most unfortunate that at this trying time Queen Alexandra should have had the Empress Marie constantly at her side and ever ready with advice. Queen Alexandra, however, was delighted to have her sister at hand and only too pleased that she should stay in England till August.

Dearer even than her sister to Queen Alexandra was her son, now King in his father's place. From now onwards King George was to be her great support and solace, remaining invariably kind, thoughtful, and affectionate, although she was sometimes to try his patience very high. All through this difficult period he had been perfect in his unselfish devotion to his mother, a devotion which she valued to the full as she made clear in a letter written the day after King Edward's funeral:

> '*How* can I thank you for what you were to me yesterday on that truly as you say terrible day! When we laid your blessed Papa to rest. I really do not know *how* I should have borne that fearful ordeal without you by my side. You were indeed my *only* consolation here on earth and your kind and affectionate support helped me through it. God was indeed merciful to me in the midst of such grief, such deep-felt sorrow and pain, to allow me to keep *one* of my darling sons, who now indeed has shown me more than ever his blessed loving and affectionate heart. *Thank* you again and again for all you ever have been and are to your poor old Motherdear.'[6]

Widowhood held special trials for Queen Alexandra over and above her natural grief for her husband, which was both deep and sincere. Every widow, no matter whether her marriage has been happy or unhappy, suffers from the curious sensation that, lacking a husband, she has become a half-person, a second-class citizen. She has lost part of her personality and the greater part of her position in the world. If this is true of ordinary widows it is far more true of a widowed Queen, who during her husband's lifetime ranked as the first lady in the land. King Edward may not have been a faithful husband, but he had been a loving and a considerate one, and round him Queen Alexandra's life had revolved for forty-seven years. She had been a girl of sixteen when they first met; now, at his death, she was a woman of sixty-five, too old to make a new life for herself, too young to sink into the inertia of old age. Of recent years two dowager Queens have made a special place for themselves in the life of the nation. Queen Alexandra was not of the calibre of Queen Mary or Queen Elizabeth the Queen Mother; she kept her hold upon the affection of the people and she continued to take her share in the charitable and representational work of the monarchy, but she had not enough resources within herself to enable her to rebuild her life satisfactorily. She had always depended too much upon her relationships with other people, and although King George was the best of sons and the unhappy Princess Victoria a very dutiful daughter, there was no one now to give a centre or a direction to her life.

In these circumstances Queen Alexandra came to rely more and more upon those two trusty friends and servants, Dighton Probyn and Charlotte Knollys. Both of them were considerably older than she was – in 1910 Probyn was in fact seventy-seven – and both might have felt that the time had now come for rest and retirement. When King Edward died Probyn gave up his office as Keeper of the Privy Purse, planning to retire altogether; Queen Alexandra, however, begged him to stay on with her as Comptroller and Treasurer. As he put it in a letter dated 1 July 1910, 'my wish to retire into private life was at once overshadowed by the greater desire to serve the poor dear lady as long as I found I had the power to do so'. In the same letter he describes himself as working as hard as ever but hoping that once matters settled down he would find his work 'easy and light'.[7] In this hope he was to be disappointed; it was never a light or an easy task to keep any sort of control over Queen Alexandra's finances.

Politically these first months of the new reign were overshadowed by the same problem of the passage of the Parliament Act which had so troubled King Edward. On 16 November 1910 King George reluctantly agreed to give the Cabinet a secret undertaking that, if the Government were returned with a majority at the forthcoming general election, he would be prepared to use his prerogative to create the necessary number of peers to ensure the Bill's passage through the Upper House. Seeing how heavily this decision weighed upon his mind, his mother did her best to convince him that he had come to the right conclusion, and on 19 December she wrote him a wise and comforting letter:

'I hope you read every word in *The Observer* yesterday. There you will see how right you acted under these very difficult circumstances, and I know for certain Papa would have been obliged to act exactly in the same way. It was unavoidable and the only course open to you so although a bitter pill for you to swallow do *not* worry about the step you were obliged to take, and pray to God, as we all do, that He will continue to lead you in the right path all through this serious and difficult crisis. Do not let any outsiders disturb you. The step you were advised to take has been taken and one must stick to it.'[8]

The good sense of this letter is the more remarkable because Queen Alexandra in no way approved of the Parliament Act, which she stigmatised as 'the odious, horrible Bill'. Where politics were concerned she remained more interested in foreign than in home affairs. In the spring of 1911 she stayed for some time in Corfu, where she met the Kaiser, enjoying himself in his prodigious villa and very full of his plan for a Berlin–Baghdad railway. 'How can we be so blind and slow?' she wrote home angrily apropos this scheme. 'E. Grey has certainly proved the worst Foreign Secretary England ever had.'[9]

The Kaiser was about to visit England to unveil the memorial to Queen Victoria. Queen Alexandra decided not to attend the ceremony; 'much the best thing', commented her wise daughter-in-law. Nor would she be present at her son's Coronation. Terribly depressed, still worried over the difficulties of settling in at Marlborough House, and troubled by a persistent cough, she had become a pitiable figure, 'hopeless and helpless', as Queen Mary described her. In such a condition she felt she could not stand the emotional strain of attendance at the Coronation. Not merely did she dread awakening painful memories of her own Coronation; her thoughts were naturally turning back to her dead son Prince Eddy, whom the rest of the world remembered, if they remembered him at all, only with a sigh of relief that it was not he who came to be crowned King of England. So she remained at Sandringham with Princess Victoria and the Empress Marie, but her heart was with her son King George at his crowning, as she clearly showed in a letter which he received from her on his Coronation Day:

'On the eve of your Coronation, the most sacred day of your life, I must send you a mother's blessing and pray God to guard and protect you and take you in His holy keeping till your life's end. May He guide you in the difficult path which you have to tread and make you a blessing to our beloved country as your beloved Father and Grandmother were before you. . . . You will feel and know that *both* our spirits are hovering near you. May God bless you both, and give a little thought to your poor sad and broken-hearted Motherdear.'[10]

In the winter following the Coronation the King and Queen were to visit India to attend the great Durbar ceremony at Delhi. Queen Alexandra doubted the wisdom of their departure; at the end of September Italy had declared war on Turkey and the situation in the Balkans and the eastern Mediterranean was very tense. In these circumstances she thought it 'hardly conceivable' that the King should leave England for as long as three months. Sir Edward Grey was again a target for her scorn – 'It is inconceivable how many blunders E. Grey always commits and our present Foreign Politics are deplorable.'[11] She was especially incensed because the right to appoint the High Commissioner in Crete had been removed from the King of Greece; 'with one stroke of the pen you have done away with what beloved Papa had taken the utmost and greatest trouble to obtain for Uncle Willy and Crete.'[12]

On 11 November the King and Queen left England for India. During their absence Queen Alexandra had the pleasure of her grandchildren's company at Sandringham. Prince John, the youngest, was now six, and to him she was particularly attached in spite of or perhaps because of the fact that he was an epileptic. As grandparents often are, she was more hopeful of a cure than ever his parents could be. Through the sad years of her widowhood this handicapped child was comfort and consolation to her; since he could never fully grow up she could 'baby' him to her heart's content. Her letters are full of references to him; whenever she was at Sandringham she would send for 'the dear and precious little boy' to have tea with her and play games, or perhaps listen to music. In 1917 it was thought wise to separate him from the rest of the family and put him to live in a house near Sandringham with his devoted nurse, 'Lalla' Bill. His grandmother acquiesced in the wisdom of this decision but she was troubled lest the child should be lonely, lacking companions of his own age. When he died at the age of thirteen and was buried in Sandringham churchyard her mind went back to that other John who had lived only for one day; 'now our two darling Johnnies lie side by side,'[13] she wrote to Queen Mary.

Whilst the King and Queen were still in India, Queen Alexandra's daughter the Duchess of Fife set out for Egypt with her family. On the way they were shipwrecked and in real danger of death when their lifeboat sank under them. Everyone behaved with commendable courage; 'Admiral Cradock told me he had *never* witnessed such *bravery* as Louise's,'[14] Queen Alexandra wrote approvingly. The holiday which had begun in such an alarming manner ended in tragedy; the Duke of Fife caught a chill and died suddenly in Cairo. Queen Alexandra had never had a very great opinion of her daughter but she was stirred to admiration by her behaviour in this crisis; 'She wanted but to be spurred into it – "a great sorrow recasts the soul" – and her *great courage* and faith have changed her into this *strong soul* and being.'[15]

The New Year had opened sadly for the Queen with the death of old Lady Macclesfield, 'whom I adored and always looked on as my second mother'.[16] In June came the death of her brother, King Frederick of Denmark, followed a few days later by the sudden death of her nephew, Prince George of Cumberland, known to his family as 'Plumpy'. After all these losses it is perhaps not surprising to find her complaining to King George that she was feeling 'low and wretched' and lamenting that for the first time she found herself solitary at Sandringham 'without any of my blessed children'.[17] Soon, however, it was time to set off on her usual round of visits to Scotland, Norway and Hvidore, where she was joined by her old friend Soveral. From Hvidore she wrote to King George on 9 October a more than usually frenzied letter on the subject of Greek and Balkan affairs. Hostilities were about to break out between Turkey on the one hand and Greece, Montenegro, Bulgaria and Serbia on the other. Queen Alexandra was perturbed by a rumour that the British were about to occupy Crete, 'one of the most unfair acts England could do towards Greece', and once again she repeated her cry, 'Remember England put my brother there and are bound to keep him there.'[18]

With or without British support King George I was not to sit very much longer on the throne of Greece; on 18 March 1913 he was assassinated in the streets of Salonika. The Queen was deeply grieved and shocked by the murder of her favourite brother, but even in these tragic circumstances she did not completely lose her sense of the ridiculous. A Danish friend sent to her at Marlborough House an outsized laurel wreath, asking her to make arrangements to have it laid on the murdered King's grave. The Queen's favourite pekinese dog had recently died, to her great distress. Faced with the problem of the laurel wreath's transportation to Greece she rang for her butler: 'Hawkins, you see that wreath? Too much trouble to send it out to Greece; put it on dear little Beauty's grave in the garden.'

Her brother's death did not cause Queen Alexandra to lose interest in the tangled politics of the Balkans; she continued to pester her son King George with ever more and more incoherent letters on this subject. During the two Balkan wars the Queen herself was able to be of some useful service to the Greek cause. The Crown Princess of Greece, distressed by the lack of provision for the sick and wounded, telegraphed personally to Queen Alexandra asking her to try to procure some help from English sources. The Queen immediately put the matter before the Council of the British Red Cross, with the result that medical units and supplies were at once sent out.

At home the great topic was Irish Home Rule, a question which had brought Ireland to the brink of civil war. Queen Alexandra, who had never had much understanding of the British constitution, was now convinced that the King could and should take matters into his own hands. On 21 March 1914, the day after the so-called Curragh Mutiny, she wrote urging him 'to use the power given you by God Himself as the *ruling sovereign* of your country'. With a typical mixture of metaphors she continued, 'You stand above all parties and *must* speak out and put your foot down! while yet there is time to save your country from such a *calamity*.'[19] Soon, however, the Irish crisis was dwarfed by a much greater catastrophe; 4 August 1914 saw the outbreak of the First World War.

THE GREAT WAR

Queen Alexandra's reactions to the Great War were typical of the average woman of her age and generation. She had always hated Germany, not without very good reason; now she believed implicitly in every story of German atrocities, and hurled abusive epithets at the head of the Kaiser. Yet underneath this sound and fury there seems to have been no comprehension of the real horror, no understanding of the magnitude and beastliness of the disaster that was overwhelming civilisation. Shallow though her attitude may have been it was by no means an uncommon one. A sentence in one of her letters dated 8 July 1916, during the Battle of the Somme, today reads like bitter irony; 'thank God,' she wrote, 'we all are doing so well in France just now'.[1] By the end of that same month of July the British had gained two and a half miles on a two-mile front and lost approximately 171,000 men; yet people still alive can well remember the exuberant feeling which swept the country at the first news of this 'advance'. We, who come after, know far more about the nature of that war than did the non-combatant population who actually lived through it; censorship was, very properly, strict, and the men who came back from the trenches for the most part preferred to keep their mouths shut. Queen Alexandra cannot fairly be blamed for a lack of comprehension which was shared by the majority of her fellow-countrymen.

Because of their complex and wide-spread family relationships, in war-time royalty suffer peculiar anxieties unknown to most ordinary families. Queen Alexandra, of course, had relations fighting on both sides. One nephew, the son of her sister Thyra, Duchess of Cumberland, was with the German army, whilst another nephew, Prince Maurice of Battenberg, was killed fighting on the British side at Mons. His death made the treatment accorded to his uncle, Prince Louis of Battenberg, seem all the more petty and unjust. Prince Louis had made his career in the British Navy and at the outbreak of war he was serving as First Sea Lord. Although he was a brilliant sailor and a loyal British subject the outcry against him on account of his German name and ancestry was so great that he was obliged to resign. Queen Alexandra had known and liked Prince Louis since the time when, as a young midshipman, he had accompanied her and her husband on their Nile journey, and now she wrote with bitter truth, 'he is of a noble character and has sacrificed himself to the country he has served so well and who has now treated him so abominably.'[2]

Prince Louis's resignation meant the return of Fisher to the Admiralty, to the consternation of King George and the delight of Queen Alexandra. On 1 November 1914 Fisher recorded in his diary, 'Queen Alexandra and Princess Victoria simply heavenly to me and they both looked quite lovely! I wish I could have married both of them!'[3] A few weeks later on 21 January Queen Alexandra wrote Fisher a letter which must have astonished even that most determined believer in unorthodox methods of warfare. Zeppelin raiders had recently appeared over Sandringham and dropped bombs in the neighbourhood. 'Please let me have a lot of *rockets* with spikes or hooks on to defend our Norfolk coast,' she demanded; 'I am sure you could invent something of the sort which would bring down a few of those rascals.'[4]

Fisher's term of office was short, for he resigned in May 1915 in consequence of a disagreement with Winston Churchill over the Gallipoli expedition. On 19 May Queen Alexandra had written him an impassioned letter begging him to stay at the Admiralty: 'Stick to your post like *Nelson*! The nation and we all have full confidence in you and *I* and they will not suffer you to go. Let the young foolhardy one* go, but you are the nation's hope and we trust you! Think of Tirpitz and his Devils how they will rejoice!!! All I say is *stick* to your *post* and God will help us all.'[5]

The national feeling of hatred against Germany had produced an almost hysterical clamour for the removal of the Garter banners belonging to enemy kings, princes and emperors which hung in St George's Chapel at Windsor. Queen Alexandra joined in the outcry, writing urgently to King George, who would himself have preferred to leave the banners in place, to urge him to take action – 'It is but right and proper for you to have down those hateful German banners in our sacred Church, St George's at Windsor.'[6] However, when the King, bowing to public opinion, had the banners duly removed she wrote again complaining that he had removed not merely 'those vile Prussian banners' but also those of the other Garter knights fighting on the German side, most of them, of course, relations of her own. 'All of them are simply *soldiers* or *vassals* under that brutal German Emperor's orders.' In this same letter she inveighs again against 'that stupid young foolhardy Winston Churchill'.[7]

Queen Alexandra's judgment of men may have been at fault, her hatred of the Germans unpleasantly strident, but her patriotism no one could call in question. She was determined that, as far as she was able to do so, she would play a real part in the effort to defeat 'those arrogant barbarians'. An old lady in her seventies, lame, bronchial, and almost stone deaf, might well have been expected to limit her war-work to patronising various war charities and to lending her name to such money-making schemes as the publication of *Queen Alexandra's Gift Book*. She, however, conceived it her duty to do something more active, and in spite of the strain and embarrassment which her deafness inevitably caused, she gave unstinted time and energy to the personal visiting which was the only form of war-work a person of her age and position could usefully undertake.

*Winston Churchill.

In some ways Queen Alexandra was ideally suited to this work of visiting, in others, not so. As a hospital visitor she had always been in her element. Doctors and nurses loved her and forgave the inevitable interruption of routine when, as almost invariably happened, her visit lasted much longer than its scheduled time. She could seldom bring herself to leave a ward until she had spoken to every patient, and to each one she spoke as if they were her own personal concern. This quick sympathy was absolutely genuine; her involvement with individual cases was the obverse side to her lack of interest in matters of organisation. In this she differed completely from Queen Mary, who took a keen, intelligent interest in the details of hospital management whilst finding it hard to make personal contact with the patients. Queen Alexandra was completely uninhibited in her approach. On one occasion, when visiting a hospital, she noticed a man looking particularly downcast and asked the nurse what his trouble might be. She was told that he had been wounded in the leg and that he had just realised that his knee would be permanently stiff and useless. Immediately the Queen was at his bedside: 'My dear, dear, man, I hear you have a stiff leg; so have I. Now just watch what I can do with it' – and lifting up her skirt she swept her lame leg clear over the top of his bed-side table.

In these more or less informal visits to simple soldiers and sailors her deafness seemed no hindrance, but on formal occasions and in dealings with more sophisticated people it reared itself into a formidable barrier. One such occasion was her visit to the offices of an organisation engaged in locating missing men and prisoners of war. She was shown round by Percy Lubbock, himself the originator of the scheme and its chief prop and support. After an hour or so spent in inspecting everything that he had to show her she turned to Lubbock with the sweetest of smiles; 'Well, it is a beautiful idea – *whoever* thought of it!'

By now Queen Alexandra had acquired quite a reputation for making such *malapropos* remarks. Some of these sayings, many of them apocryphal, are still quoted as proof of her stupidity; they should rather be quoted as proof of her courage. No one would have thought to blame her had she retired completely from public life; instead, in spite of deafness, lameness, and increasing delicacy, she continued to do what she conceived to be her duty.

The effort was a costly one. She no longer enjoyed her public appearances; what had once been a pleasure had now become a penance. Nowadays her name is most often remembered in connection with Alexandra Rose Day, the prototype of all the flag-days which now beset us. Rose Day is popularly believed to have provided Queen Alexandra with a pleasant interest in her declining years; in fact it was an occasion which she acutely disliked. She referred to 'that tiresome Alexandra Day, *which I dread*',[8] and again to 'that horrible Rose Day drive'.[9] No one, however, who saw her on what was once described as 'her radiant progress' through London, stopping here and there to speak to the various rose-sellers, could have guessed at the real nature of her feelings.

She still maintained a close connection with the Military Nursing Service. When there was talk of changing its constitution, which had remained unaltered since its beginning, she wrote to Sydney Holland, now Lord Knutsford, what she described as 'a scrawl of despair', protesting that '*nothing* will I *allow* to be touched without *our mutual* approval and sanction', sure that 'this new plan will soon upset all our old work'.[10] Believing implicitly in every atrocity story she was anxious to do something to help Belgian women refugees who had been, or said they had been, raped by German soldiers. Fortunately, Lord Knutsford had tact enough to point out the difficulties in the way and to persuade her to abandon this idea; 'You do not want to help women who have willingly surrendered themselves to German soldiers and then, when they find they are *enceinte*, declare they have been outraged.'[11]

By the summer of 1915 Queen Alexandra was a very tired woman. Not merely was she exhausted by the nervous strain of her own public appearances; she shared to the full in the general feeling of overwhelming anxiety and grief as the enormous casualty lists lengthened. True, she lost none of her immediate relatives, but in almost every one of her letters she grieves for someone, perhaps the son of a friend or one of the Sandringham tenants whom she knew so well. She was also full of anxiety for her many relations abroad. Whilst the war lasted she could not hope to see her daughter, Queen Maud of Norway, or any of her Danish relatives, and of course she could not visit her beloved home at Hvidore. She was completely cut off from her sister in Germany, but since Russia was England's ally she could still write freely to the Empress Marie, sometimes passing on information which she hoped might be of use to the Russian authorities. For instance, on 14 February 1915 the Empress told her son, Nicholas II, 'Aunt Alix wires to say that they know for certain that the Germans intend to attack Warsaw this week and she hopes we are aware of it,' adding the comment, 'her information has usually been correct'.[12]

By devious means Queen Alexandra succeeded in keeping up a private correspondence with her nephew, King Christian X of Denmark. Many of these letters were carried by a Danish ship-owner called Andersen, 'the great man who invented and owns all those beautiful oil ships with no funnels', who apparently was on friendly terms not only with the English, the Danish, and the Russian royal families, but also with the Kaiser – 'he has just been in Russia, seen Minny and Nicky, and on his way back he actually went to see WILLIAM.'[13] In her letters the Queen encourages King Christian in his anti-German attitude – 'God protect the three Northern Kingdoms from their clutches! The courage of the three Kings was fine, and I hope to God they will firmly maintain their neutrality.'[14] Apparently, as early as 1915, King Christian had suggested to her that Copenhagen would be a suitable place for a peace conference, for on 15 April she writes to her son, King George: 'I think myself it would be an excellent plan and a first-rate idea if peace could be discussed and signed at Copenhagen. But it is *too* soon for *us* to think of peace yet. We must thrash them first of all.'[15]

In this same letter the Queen complains of colds and influenza and 'a most hacking cough which I feel will really soon finish me off'. Throughout the summer, however, she remained in London, busy with her various activities, going somewhere nearly every day. To the outside world she preserved a cheerful face; her own family, however, were only too well aware of her state of nerves and depression. In spite of the devotion and sympathy shown to her not only by her son, her daughter, and her daughter-in-law, but also by her faithful friends in her own household, she was forever complaining of her 'utter loneliness'; then, in contrary mood, she would grumble because 'in London I never have a moment's peace'. Finally, early in September, feeling like 'a poor old carthorse when it cannot go any further', she fled to Sandringham, leaving her standard still flying over Marlborough House. She took no one but Charlotte Knollys with her, and she refused to let even the faithful Dighton Probyn know that she had left London, insisting that 'I shall go mad if not left alone by myself'.[16]

Clearly this flight to Sandringham indicates some sort of breakdown, the beginning of a physical and mental decline. From now onwards her letters become those of a very old woman, growing more and more plaintive and incoherent. She complains of 'weariness of spirit' and describes herself as feeling 'utterly collapsed' and 'so horribly low-spirited'. Such letters can only have added to the heavy burden already resting on the shoulders of her son King George who nevertheless remained unalterably patient and affectionate. Did she reproach him for not writing to her more frequently? Somehow he found time to do so in spite of the ever-increasing weight of his official correspondence. She then complained that even though they could never now enjoy a private little lunch together at least he might have spared her a minute or two – 'If only you had sent for me when you were putting on your coat, as you did once or twice before, so that I could have seen you, my precious boy!'[17] Despairing of making her understand his over-loaded time-table he wrote back a letter of warmest affection, 'Rest assured, darling Motherdear, that you have the same place in my heart that you have had ever since I was a little child.'[18]

Most trying of all must have been her frequent letters attempting to influence him in favour of her nephew, King Constantine of Greece, whom the British people regarded as a pro-German weakling and contemptuously nicknamed 'Tino'. King Constantine's sister Marie, wife of a Russian Grand Duke, in 1917 fled to England, where she naturally spent much of her time with her aunt. Great was Queen Alexandra's indignation when she was told that 'little Minny's' continued presence at Marlborough House and Sandringham had aroused suspicions that she was intriguing there on behalf of her brother. 'I will do my best not to be seen in public with the poor child,' the Queen wrote in righteous anger, 'but will not give her up or [refuse to] see her in private here as that would indeed be too cruel and hard.'[19]

On 25 October 1915 came the news of King George's accident whilst visiting the troops in France. Neither Queen Mary nor Queen Alexandra at first realised the serious nature of his injuries; Queen Mary wrote that 'no bones had been broken'[20] – he had in fact fractured his pelvis in two places – whilst Queen Alexandra suggested that 'he may have had a slight concussion and that is why the doctors order a complete rest.'[21]

The early summer of 1916 was an anxious period, darkened by two events which at the time seemed catastrophic although posterity has judged of them differently. Queen Alexandra had always had a great admiration for Lord Kitchener. She was told beforehand of his secret journey to Russia, a plan which as she told King George she regarded as both unnecessary and dangerous. 'My dear Queen was furious when she heard he was going,' Dighton Probyn wrote afterwards, 'and said he ought not to be allowed to go.'[22] The 'fearful news' of the loss of H.M.S. *Hampshire* and Kitchener's death by drowning left her 'quite stunned and collapsed', following as it did so closely upon the first over-pessimistic report of the Battle of Jutland and the news of the heavy British losses in that battle.[23]

The worst personal distress which the war brought to Queen Alexandra was still to come. For nearly forty years, ever since the murder of the Czar Alexander II, she had gone in constant fear for the lives of the members of the Imperial Family. The Queen had never been deceived as to the situation in Russia; she knew well enough that a storm was brewing whose magnitude no one could guess. She had been especially troubled by what she heard of the Czarina's interference in political affairs and the evil influence exercised over her by the 'holy man' Rasputin. On receiving news of Rasputin's murder the Queen wrote to King George, 'The wretched Russian monk caused a tremendous sensation in the world but [is] only regretted by poor dear Alicky who might have ruined the whole future of Russia through his influence.' She added the not inapt comment, 'I am sure she thinks herself like their Empress Catherine.'[24]

Events moved quickly after Rasputin's murder. On 8 March 1917 rioting broke out in the streets of Petrograd and on 15 March Nicholas II abdicated. A week later at Mogilev he said goodbye to his mother the Empress Marie. Neither of them realised that this was their final farewell, but nevertheless the Empress telegraphed to Queen Alexandra that the parting had been 'heart-crushing'. From now onwards communications between the sisters became more and more difficult and uncertain. The Czar and his family were taken first to Tobolsk and then to Ekaterinburg whilst the Empress Marie made her way to the Crimea, not yet in Bolshevik hands. On 5 September 1918 King George wrote to Queen Alexandra to tell her that the rumours she had heard about the Czar's fate were all too true and that he and his whole family had been shot at Ekaterinburg on 16 July. Shocked and horrified as she was by this news the Queen's chief preoccupation seems to have been with her sister and the relations and friends with her in the Crimea – 'I can hear *nothing* and they are quite cut off from the world and alone in their misery and despair. God help them all.'[25]

At home in England Queen Alexandra had been herself exposed to the dangers of war, an experience which she seems to have enjoyed considerably. On 17 September 1916 she wrote to her son describing a Zeppelin raid over Sandringham:

> 'We have been living through some gruesome moments here – just a fortnight ago we had those beastly Zepps over us. At 10 o'clock that Saturday evening they began. We were all sitting upstairs in Victoria's room when we suddenly were startled by the awful noise! and lo and behold, there was the awful monster over our heads. Everybody rushed up and wanted us to go downstairs. I must confess I was not a bit afraid – but it was a most uncanny feeling – poor Victoria was quite white in the face and horror-struck – but we all wanted to see it – the house was pitch dark and at last Charlotte and I stumbled down in the darkness and

found Colonel Davidson and Hawkins scrambling about outside so I also went out, but saw nothing and for the time the Zepps had flown off somewhere but came back about four o'clock in the night and dropped bombs all over the place!!'[26]

Next morning the Queen's first thought was for the villagers at Dodhill on whom those bombs had dropped; she went immediately to visit them and to see the damage for herself, 'an *awful* sight, everything destroyed both inside and out'.

Because he was married to Dorothy Vivian, her one-time Maid-of-Honour, Queen Alexandra took a special interest in the career of Sir Douglas (afterwards Lord) Haig, who had by this time succeeded French as Commander-in-Chief of the British Forces in France. On 23 April 1917, after the capture of Vimy Ridge, an action described by Churchill as 'a brilliant preliminary operation' to the bloody and inconclusive battle of Arras, she wrote warmly to Lady Haig, whom she always addressed as 'dearest Dorris': 'I must send you a few lines to say *how* proud you must feel about your beloved husband and his splendid deeds and leadership in this awful war. What a glorious success he has been – and how proud every English heart is of him! His name has indeed become famous all over the world – I pray to God that he may lead us on to victory and that we may soon see the end of this cruel and terrible war.'[27]

In spite of her passionate desire to see 'those beastly Germans' defeated Queen Alexandra could not be brought to realise that if the war were to be won, everybody in Britain, including even the Queen Mother, must make certain economies and sacrifices. To any idea of economising on petrol she turned a conveniently deaf ear, even when her old friend Soveral joined with Queen Mary in urging upon her the necessity of such saving. Economies in money were, of course, even more distasteful; where finance was concerned she reduced the faithful Dighton Probyn almost to despair. Ever since King Edward's death he had waged a gallant but losing battle with the Exchequer on the subject of taxation. As the King's widow Queen Alexandra had been given a Parliamentary annuity which was subject, however, to taxation. So great was the wartime increase in taxation that by 1920 her net income was rather less than half what it had been in 1911.

This drop in income made no impression at all upon Queen Alexandra's mind. The war, of course, had given her ample excuse to indulge her charitable impulses to the full. Within three days of the outbreak of war she had given away £1,000 in bank notes to various charities, and at Christmas 1914 she distributed another £1,000 in notes. 'The Blessed Lady's generosity knows no bounds,' Probyn wrote in January 1915, 'hundreds and thousands of pounds she is spending on all sorts of war charities.'[28] It is not surprising to find that he reckoned, were her expenditure to continue at this rate, by the end of 1915 it would be vastly in excess of her annual income.

Not only did the Queen refuse to cut down the charitable spending; she refused absolutely to make even the most necessary economies in the running of Sandringham and Marlborough House. Did Queen Mary suggest that she might save both money and labour by having less profusion of cut flowers? 'It is very difficult as I do like a lot of lovely flowers about the house and in my rooms.'[29] Had Probyn told her that she really could not afford to equip and run a house on the Sandringham estate as a convalescent home for wounded officers? 'All right, beloved General Probyn, then I will not offer my house to the officers particularly as they did not like it and found it dull;'[30] instead, she would invite a few tired nurses to rest and relax there at her expense. Did anyone, greatly daring, attack her seriously on the subject of finance? All she would do was to wave her hand airily and reply, 'I don't care, I shall do as I please; if I get into debt *they* can pay.' On one such occasion King Edward's old friend, Arthur Davidson, was not to be thus lightly put off. '*Who* will pay, Ma'am?' he countered. 'Certainly not the nation for they won't pay a penny. It will all fall on King George or Princess Victoria and it isn't either right or fair on them.' Thus driven into a corner the Queen took unfair advantage of her deafness; she broke off the conversation, protesting that she had not heard a word.[31]

Most of all did she dislike any talk of economies in her

stables or kennels. Probyn was urgent with her to allow him to have some of her worn-out horses and dogs put down, arguing that this was necessary not merely for the sake of financial economy but also because so many men had gone off to the Services that there were no longer sufficient staff to look after all her animals. 'It breaks my heart,' she replied, 'that this cruel wicked beastly war should be the cause of so many of my *precious* old friends my *horses* being *slaughtered* after all these years of faithful service.' She nevertheless agreed that some of the horses should go but she refused absolutely to have any of her old dogs put down. 'My kennels and dogs I will not have touched; I will rather keep them out of my own pocket,'[32] she declared, oblivious of the fact that they had never been paid for in any other way.

'Thank God the news from the Front continues splendidly and Haig is one of the best and grandest leaders and generals we ever had,'[33] Queen Alexandra wrote on 29 October 1918. On Armistice Day itself Queen Alexandra chanced not to be in London; 'a real heartbreak and bitter disappointment not to have shared in our people's rejoicing and happiness'.[34] She insisted on being present at Haig's official entry into London and when his carriage paused for a moment outside Marlborough House she stepped forward and pressed a flower into his hand.

In the hour of victory Queen Alexandra did not forget another wartime leader. When Asquith had been forced to resign in December 1916 the Queen had written him a warmly sympathetic letter assuring him that he had never lost the confidence either of King Edward or King George, and declaring that 'the whole of England owes you a debt of gratitude it can never adequately repay'.[35] Now she made sure that the fallen statesman should know that one person at least had not forgotten him. On Armistice Day she telegraphed to Margot Asquith, 'In the great rejoicings which we share with you and the people all over our Empire we do not forget your husband today.'[36] Queen Alexandra never liked Asquith's rival, Lloyd George, who swept the country in the 'khaki election', Asquith himself losing his seat. When he was returned two years later to the House of Commons at the Paisley by-election Queen Alexandra threw aside all pretence of royal impartiality in politics and sent him an excited telegram of congratulation: 'Perfectly delighted at your grand success which I never doubted for a moment. How my beloved husband would have rejoiced with the whole country at your splendid achievement!'[37]

Queen Alexandra attended one of the very first official victory celebrations, a review of disabled ex-service men held in Hyde Park on 23 November. King George rode down the lines on horse-back, followed by Queen Mary and Queen Alexandra in an open landau. Everyone was keyed to a very high pitch of emotion and excitement. Suddenly the tension became too great; discipline cracked, and in a moment the King had disappeared among a mass of enthusiastic men, who all but succeeded in pulling him off his horse. The two Queens found themselves surrounded by an excited mob, some of the men even attempting to climb into their carriage. To prevent this happening the officer of the escort forced his horse close up against the carriage so that its head was actually in Queen Alexandra's lap. She took its nose between her white-gloved hands, stroking and soothing the nervous animal whilst she smiled and bowed with complete calmness to the crowd milling all around. For a moment it had seemed as if a nasty accident must occur but now the danger was avoided. As the carriage drove on again perhaps she remembered a long-ago occasion when another enthusiastic crowd had surged around her carriage and only her quick wits and skill at handling another cavalry charger had averted catastrophe.

EPILOGUE

Few indeed are the fortunate people who enjoy 'an old age serene and bright and lovely as a Lapland night'. Queen Alexandra was not among them. For a famous beauty old age is bound to be a particularly hard trial, and so the Queen found it. 'Ugly old woman,' she would say again and again of herself, 'nobody likes me any more.' For her the years from 1918 till her death in 1925 were anything but a happy period.

As early as October 1919 Queen Mary reported 'a great change in her, she looks so frail, and the deafness is awful'.[1] That year had, however, brought her great happiness in her reunion with her beloved sister. When the French evacuation of Odessa brought the Bolshevik forces within striking distance of the Crimea a British warship was sent to Yalta with orders to bring off the Empress Marie. Queen Alexandra sent an urgent letter to her sister begging her to leave while yet there was time; the Empress agreed to do so, but only on condition that the relatives and friends who were with her in the Crimea should also be taken on board.

At Malta the party trans-shipped from H.M.S. *Marlborough* to H.M.S. *Lord Nelson*. The voyage to England was an unexpectedly gay one; the ship's officers were surprised to find that the Empress was 'great fun', appearing to be in no way depressed by her tragic experiences. One fine evening she sent for the Captain and demanded that there should be dancing on the quarter-deck. In vain to point out to her that wartime routine was still being observed and that all officers were already in bed or on watch; brushing aside every objection she insisted that the officers be collected and the Marine band routed out to play dance music whilst she herself supervised the festivities from a perch on the after-capstan.

On 9 May H.M.S. *Lord Nelson* arrived at Portsmouth in brilliant sunshine. So many tragic happenings had occurred since the two royal sisters had last seen each other that their meeting was bound to be a poignant occasion; it was, nevertheless, to take place in public and accompanied by full royal ceremonial. The ship's company were paraded on deck whilst the little group of Russian exiles waited on the quarter-deck, the Empress standing slightly apart with her daughter and her grandsons. At last came the shrill sound of whistles as Queen Alexandra was piped on board. Each with her daughter by her side the two sisters moved forward to greet one another, the Empress appearing very excited, the Queen strangely calm. They embraced, but even now they were not free of ceremonial and formality; there were still presentations to be made, first of the Empress's Russian friends, afterwards of the ship's officers, before these two sisters, so long parted, could go off together to talk and laugh and cry quietly in privacy.

For a while the Empress lived at Frogmore, and then finally made her home in Denmark, frequently visiting England to see Queen Alexandra, who was no longer fit to travel abroad.

At first the sisters' old home at Hvidore was allotted to the Empress's daughter, the Grand Duchess Olga, the Empress herself being lodged in a wing of the Amalienborg Palace. This arrangement was not a happy one. King Christian X was paying all his aunt's expenses, and, living at such close quarters to her, he found himself constantly irritated by signs of her blatant extravagance. One evening his patience gave way; he sent a message asking her to turn out some of the unnecessary electric lights that were blazing away at his expense.

Immediately she ordered every light in her apartments to be turned on and to be left burning all night. Ultimately it was decided that the Empress must leave the Amalienborg and make her home at Hvidore, Queen Alexandra undertaking to pay £1,000 annually towards the upkeep of the house. King George generously made his aunt a yearly allowance of £10,000 to which Queen Alexandra intended to add another £850, but such was the precarious state of her own finances that this sum was never paid.

Although she was never again to visit Denmark, Queen Alexandra maintained her interest in Danish affairs. In 1920, following a plebiscite, north Schleswig once again became Danish, with the exception of the town of Flensborg, which remained in German hands. The Queen vehemently protested against this exception, arguing that Flensborg had voted for Germany only because the German authorities 'had for years prepared for this and kicked every Danish-speaking man out'. 'Do look at the map,' she begged of King George, 'and see what Flensborg means to that vile nation.'[2]

The fortunes of her nephew Constantine, the ex-King of Greece, were becoming an obsession with her; she was forever demanding that King George V should interfere personally on behalf of 'poor, excellent, *honest* Tino'.[3] In vain did the King point out to her that it was not in his power to do anything; 'I am not prepared now on account of the strong feeling which certainly exists in this country against him, to do anything, in fact no one would listen to me if I did.'[4] Queen Alexandra was not to be convinced. Time and again after visiting her at 'the Big House', King George would return to York Cottage exclaiming in despair, 'I simply cannot make Motherdear hear, much less understand, anything at all about Greece.'

Sir Harold Nicolson writes that 'the King was not by temperament an equable man';[5] all the more admirable then was the unfailing good-temper which he displayed towards his mother, even at her most trying moments. He wrote to her regularly, careful to tell her any piece of news which he thought might please or interest her. Knowing that she longed to feel herself still in touch with affairs of state he would write about the 1920 coal strike or the Sinn Fein troubles in

Ireland and the hunger-striking Mayor of Cork, receiving in reply a muddled tirade insisting that 'Mr Smillie* tries to upset everything through his vanity and audacity',[6] or inveighing against Mr de Valera, who in her opinion should not be allowed to disturb the peace of what she still remembered as 'that dear and lovely country'.[7] Her fiercest anger was reserved for what she chose to regard as personal insults to herself. She was particularly hurt by the disbandment of the Nineteenth Hussars, whose Colonel-in-Chief she was. In vain did King George offer her in exchange the Colonelcy of the Ninth Queen's Royal Lancers – 'I can *never* accept a new one after having been robbed of the dear old one given me by Papa and of which I was so proud.'[8] Another bitter grievance was the sale of the royal yacht which bore her name. The King might write a kind and patient letter pointing out that the upkeep of the vessel cost the nation £26,000; she was not to be placated.

Her attitude was in part due to the querulousness of old age, in part to failing health both physical and mental. In 1920 she broke a blood-vessel in her eye and was for a time half-blind; a year or so later she was complaining of 'everlasting pain and *noises* in my wretched old head'.[9] It was during this twilight period that T. E. Lawrence was bidden to an audience with her at Marlborough House, an occasion which he described in *The Mint* in a passage of carefully calculated brilliance, wholly lacking in the quality of compassion.

She, who had been a Queen and a beauty, was now 'your poor old blind and deaf old loving Motherdear'.[10] For she was still loving; her worst moods of depression could be charmed away by a letter or, better still, a visit from her son or daughter-in-law, or from one of the grandchildren in whose doings she took so keen an interest. Having been a fine horse-woman herself she was full of pride that her grandsons should show themselves good enough riders to compete successfully in point-to-point races although she worried over the risk that the Prince of Wales, the precious 'David', ran by so doing. She was eager for news of his visits to Canada and India and she was much concerned that he should show no signs of wishing to marry – 'May God grant him a perfect wife!'[11]

***Robert Smillie, miners' leader.**

The Duke of York, as 'beloved Bertie' had now become, gave her special pleasure by writing to her to describe his visit to Laeken. In her reply she told him how another 'Bertie' had long ago proposed to her there: 'We were walking together in the pretty garden following my mother and the late Queen of the Belgians when he suddenly proposed to me! My surprise was great and I accepted him with *greatest* delight!'[12]

The Duke of York's engagement to Lady Elizabeth Bowes-Lyon gave her great pleasure and so did the birth of her first great-grandson, Princess Mary's elder child.

Other relations came and went, among them the Queen of Denmark, always known as 'Adine', and the Grand Duchess Marie, 'little Minny', now repaying by her kindness and devotion all that Queen Alexandra had done for her during the difficult war years. In letter after letter the Queen sadly recorded the death of old friends, such as Fisher, Beresford, and Soveral. A few faithful friends still remained, Julie Stonor in particular, who had married the Marquis d'Hautpoul. She was a frequent visitor to Sandringham, and occasionally the Queen would spend a quiet week or so with her at her charming little house on the Chilterns. Most important of all, there were dear Charlotte Knollys and of course Sir Dighton, a physical wreck but still struggling on in the service of his 'Blessed Lady'.

Life at Sandringham with 'the Old Ones', to use Queen Maud of Norway's expression, was not very entertaining for the younger members of Queen Alexandra's household. Every afternoon there would be a drive along the road towards King's Lynn, varied only occasionally by an expedition to a little chalet by the sea-shore. The evening was the worst time of all, conversation being almost impossible, partly because of the Queen's deafness, partly because in that small, enclosed group of people, no one could think of anything fresh to say. One evening, as they waited for Queen Alexandra to appear – she was, as usual, very late – her private secretary, Sir Henry Streatfeild, congratulated himself that for once in a way he had a piece of news to recount; King George had bought a new car. He decided not to tell his companions this exciting fact but to keep it as a titbit for the Queen herself. At last she arrived and led the way to dinner. Sir Henry's moment had come.

'Did you know, Ma'am, that His Majesty has a new car?'

'A new cow?'

'No, Ma'am, a new *car*.'

'Yes, yes,' in a triumphant voice, 'I hear you, I understand, the old one has calved.'

The person who suffered most from the sad monotony of Sandringham existence was, of course, Princess Victoria. In 1922 the King gave her a set of apartments in Kensington Palace so that at last she had a place of her own to which she could, and did, retreat. Queen Alexandra, however, hated being without her daughter and complained bitterly whenever she was deprived of Princess Victoria's company. She herself now found London life too exhausting, but nevertheless she was obliged to spend most of the summer of 1923 at Marlborough House. Early in the spring the Empress Marie had come over to see her sister, and falling ill, she had remained in London until the end of August when at last she felt herself sufficiently recovered to be able to return to Denmark. Queen Alexandra, of course, had stayed in London to keep the Empress company. The effort was too much for her; 'I have been too long here,' she wrote to Queen Mary, 'and feel every day worse.'[13] She knew all too well that her memory was failing and over and over again she describes herself as 'feeling a perfect idiot'. However, she was well enough that autumn to receive King Gustav of Sweden and to attend the wedding of her grand-daughter Maud to Lord Carnegie. As late as 1 December, after paying her a birthday visit, the King could write that he had found her 'looking wonderfully well and in better spirits, one cannot realise she is 79'.[14]

But mind and body were failing fast. She could still enjoy small pleasures, paying a daily visit to her kennels and stables, amusing herself with jigsaw puzzles, feeding the sea-gulls and the white pheasant which the King was at pains not to kill when out shooting. This most devoted of sons wrote to her regularly, giving her his impressions of his first Labour Cabinet, describing the Wembley Exhibition or the Trooping the Colour, telling her of Ascot Week and 'the ladies in very smart frocks'. 'You are always in my thoughts', he assures her, not once but many times, and in her pathetically incoherent replies she thanks him for his letters which give her '*such pleasure* I cannot describe'.[15] The practice of religion had always been a comfort to her and so it was now; several times she tells him that she has been to Communion and prayed for him and his family. She was still regular in her attendance at Sandringham Church, too regular, in fact; when she was ill with a bad cough the King must needs send round a hasty note from York Cottage begging her, for his sake, not to go to service that Sunday. He would sit beside her in church at Sandringham, finding the places for her in her prayer-book just as she might have done for him when he was a little boy.

For Queen Alexandra Dighton Probyn's death on 20 June 1924 meant the loss of a friend who for fifty years or more had given her unstinting service and devotion. Still she lived on, stone deaf, her memory clean gone, her speech badly impaired. 'Think of me as I used to be, now I am breaking up,'[16] she wrote sadly to her old friend, Lord Knutsford. Her last letter to King George is dated 9 March 1925. She is obviously writing with great difficulty, but she can still assure him that 'you and my darling May are in my thoughts all day long, and all your children'.[17] On 19 November she had a sudden heart attack. The King and Queen were already at Sandringham; next day her grandsons were sent for in haste, but too late. She died in the early evening of 20 November before they could reach her bedside.

Two days later some of the Sandringham servants and estate workers carried her coffin to the little church in the park so that her body might lie there quietly for a while among her own people before being taken to Westminster for the pomp and ceremony of a state funeral. Although the afternoon was cold and cheerless Charlotte Knollys had flung a window wide open, the better to watch the little procession. As the bearers crossed the wintry lawns they heard her crying aloud, like a little child.

LIST OF ABBREVIATIONS

RA	Royal Archives, Windsor Castle
BM	British Museum
NLS	National Library of Scotland
Journal	Queen Victoria's Journal, Royal Archives
Somerset	Lady Geraldine Somerset's personal diary, also for years when this diary is missing, the journal kept for the Duchess of Cambridge by Lady Geraldine. Property of the Duke of Beaufort, now deposited in the Royal Archives. Uncatalogued; all references by dates
Magnus	*King Edward the Seventh*, by Philip Magnus. (John Murray Ltd., 1964)
Dearest Child	*Dearest Child*, Letters between Queen Victoria and the Princess Royal, 1858–1861; edited by Roger Fulford. (Evans Brothers Ltd., 1964)
Dearest Mama	*Dearest Mama*, Letters between Queen Victoria and the Princess Royal, 1861–1864; edited by Roger Fulford. (Evans Brothers Ltd., 1968)

CHAPTER ONE

Danish Childhood

1 Palle Lauring, *A History of the Kingdom of Denmark* (1963), p. 210.
2 Hans Madol, *Christian IX* (Collins, 1939), p. 66.
3 RA/Add/U/32, 6 November 1872.
4 Peter Carew, *Combat and Carnival* (Constable, 1954), p. 147.
5 Madol, op. cit., p. 100.
6 RA/Z/462/14, 15 February 1861.

CHAPTER TWO

The Prince of Wales

1 Roger Fulford, ed., *Dearest Child*, (Evans), p. 187.
2 RA/Z/455/17 (Magnus, *King Edward VII*, Murray).
3 RA/Z/462/1
4 RA/Z/462/5
5 RA/Z/462/7
6 *Dearest Child*, p. 223.
7 RA/Z/462/13
8 RA/Z/462/18
9 RA/Z/462/8
10 *Dearest Child*, p. 223.
11 RA/Z/462/11
12 RA/Z/462/7
13 *Dearest Child*, p. 39.
14 Ibid., p. 354.
15 Walburga Paget, *Embassies of Other Days* (Hutchinson, 1923), p. 139.
16 *Dearest Child*, p. 289.
17 RA/Z/13/49
18 *Dearest Child*, p. 291.
19 RA/Z/10
20 *Dearest Child*, p. 308.
21 Ibid., p. 323.
22 Ibid., p. 322.

23 RA/Z/4/16
24 RA/Z/462/26
25 *Dearest Child*, p. 337.
26 Ibid., pp. 337–8.
27 Ibid., p. 338.
28 Ibid., p. 338.
29 RA/Z/462/43
30 RA/Z/4/15
31 *Dearest Child*, p. 341.
32 Magnus, p. 46.
33 *Dearest Child*, p. 342.
34 RA/Z/462/47
35 *Dearest Mama*, p. 39.
36 RA/Z/141/85
37 RA/Z/462/73
38 RA/Z/462/86
39 *Dearest Child*, pp. 350–1.
40 RA/Z/462/85
41 *Dearest Child*, p. 357.
42 Ibid., p. 356.
43 RA/Z/141/91
44 RA/Z/446/18

CHAPTER THREE

Engagement and Marriage

1 RA/Add/U/32, 22 January 1862.
2 *Dearest Mama*, p. 38.
3 Ibid., p. 38.
4 Ibid., p. 53.
5 RA/Z/463/14
6 *Dearest Mama*, p. 53.
7 RA/Add/U/32, 16 April 1862.
8 RA/Z/12/14
9 RA/Z/12/64
10 RA/Z/463/9
11 RA/Z/463/18
12 Journal, 3 September 1862.
13 RA/T/3/88
14 RA/T/3/88

15 RA/Z/463/56
16 RA/Z/463/67
17 RA/Z/463/72
18 RA/Z/463/83
19 RA/Z/4/22
20 RA/Z/463/46
21 RA/Y/84/51
22 RA/Y/84/53
23 RA/Y/84/55
24 RA/Z/14/13
25 RA/Z/463/96
26 BM/Paget Papers, 51237.
27 *Letters of Lady Augusta Stanley*, edited by A. V. Baillie and Hector Bolitho (G. Howe, 1927), p. 271.
28 George Bell, *Randall Davidson* (Oxford Univ. Press, 1935), p. 119.
29 Stanley, op. cit., p. 273.
30 Ibid., p. 272.
31 RA/Z/463/135, 132
32 RA/A/8/384
33 RA/Add/U/32, 12 November 1862.
34 *Dearest Mama*, p. 126.
35 RA/Z/447/47
36 RA/Z/463/127
37 RA/Z/463/145
38 RA/Z/463/127
39 RA/Z/463/134
40 RA/Y/109/10
41 RA/Z/463/123
42 BM/Paget Papers, 51237.
43 Somerset, 7 March 1863.
44 Journal, 7 March 1863.
45 A. G. C. Liddell, *Notes from the Life of an Ordinary Mortal* (Murray, 1911), p. 46.
46 Letter in the possession of Mrs Eleanor Vigor.
47 Liddell, op. cit., pp. 46–7.
48 Somerset, 5 March 1863.
49 *My Dear Duchess, Letters to the Duchess of Manchester*, edited by A. L. Kennedy (Murray, 1956), p. 210.
50 Somerset, 10 March 1863.

51 Vigor letter as above.
52 Journal, 10 March 1863.

CHAPTER FOUR

A young wife and mother

1 *Dearest Mama*, p. 180.
2 Ibid., p. 182.
3 Somerset, 20 March 1863.
4 Sir William Hardman, *A Mid-Victorian Pepys* (Cecil Palmer, 1923), p. 280.
5 Ibid., p. 281.
6 Lord Esher, *Cloud Capp'd Towers* (Murray, 1927), p. 163.
7 Augustus Hare, *The Years With Mother*, Allen & Unwin (Abridged edition 1952), p. 92.
8 *Diary of Lady Frederick Cavendish*, edited by John Bailey (Murray, 1927), Vol. I, p. 163.
9 Somerset, 22 May 1863.
10 *Journals of Lady Knightly of Fawsley*, edited by J. Cartwright (Murray, 1915), p. 56.
11 Knollys Papers.
12 Macclesfield Papers.
13 A. V. Baillie and Hector Bolitho, *A Victorian Dean* (Chatto & Windus, 1930), p. 218.
14 Ibid., pp. 24, 292.
15 J. G. Lockhart, *Viscount Halifax* (Centenary Press, 1935), p. 104.
16 Ibid.
17 RA/Y/109/20
18 RA/Add/U/32, 27 March 1863.
19 *Dearest Mama*, p. 186.
20 Ibid., p. 236.
21 Ibid., p. 247.
22 Ibid., p. 212.
23 Ibid., p. 226.
24 RA/Z/447/60
25 *Dearest Mama*, p. 213.
26 RA/Y/111/22
27 RA/Z/447/80

28 RA/Z/447/80
29 *Dearest Mama*, p. 278.
30 Bell, op. cit., p. 119.
31 Rigsarkivet, Archives of Christian VIII, Appendix A.
32 RA/Y/110/22
33 RA/Z/447/90

CHAPTER FIVE

Denmark and Prussia at War

1 RA/Z/447/121
2 *Dearest Mama*, p. 306.
3 Macclesfield Papers.
4 Cavendish, op. cit., I, p. 216.
5 RA/Y/111/24
6 RA/Y/113/18
7 RA/Y/112/17
8 RA/Add/U/32
9 Magnus, p. 83.
10 George Villiers, *A Vanished Victorian* (Eyre & Spottiswoode, 1938), p. 325.
11 Letters of Queen Victoria, Second Series, Vol. I, p. 207.
12 Ibid., p. 219.
13 RA/Y/112/2
14 *Dearest Mama*, p. 350.
15 Rigsarkivet, Copenhagen.
16 RA/Z/448/54
17 RA/Add/U/32, 3 October 1864.
18 RA/Add/U/32, 11 October 1864.
19 RA/Y/113/2
20 RA/Add/U/32, 19 November 1864.
21 W. Paget, *The Linings of Life* (Hurst & Blackett, 1928), p. 101.
22 RA/Z/449/94
23 RA/Z/448/130
24 RA/Z/448/118
25 Somerset, 31 August 1865.
26 RA/Y/113
27 RA/Y/114/9
28 Macclesfield Papers.

29 RA/Y/114/31
30 RA/Y/114/32
31 RA/T/4/74
32 RA/T/4/78
33 RA/T/4/78
34 RA/L/25/16
35 Somerset, 2 December 1865.
36 RA/Add/U/32, 20 December 1865.

CHAPTER SIX

The Princess's illness

1 RA/Y/178/34
2 RA/Y/178/1
3 RA/Y/178/2
4 RA/Add/U/32, 31 March 1866, 11 April 1866.
5 RA/Add/U/32, 9 November 1866.
6 RA/Add/U/32, 14 November 1866.
7 For the correspondence with Princess Louise see RA/Add/A/17.
8 RA/Z/448/32
9 Journal, 23 March 1867.
10 RA/Add/Vic/C/7, 18 March 1867.
11 All extracts describing the Princess's illness are from the Macclesfield Papers.
12 RA/Add/C/7/28
13 RA/Add/C/7/32
14 RA/Add/C/7, 5 July 1867.
15 Journal, 2 July 1867.
16 Esher, *Journals & Letters* (Nicholson & Watson, 1934), Vol. I, p. 345.
17 Magnus, p. 159.
18 RA/Add/C/7, 19 August 1867.
19 RA/Vic/Add/C/7, 5 October 1867.
20 RA/Vic/Add/C/7, 7 October 1867.
21 RA/Add/Vic/C/7, 11 October 1867.
22 RA/Add/U/32, 5 October 1867.
23 RA/J/65/6
24 RA/D/23/46
25 RA/D/23/65

26 RA/Z/449/13
27 RA/Z/449/7
28 RA/A/17/276
29 Somerset, 30 April 1868.

CHAPTER SEVEN

The gorgeous East

1 RA/Z/449/24
2 RA/Z/449/27
3 Edward, Earl of Sandwich, *Memoirs* (Murray, 1919), p. 81.
4 Sir George Arthur, *Queen Mary* (T. Butterworth, 1934), p. 85.
5 Lady Antrim, *Recollections* (1937), p. 221.
6 Sandwich Papers at Mapperton.
7 RA/Z/448/50
8 RA/Y/85/14
9 RA/Z/449/28
10 RA/A/17/288
11 RA/A/3/121
12 RA/Z/449/44
13 RA/A/3/129
14 Lord Redesdale, *Memories* (Hutchinson, 1915), p. 311.
15 RA/Z/449/51
16 RA/Z/449/51
17 RA/Z/449/70
18 RA/Z/449/66
19 *Illustrated London News*, 26 February 1870.
20 Cavendish, op. cit., II, p. 80.
21 *Observer*, 27 February 1870.
22 RA/Add/U/32, 2 March 1870.
23 RA/Z/449/5
24 RA/Z/449/96

CHAPTER EIGHT

A time of trouble

1 Magnus, p. 110.
2 RA/A/17/384
3 RA/Add/U/32, 1 November 1870.

4 RA/Z/449/132
5 RA/AA/29/19
6 RA/T/5/43
7 RA/A/17/512
8 *The Times*, 11 December 1871.
9 This account of the Prince of Wales's illness, together with all quotations not otherwise marked, is taken from the Macclesfield Papers.
10 RA/A/17/512
11 RA/Dalton Papers, 23 December 1871.
12 RA/A/17/532
13 RA/Z/451/114

CHAPTER NINE

Life at Sandringham

1 RA/Add/A/3/131
2 RA/Z/449/26
3 RA/AA/28/47
4 RA/AA/29/26
5 RA/Add/U/32, 8 April 1874.
6 RA/Add/U/32, 17 March 1872.
7 Somerset, 17 April 1871.
8 Ibid., 16 April 1871.
9 RA/Z/450/148
10 RA/Add/U/32, 16 December 1874.
11 RA/AA/29/2
12 H.R.H. Princess Alice of Athlone, *For My Grandchildren* (Evans, 1966), p. 116.
13 RA/D/3/91
14 RA/AA/30/2
15 Lady Randolph Churchill, *Reminiscences* (E. Arnold, 1908), p. 144.
16 Ponsonby Papers.
17 Cavendish, op. cit., II, p. 146.
18 Ibid., p. 145.
19 Sandwich Papers at Mapperton.
20 Antrim, op. cit., p. 218.
21 RA/Dalton Papers, 1 February 1874.
22 Esher, *Cloud Capp'd Towers* (Murray, 1927), p. 163.

23 Ponsonby Papers.
24 RA/AA/33/29
25 RA/CC/42/66
26 Magnus, p. 135.
27 Ponsonby Papers.
28 RA/O/12/127
29 RA/Add/A/2/19
30 Magnus, p. 145.
31 For this episode see Magnus, p. 145 and RA/CC/47/1896.
32 RA/S/31/35
33 RA/Add/A/2/22
34 Magnus, p. 147.
35 RA/S/31/36
36 RA/Add/A/12/30/2

CHAPTER TEN

Husband and sons

1 RA/AA/36/21
2 Lillie Langtry, *The Days I Knew* (Hutchinson, 1925), p. 77.
3 RA/Add/A/17/882
4 Ponsonby Papers.
5 Sandwich Papers at Mapperton.
6 RA/AA/28/17
7 Somerset, 13 September 1879.
8 RA/AA/28/6
9 RA/Dalton Papers, 20 April 1877.
10 Ibid., 20 November 1877.
11 Ibid., 21 September 1877.
12 RA/Z/452/108
13 RA/AA/28/11
14 RA/AA/39/60
15 RA/AA/28/28
16 RA/AA/29/44
17 RA/AA/36/38
18 RA/AA/36/10
19 RA/AA/36/14
20 RA/A/15/2852
21 RA/Add/A/15/3268
22 This account of the negotiations preceding Princess

Thyra's marriage, with all quotations, is taken from papers in the Archives of the House of Hanover at Gmunden.

23 RA/Add/U/32, 22 October 1878.
24 Somerset, 13 January 1878.
25 RA/Add/U/32, 11 April 1886.
26 RA/Z/452/191

CHAPTER ELEVEN

Russian involvements

1 *Cambridge Modern History* (Cambridge Univ. Press, 1934 Edition), Vol. XII, p. 398.
2 Magnus, p. 154.
3 RA/B/59/21
4 BM.Add.MSS. 46219/122
5 BM.Add.MSS. 46219/116
6 RA/Dalton Papers, 11 December 1878.
7 RA/AA/28/30
8 RA/AA/28/37
9 RA/AA/36/1
10 RA/AA/36/16
11 RA/AA/28/38
12 RA/AA/28/50
13 RA/AA/28/38
14 RA/AA/29/2
15 RA/Dalton Papers, 15 January 1880.
16 Ibid., 18 January 1881.
17 Ibid., 10 February 1881.
18 RA/H/43/84
19 RA/H/44/9
20 Lord Frederick Hamilton, *The Vanished Pomps of Yesterday* (Hodder, 1919), p. 168.
21 RA/H/43/121
22 RA/Dalton Papers, 7 November 1882.
23 Ibid., 11 March 1883.
24 Ibid., 13 July 1883.
25 RA/Add/U/32
26 Ponsonby Papers.
27 Harold Nicolson, *King George V* (Constable, 1952), p. 22.

28 Ponsonby Papers.
29 RA/Z/162/7
30 RA/AA/29/35
31 RA/AA/29/39
32 RA/AA/29/41
33 RA/AA/29/41
34 RA/AA/29/42

CHAPTER TWELVE

Jubilee and Silver Wedding

1 Lincolnshire Papers.
2 RA/Z/455/7
3 RA/Z/455/9
4 RA/AA/30/11
5 RA/Z/455/11
6 Ponsonby Papers.
7 RA/AA/29/45
8 RA/AA/30/9
9 Dame Beryl Oliver, *The British Red Cross in Action* (Faber, 1966), p. 152.
10 RA/AA/30/22
11 Ponsonby Papers.
12 RA/Z/162/11
13 RA/AA/30/27
14 RA/AA/30/33
15 Somerset, 21 February 1886.
16 Nicolson, op. cit., p. 39.
17 RA/AA/30/17
18 RA/AA/30/21
19 Somerset, 5 July, 1 August, 21 November 1885, 8 January 1886.
20 RA/Add/U/32, 27 May 1887.
21 RA/AA/30/39
22 RA/AA/30/40
23 RA/AA/30/36
24 RA/Add/U/32, 17 January 1885.
25 James Pope-Hennessy, *Queen Mary* (Allen & Unwin, 1959), p. 192.
26 RA/AA/31/11

27 RA/AA/31/23

28 RA/AA/31/11

29 NLS/Rosebery Papers.

30 BM/Gladstone Papers, 44289 f. 19.

31 NLS/Rosebery Papers.

32 R. C. K. Ensor, *England 1870–1914* (Oxford Univ. Press, 1936), p. 194.

CHAPTER THIRTEEN

The Duke of Clarence

1 RA/AA/31/16

2 RA/AA/31/17

3 RA/AA/31/18

4 RA/Add/U/32, 16 June 1891.

5 Frances, Lady Warwick, *Afterthoughts* (Cassell, 1931), p. 37.

6 RA/Z/475/17

7 RA/Z/475/18

8 Ponsonby Papers.

9 Magnus, p. 234.

10 RA/Add/A/4/78

11 Magnus, p. 235.

12 Ponsonby Papers.

13 RA/Z/475/49

14 RA/Z/450/148

15 This account of the Duke of Clarence's death, together with all quotations, is taken from a letter from the Princess to her parents now in the Rigsarkivet, Copenhagen.

16 RA/Add/A/5/40

17 RA/Z/475/156

18 RA/Z/475/200

19 NLS/Rosebery Papers.

20 Ibid.

21 RA/L/4/20

22 RA/AA/31/23

23 Sandwich Papers at Mapperton.

24 Ibid.

25 Ibid.

26 Ibid.

27 RA/AA/31/27
28 RA/CC/342/35

CHAPTER FOURTEEN

The end of the Old Order

1 Bing, *Letters of Nicholas II to the Empress Marie* (Nicholson & Watson, 1938), p. 260.
2 RA/CC/5/57
3 RA/CC/27/53
4 Ponsonby Papers.
5 RA/Z/55/73
6 RA/Add/U/32, 5 June 1894.
7 Esher, *Journals & Letters* (Nicholson & Watson, 1934), Vol. I, p. 345.
8 RA/AA/36/15
9 Esher, *Journals & Letters* (Nicholson & Watson, 1934), Vol. I, p. 186.
10 Magnus, p. 245.
11 Ian Vorres, *The Last Grand Duchess* (Hutchinson, 1964), p. 53.
12 RA/AA/32/5
13 BM/Balfour Papers, 49685/786A. f. 126.
14 RA/Z/499/163
15 RA/Z/499/145
16 RA/Z/499/114
17 Carroll Papers.
18 *Mary Gladstone's Diaries & Letters*, edited by Lucy Masterman (Methuen, 1930), p. 422.
19 Lincolnshire Papers.
20 RA/AA/32/12
21 RA/CC/6/60
22 RA/CC/2/96
23 For quotations in this and preceding paragraph see T. Lang, *My Darling Daisy* (Joseph, 1966), pp. 79–81.
24 Magnus, p. 260.
25 RA/CC/7/32
26 RA/CC/3/29
27 RA/CC/7/68
28 RA/AA/32/9

29 Lincolnshire Papers.
30 Sir Victor Mallet (Editor), *Life With Queen Victoria* (Murray, 1968), p. 103.
31 Ibid., p. 111.
32 Morley, *Gladstone* (E. Lloyd, 1908 Edition), Vol. II, p. 562.
33 Mary Gladstone Papers. BM.Add.MSS. 46219 f. 184.
34 RA/AA/32/1
35 Knutsford Papers.
36 Ibid.
37 Ibid.
38 Carroll Papers.
39 RA/Add/A4/175

CHAPTER FIFTEEN

Edwardian Queen

1 Esher, *Journals & Letters* (Nicholson & Watson, 1934), Vol. I, p. 279.
2 Magnus, p. 457.
3 Margot Asquith, *Autobiography* (T. Butterworth, 1922), Vol. II, p. 128.
4 RA/CC/33/30
5 Macclesfield Papers.
6 Esher, *Journals & Letters* (1934), Vol. I, p. 373.
7 Ibid., p. 318.
8 Ibid., p. 285.
9 RA/AA/32/28
10 Pope-Hennessy, op. cit., p. 355.
11 RA/AA/32/31
12 Mary Gladstone Papers. BM.Add.MSS. 46219 f. 219.
13 Macclesfield Papers.
14 RA/CC/42/81
15 RA/CC/24/24
16 Rigsarkivet, Copenhagen.
17 Mabelle, Countess of Airlie, *Thatched With Gold* (Hutchinson, 1962), p. 106.
18 F. Ponsonby, *Recollections of Three Reigns* (Eyre & Spottiswoode, 1951), p. 105.
19 Somerset, 8 August 1883.
20 Ibid., 1 August 1884.

21 Ponsonby, op. cit., p. 209.
22 Daisy, Princess of Pless, *My Private Diary* (Murray, 1931), p. 127.
23 L. V. Fildes, *Luke Fildes, R.A.* (Joseph, 1968), p. 160.

CHAPTER SIXTEEN

Naval and Military

1 Pope-Hennessy, op. cit., p. 361.
2 Lincolnshire Papers.
3 Frances, Lady Warwick, op. cit., p. 275.
4 Mabelle, Countess of Airlie, op. cit., p. 106.
5 Magnus, p. 370.
6 Blackford Papers.
7 Ibid.
8 Admiral Sir R. H. Bacon, *Life of Lord Fisher of Kilverstone* (Hodder, 1929), p. 72.
9 *Fear God and Dread Nought*, Correspondence of Admiral of the Fleet Lord Fisher, edited by A. J. Marder (Cape, 1952/9), p. 490.
10 Fisher Papers.
11 Fisher, op. cit., p. 166.
12 Ibid., p. 166.
13 Fisher Papers.
14 Ibid.
15 Fisher, op. cit., p. 166.
16 Ibid., p. 187.
17 Knutsford Papers.
18 NLS/Haldane Papers, Vol. 6020, f. 25.
19 Ibid., Vol. 6019, Lady Roberts to Miss Haldane, 19 June 1906.
20 Ibid., Vol. 6022, f. 104.
21 Ibid., Vol. 6022, f. 164.
22 Ibid., Vol. 6020, f. 161.
23 Knutsford Papers.
24 Oliver, op. cit., p. 192.
25 RA/AA/33/5

CHAPTER SEVENTEEN

Coronation postponed

1 RA/AA/32/25
2 RA/CC/3/73
3 Nicolson, op. cit., p. 20.
4 RA/CC/42/50
5 RA/CC/42/52
6 RA/AA/32/30
7 RA/CC/42/53
8 RA/AA/37/1
9 Queen Marie of Rumania, *The Story of My Life* (Cassell, 1934), p. 460.
10 RA/Add/U/28
11 RA/Charlotte Knollys's Diary, 7 July 1902.
12 Esher, *Journals & Letters* (Nicholson & Watson, 1934), Vol. I, p. 345.
13 RA/Add/U/28. The description of King Edward's illness and convalescence is chiefly taken from the unpublished account by Sir Frederick Treves.
14 Mary Gladstone Papers. BM.Add.MSS. 46219 f. 219.

CHAPTER EIGHTEEN

The reign of King Edward VII

1 RA/AA/32/39
2 RA/CC/7/85
3 RA/CC/29/8
4 RA/CC/30/68
5 RA/CC/24/12
6 RA/AA/33/7
7 RA/AA/33/10
8 RA/CC/33/10
9 RA/AA/33/1
10 RA/AA/33/37
11 RA/AA/33/7
12 RA/AA/33/19
13 E. Dugdale, *Maurice de Bunsen* (Murray, 1934), p. 204.
14 RA/AA/33/4

15 RA/AA/33/4
16 RA/CC/42/6
17 Knutsford Papers.
18 RA/AA/33/7
19 RA/CC/7/159
20 RA/CC/42/75
21 RA/CC/42/57
22 RA/CC/42/62
23 RA/CC/33/27
24 RA/CC/42/68
25 RA/AA/33/27
26 RA/AA/33/8
27 RA/CC/42/66
28 Kenneth Young, *A. J. Balfour* (G. Bell, 1963), p. 252.
29 RA/AA/33/20
30 RA/AA/33/20
31 Asquith, op. cit., I, p. 58.
32 RA/AA/33/26
33 Lord Hardinge, *Old Diplomacy* (Murray, 1947), p. 152.
34 Baroness de Stoeckel, *Not All Vanity* (Murray, 1950), p. 114.
35 Bing, op. cit., p. 221.
36 Fisher, op. cit., p. 180.
37 RA/CC/25/19
38 Ponsonby, op. cit., p. 258.
39 Ponsonby, op. cit., pp. 262–3.
40 Bing, op. cit., pp. 244–7.
41 RA/AA/33/41
42 RA/CC/4/39
43 RA/AA/33/42
44 RA/CC/8/113
45 RA/CC/3/246
46 RA/AA/37/16

CHAPTER NINETEEN

Widowhood

1 Esher, *Journals & Letters,* (Nicholson & Watson) Vol. III, p. 1.
2 Ibid., p. 2.

3 RA/CC/35/22
4 RA/CC/47/209
5 RA/CC/47/212
6 RA/AA/33/45
7 Probyn Letters, property of Mrs Campbell Ellis.
8 RA/AA/33/53
9 RA/AA/34/5
10 RA/AA/34/6
11 RA/AA/34/11
12 RA/AA/34/11
13 RA/CC/42/135
14 RA/CC/42/98
15 RA/AA/34/24
16 RA/AA/34/18
17 RA/AA/34/26
18 RA/AA/34/29
19 RA/AA/34/38

CHAPTER TWENTY

The Great War

1 RA/AA/35/1
2 RA/AA/34/41
3 Fisher, op. cit., II, p. 65.
4 Fisher Papers.
5 Ibid.
6 RA/AA/34/47
7 RA/AA/34/48
8 RA/CC/42/102
9 RA/CC/42/130
10 Knutsford Papers.
11 Ibid.
12 Bing, op. cit., p. 292.
13 RA/AA/34/46
14 Rigsarkivet, Copenhagen.
15 RA/AA/34/46
16 RA/AA/34/51
17 RA/AA/35/17
18 RA/AA/37/74
19 RA/AA/35/9

20 Pope-Hennessy, op. cit., p. 501.
21 RA/CC/42/114
22 Probyn Papers.
23 RA/AA/34/54
24 RA/AA/35/6
25 RA/AA/35/22
26 RA/AA/35/4
27 NLS/H/248
28 Probyn Papers.
29 RA/CC/42/108
30 RA/Add/A/21/228/140
31 RA/Add/A/21/228/184
32 RA/Add/A/21/228/164
33 RA/AA/35/23
34 Mary Gladstone Papers. BM.Add.MSS. 46219 f. 263.
35 Asquith Papers, Bodleian 17/271.
36 Asquith, op. cit., II, p. 284.
37 Asquith Papers, Bodleian 62/10.

EPILOGUE

1 RA/CC/50/1443
2 RA/AA/35/28
3 RA/AA/35/32
4 RA/AA/38/34
5 Nicolson, op. cit., p. 433.
6 RA/AA/35/30
7 RA/AA/35/37
8 RA/AA/35/34
9 RA/AA/35/43
10 RA/AA/35/29
11 RA/AA/35/53
12 RA/Add/A/21/159
13 RA/CC/42/154
14 RA/CC/4/234
15 RA/AA/35/59
16 Knutsford Papers.
17 RA/AA/35/61

INDEX

In this index A=Queen Alexandra, E=King Edward VII and V=Queen Victoria

Richard III

PAUL MURRAY KENDALL

An impressive biography of Richard III by an author with a keen sense of background. A plausible, human and convincing picture of Richard told with infectious enthusiasm and dramatic skill.

"A first class piece of historical writing; and if it is as interesting as a novel that does not mean that it is in any sense a work of fiction" – *Liverpool Daily Post*

"Brilliantly successful . . . Richard III is displayed as a sombre and intelligible figure . . . this book, based throughout on original authorities combines sound scholarship with literary distinction" – *The Times Literary Supplement*

"His sources are unimpeachable, his handling of them impeccable" – *Glasgow Herald*

A Sphere Book 75p

Warwick the Kingmaker and the Wars of the Roses

PAUL MURRAY KENDALL

Richard Neville, Earl of Warwick, has been relegated to a famous oblivion. Is there any other man in English history so well known and so little known about?

Tudor writers were so intent on depicting the victory of Henry Tudor as part of the pattern of God's justice, that Warwick was regarded only as a bellicose baron in the hurly-burly of civil strife from which England had been rescued.

Paul Kendall, whose biography of Richard III received such high praise, has attempted to make good this deficiency. The result is a work of historical biography every bit as colourful and dynamic as its predecessor. For the first time in literature Warwick, the last of the barons, becomes a figure of flesh and blood, and a memorable human being.

A Sphere Book 75p

For the Good of the Cause

ALEXANDER SOLZHENITSYN

'By common consent, Alexander Solzhenitsyn is by far Russia's greatest living writer." – *The Observer*

FOR THE GOOD OF THE CAUSE is set in a school in a provincial Russian town – it is a scathing indictment of the victimization of ordinary, decent people by Soviet careerist bureaucrats. Solzhenitsyn presents the conflicts between right and wrong, between the freedom of the individual and the harshness of the system with absolute sincerity and conviction.

Superbly translated by Max Hayward and David Floyd, this novel shows again the author's unique genius in presenting through the eyes of brilliantly memorable characters, a whole unfamiliar world and system which affects the reader as much as his own familiar reality.

A Sphere Book 25p

The Tomb of Tutankhamen

HOWARD CARTER

Tutankhamen's tomb, discovered in 1922, is an archaeological landmark. The tomb of the boy-king had lain unmolested by graverobbers for more than three thousand years, and it yielded a treasure of unimagined magnificence.

The story of the discovery is told by Howard Carter who led the work of excavation. Not only does he provide a brilliant portrait of an 18th Dynasty Pharaoh, but he also communicates the feeling of awe and excitement which spurred the explorers as the tomb revealed its extraordinary riches.

The text is complemented by Harry Burton's contemporary photographs, and a selection of more recent colour plates.

A Sphere Book £1.50

Ulysses Found

ERNLE BRADFORD

ULYSSES FOUND is the story of Ernle Bradford's quest for the reality behind the legend of Homer's Odyssey. His curiosity was first aroused as a seaman serving in the Mediterranean during the Second World War. Later he took a small sailing boat around the shores of the tideless sea, checking capes, islands, caves and harbours against Homer's descriptions of Ulysses' many landfalls.

The Land of the Lotus Eaters, the Cave of Polyphemus, the island of Circe, Scylla and Charybdis and the Pillars of Hercules. All are described and identified. And whether we read ULYSSES FOUND as a work of scholarship or as an adventure of discovery, it surely remains one of the best books to have been written about the Mediterranean.

A Sphere Book 25p

A Trail of Blood

JEREMY POTTER

Brother Thomas was entrusted with a frightening task – to save the Church party that opposed the dissolution of the monasteries, he had to find evidence that could (in the words of Robert Aske, the one-eyed rebel) "topple the fat Tudor".

Such evidence could be found if there were heirs to the Yorkist line – the princes supposedly murdered in the Tower . . .

In desperation, Robert Aske raises the Northern counties against the King, but the "fat Tudor" is not toppled and the great abbeys fall. In the death throes of the Old Faith, Brother Thomas has one consolation: he has solved the most famous mystery in British history.

A Sphere Book 35p